CHINESE EMPRESSES
The Nature of Female Power

BRET HINSCH

ROWMAN & LITTLEFIELD
Lanham • Boulder • New York • London

Acquisitions Editor: Ashley Dodge
Acquisitions Assistant: Laney Ackley
Sales and Marketing Inquiries: textbooks@rowman.com

Credits and acknowledgments for material borrowed from other sources, and reproduced with permission, appear on the appropriate pages within the text.

Published by Rowman & Littlefield
An imprint of The Rowman & Littlefield Publishing Group, Inc.
4501 Forbes Boulevard, Suite 200, Lanham, Maryland 20706
www.rowman.com

86-90 Paul Street, London EC2A 4NE

Copyright © 2024 by The Rowman & Littlefield Publishing Group, Inc.

All rights reserved. No part of this book may be reproduced in any form or by any electronic or mechanical means, including information storage and retrieval systems, without written permission from the publisher, except by a reviewer who may quote passages in a review.

British Library Cataloguing in Publication Information Available

Library of Congress Cataloging-in-Publication Data
Names: Hinsch, Bret, author.
Title: Chinese empresses : the nature of female power / Bret Hinsch.
Description: Lanham : Rowman & Littlefield, [2024] | Includes bibliographical references.
Identifiers: LCCN 2023041561 (print) | LCCN 2023041562 (ebook) | ISBN 9781538186152 (cloth) | ISBN 9781538186169 (paperback) | ISBN 9781538186176 (epub)
Subjects: LCSH: Empresses--China. | Women--Political activity--China. | China--Kings and rulers. | China--Politics and government.
Classification: LCC DS740.2 .H54 2024 (print) | LCC DS740.2 (ebook) | DDC 951–dc23/eng/20231101
LC record available at https://lccn.loc.gov/2023041561
LC ebook record available at https://lccn.loc.gov/2023041562

Contents

Chronology v
Introduction: The Nature of Female Power 1
Chapter 1: Neolithic Beginnings. 41
Chapter 2: Ancient Consorts. 57
Chapter 3: The Imperial System 91
Chapter 4: Medieval Empresses 127
Chapter 5: Empresses Contained 167
Chapter 6: Palaces and Harems 203
Chapter 7: Strategies of Restraint 231
Conclusion: The Power of Chinese Empresses 247
Glossary 255
Index 265

CHRONOLOGY

Shang	ca. 1600 BCE–ca. 1046 BCE
Zhou	ca. 1046 BCE–256 BCE
Qin	221 BCE–206 BCE
Han	206 BCE–220 CE
Jin	265–420
Northern Wei	386–535
Sui	581–618
Tang	618–907
Liao	907–1125
Song	960–1279
Jin	1115–1234
Yuan	1271–1368
Ming	1368–1644
Qing	1644–1912

Introduction

The Nature of Female Power

THIS BOOK IS NOT A COMPENDIUM OF BIOGRAPHIES OF CHINESE empresses. There are already works in Chinese and English that recount the lives of various imperial consorts in detail. The objective of this book is more fundamental: to understand the nature of women's power in China and beyond. By analyzing details from the lives of representative empresses it is possible to comprehend how women gained and used political power and how male rivals opposed them. The significance of this topic extends far beyond the scope of Chinese studies. In China, monarchy stretches back to high antiquity providing hundreds of case studies that expose the nature and applications of female power. Whereas the histories of most countries describe only a few powerful women, Chinese chronicles offer numerous examples that reveal how rulers' consorts gained, maintained, and used power. The length and richness of Chinese history make it the best historical field for exploring female power in detail.

Surviving records from most parts of the world include relatively little evidence of ancient and medieval female rulers.[1] Much of the writing about powerful woman mixes facts with imaginative storytelling so accounts are often misleading. Views of normative gender also colored the writings of traditional historians, who usually had an ambivalent or even hostile attitude toward powerful women. They often portrayed queens and empresses as illegitimate, incompetent, and immoral. Some stories of influential women were suppressed while others were exaggerated into myths.[2] Even when a historian praised a woman, it was often an implicit rebuke of contemporary men.³ Fortunately in the last few decades numerous historians have reassessed the place of royal consorts in world history, creating a vibrant academic field known as queenship studies. This undertaking emerged as a critique of established representations of female rulers and consorts and has led to a re-evaluation of female roles in government.

Although there are far more cases of powerful women in Chinese records than in any other region of the world; even in China female authority was exceptional. Most imperial consorts were political non-entities. They led uneventful lives and little is known about them. Yet accounts of politically inactive empresses still have value as they provide foils for understanding their dynamic counterparts. If most of the wives and mothers of emperors lacked power, why did some become prominent? Juxtaposing the puissant against the passive reveals which circumstances were congenial to female authority and highlights the strategies that ambitious women used to empower themselves. Empresses gained authority in a limited number of ways. The purpose of this book is to uncover these techniques.

Gender hierarchies condition many aspects of social interaction.⁴ One study recognized fifty-two variables that contributed to gendered status.⁵ With so many factors involved, it is impossible to simplistically sum up women's status in a particular society as high or low. Preoccupation with general female status can even lead investigators to ignore women's unique roles and define their worth solely according to their level of involvement in male-dominated activities.⁶

Instead of quixotically searching for a unitary status of all women, investigators can try to gauge the agency of individuals or groups. A person's capacity for action does not arise in a vacuum. Collective rules, identities, and norms inform and bound behavior.⁷ Measuring the amount of agency within these limitations can expose the degree of female autonomy within a patriarchal power structure. It also highlights the ingenuity of individual women who managed to expand their potential for action.⁸ Yet, employing the concept of agency also raises questions.⁹ Does one measure female agency by a woman's capacity to act like a man? Does

INTRODUCTION

it refer to behavior independent of male control? Or is it simply a catchall term for the capacity to make personal choices in life?

However much the historian focuses on personal agency, it is impossible to ignore the hierarchies that structure society. Although power underpins hierarchy, unequal relations are never absolute, as people constantly contest and renegotiate them.[10] Hierarchies encompass different types of power of varied scope. At the largest scale, leaders exert control over society.[11] But power also shapes interactions between individuals, most fundamentally among kin.

Scholars frequently use two major theories to explain the origins of inequality.[12] Functionalists hold that social stratification arises to serve common interests, as it can motivate people to carry out necessary but difficult duties. Stratification provides systematic rewards such as authority, prestige, and wealth for undertaking important duties.[13] For this reason, useful but tedious or dangerous undertakings such as hunting, plowing, and war accrued prestige in prehistoric societies. Celebrating vital tasks encouraged people to carry out essential tasks that they might otherwise avoid.

In contrast to this functionalist approach, conflict theorists emphasize the opposing interests of different social groups. Social divisions lead some groups to benefit their members by coercing outsiders. Group leaders also dominate others to empower themselves. Although functionalism and conflict theory explain the origins of inequality differently, the outcome is the same. In remote prehistory, social hierarchy gave rise to leaders who dominated those around them. Leaders used their powers to pursue their own interests, elevating their own position even further.

As a starting point for this investigation, it is necessary to comprehend what is meant by the term *power*. In all complex societies, power is distributed unequally. However, inequality has social benefits. The dominant elite enforces order and coordinates activities, allowing society to become increasingly complex.[14] Hierarchies of power take many forms. Authority, prestige, and resources can be allocated according to age, race, gender, and many other factors.

Historians use the term *power* to describe various social connections. Most importantly, they often distinguish authority from power. Authority is the socially sanctioned right to make decisions that others must follow. In contrast, power is a far broader term that encompasses both informal influence and formal authority. Power might constitute the ability to control a setting where people interact, such as the home. It can also be the capacity to privilege something as true, beautiful, or important and have others accept this assessment.[15] An inclusive view of power appeals to specialists in women's history as it embraces a wide range of gender asymmetries.[16] Feminist historians have further expanded the discussion by redefining the political realm in very broad terms.[17] Because ideology constrains gendered behavior, they see politics as not just the activities of the government but also family, work, and general social relations.

The pioneering sociologist Max Weber studied the nature of power in detail, and his writings have profoundly influenced discussions of the subject.[18] Weber saw power as the possibility of affecting the behavior of others.[19] The precise nature of power varies depending on the types of relationships or activities involved.[20] And he defined authority as a recognized right and responsibility to lead that can be exercised without recourse to physical coercion. People willingly obey leaders they consider legitimate, so leaders go to great lengths to create an aura of legitimacy.[21] Significantly, Weber saw power as omnipresent. He believed that it emerges from the interplay between different individual interests and conditions all social interactions.

Power relations are a fundamental aspect of social structure. A society's members possess a common body of knowledge about the normative order, including whom they ought to obey and why.[22] Although a society founded on unequal relationships might seem unfair, sociologists consider inequality necessary for the emergence and development of the complex societies referred to as civilizations. Hierarchical power networks allow people to create effective forms of social organization, efficient governments, prosperous economies, and formidable militaries.[23]

Legitimation determines how power is exercised. In the absence of legitimation, leaders must rely on the threat of violence or the actual use of force to compel obedience. Simple societies such as chiefdoms lack sophisticated mechanisms of legitimation so warriors become dominant.

However, rule by violence is highly uncertain, and this sort of society tends to be highly unstable.[24]

People willingly obey authorities they consider legitimate, reducing dependence on violence, so Weber saw legitimation as fundamental to political success. The concepts used to legitimate a ruler or system can be systematized into an ideology.[25] This intellectual framework justifies social hierarchy and institutionalizes the exercise of authority by explaining the existence of rights and obligations. Ideologies are embedded in culture and associated with the beliefs, behaviors, rites, and objects specific to a particular place. Rulers often strengthen ideology by associating it with prestigious objects, thereby making it tangible. In ancient China, bronze vessels and jade ritual items had particularly rich ideological associations. By controlling objects associated with the ideology of power, powerful men could exclude women from formal political dealings. Yet, in spite of these patriarchal ideologies, women still managed to exercise some agency. The social ideals expressed in ideology often differed from the reality of gender relations.[26]

Weber's theory of legitimation is particularly useful for understanding women's powers, as men usually declared female participation in public matters illegitimate. For an ambitious woman to succeed, she had to make her power seem legitimate. Weber saw three ways of attaining legitimacy. Some authorities, such as rulers in an established monarchy, are considered legitimate because the institution's long history has made obedience customary. Weber called this *traditional domination*. Other authorities exercise *legal domination*, gaining legitimacy by enforcing a system of rules. The third kind of domination is *charismatic*. People willingly obey a compelling leader who exhibits special qualities such as success in war or a link to the supernatural. Weber stressed that these three types of legitimacy are never singular. In every society, leaders use a combination of legitimation strategies. Weber's tripartite theory of legitimacy helps explain the behavior of Chinese empresses. Many of their actions, such as public displays of piety or virtue, can be understood as pragmatic gambits for legitimizing their powers and reducing opposition.

Although men almost always monopolize positions of authority, women sometimes find ways to exert power outside the formal political process. This is easiest in societies with the simplest modes of organization. In societies with rudimentary institutions, power is largely patrimonial.[27] People recognize the authority of family or lineage elders who keep order by enforcing customary rules so there is little distinction between family and government. As mothers and wives, women have important kinship roles, so patrimonialism often allows them to accrue power. Even if men dominate roles with formal authority, they live with women and are bound to them through kinship ties. This propinquity allows women to influence men's decisions.[28] In every time and place, the influence of women on powerful men constitutes one of the most important forms of female power.

Informal female power usually grows out of women's prominence in the domestic sphere.[29] Whereas men dominate decisions in the public realm, women make many decisions that affect home life. In agricultural societies, the household is the primary unit of production, consumption, and social activity, so many important interactions occur in a domestic context. Because peasants have most authority over home life, they try to maximize the autonomy of the domestic sphere. On the surface it might seem that men are in almost complete control of important matters, yet women make many of the decisions that affect the well-being of their families. Women thus end up wielding power even as gender ideology stresses the importance of male decision making.

Social image is also a factor determining power. Prestige refers to the amount of deference that a person receives, often from occupying a respected social role.[30] Under capitalism, prestige tends to be correlated with wealth. In historic societies, however, deference did not automatically confer wealth nor was wealth the primary foundation of prestige.[31] Overall, prestige is often closely associated with power. Men usually dominate the most prestigious roles and settings but women can also receive deference in certain circumstances. Even if a woman occupies a low place in the public realm, she can still enjoy considerable prestige in the home. Most importantly, motherhood imbues a woman with prestige. Not only do her children see her as an authority figure, but most societies celebrate motherhood. In China, parenthood became especially prestigious as the ideology of filial piety presented the mother as an almost holy figure deserving veneration and obedience.[32]

Control of key resources marks another key aspect of power.[33] Wealth can buy compliance so ambitious people use economic resources to obtain and exercise power. A powerful person can hand out resources to reward obedience and withhold them to punish defiance. The degree of resource inequality differs according to the amount of surplus production. In the simplest societies, people usually receive resources according to their needs. As the administrative system becomes more developed, leaders gain more power over the allocation of goods and services.[34] The most valuable resources that allow large-scale political control, such as taxation and military force, tend to be the purview of men. Women usually had less wealth than men, making it difficult for them to gain power in the public sphere through economic means.

People today are extremely interested in powerful women of the past. This theme has become a staple of popular culture as Hollywood movies and romance novels pander to this fascination. But by giving audiences what they want, directors and authors often end up distorting history. They promote the false impression that powerful women used to be common when in fact female monarchs were extremely rare. In all but the simplest societies, men dominate public life. The anthropologist Ruth Benedict declared patriarchy a basic social fact, noting that the prerogatives of adult men exceed those of women "in every culture."[35] Subsequent research has repeatedly confirmed this assertion.[36]

Although most anthropologists study small-scale societies, male supremacy holds true for large states as well. Men have dominated state societies at every level of complexity throughout history, and this trend has continued into the modern era. From 1945 until 1980 women led only about 0.5 percent of organized states.[37] However, imperial China presents a notable exception to the prevailing pattern of male rule. Due to particularities of China's system and family ethics, an unusually large number of women gained control of the government. In this respect, China is an outlier in world history.

Introduction

To appreciate the nature of female power in China, it is necessary to understand the origins and development of gendered power relations in world history. The patriarchal ideas and institutions that blocked women's rise emerged very early. Simple prehistoric societies, with people grouped into small bands consisting of no more than a few dozen families, were relatively egalitarian. Even so, they were not completely equal. No two individuals are identical, so absolute social equality has always been an impossibility.[38] During the Stone Age, for example, some people were better at hunting and others had better luck finding edible wild plants, affecting how the community perceived them. When anthropologists call a society *egalitarian*, they mean that it lacks social strata or other types of fixed hierarchy.[39] Yet, individuals still occupy kinship roles with different degrees of domestic authority. They also have different degrees of dominance over others in the community depending on their relative strength, skill, intelligence, and other personal qualities.[40]

In an egalitarian society, individuals have considerable leeway to make decisions regarding their own labor and other important matters.[41] People perform various tasks, and the community considers their contributions significant, as different types of labor are necessary for the group to thrive. Most decisions in an egalitarian society are made within the family.[42] In the wider community, leadership is transient. Different people take the lead depending on the activity being undertaken. This sort of alternating leadership is only feasible when the population is low. As a community grows, stable forms of leadership emerge.[43]

In egalitarian societies, women are not required to defer to men nor does the community prioritize men's needs and desires.[44] Skillful and charismatic women exercise leadership in certain situations. The Kutse Bushmen (or San) of the Kalahari exemplify an egalitarian society that recognizes the biological differences between men and women but lacks gender hierarchy.[45] The Kutse believe that women and men tend to have different traits but they do not emphasize gender stereotypes. Although they associate many tasks with one sex or the other, men and women help each other with their work. Men sometimes fight men but they also fight women. However, they do not do so out of a sense of male privilege. A man hits a woman for the same reason that he would hit a man. The

Kutse present an extreme example of relative gender equality. Most other so-called egalitarian societies put far more stress on differences between the sexes. For example, in many Melanesian societies, while relations between adult men are predominantly egalitarian, those between men and women or people of different generations are unequal.[46] In these egalitarian societies, equality usually only occurs between adults of the same sex.

In recent years, anthropologists have begun describing gender difference in relatively simple societies as *heterarchy* rather than hierarchy.[47] Men and women perform different tasks, but the labors of each are recognized as essential and respected. In preindustrial societies, work tends to be assigned according to gender.[48] Due to the burdens of childcare, women usually focus on tasks within the home and men undertake activities farther afield. Both sexes must carry out their appointed tasks for the community to thrive. The production of a loaf of bread illustrates this cooperation.[49] In many places, men grow the grain and women grind it into flour, make dough, and bake loaves. Both women and men are respected for carrying out necessary work roles.

Heterarchy gives women opportunities to exercise power outside the domestic sphere. In both Bronze Age Denmark and the Mississippian society of North America, men served in elite positions most frequently but women could also hold leadership roles.[50] Moreover, chiefs were not the only people with power. The manipulation of crops, handicrafts, trade goods, combat, and ritual could all confer authority. Both sexes conducted important rituals and controlled prestigious articles. This arrangement benefited both sexes. Women in Bronze Age Denmark were taller than at any time before the twentieth century attesting to a good diet and beneficial circumstances. Yet, even in a heterarchal society men still enjoy considerable privileges. Although women have significant social roles, people are still taught that men are fundamentally superior to women in key respects, and men almost always occupy the most important positions.

Heterarchy is a useful analytic tool that can help account for certain types of female power in imperial China. Chinese never regarded their society as purely patriarchal. They always acknowledged the importance of women's contributions to the family and community. Thinkers of various schools described the well-functioning society as one in which men plow and women weave, a heterarchal vision of ideal social order.[51] Empresses could associate themselves with respected female endeavors such as cloth production or devoted motherhood to gain respect.

As a society becomes more complex, increasingly steep hierarchies emerge. Adults have more control over youths, and people have different degrees of wealth and public authority. Stratification intensifies gender inequality, a condition that has been variously described as patriarchy, sexual stratification, sexual asymmetry, and gender hierarchy.[52] As social hierarchy increases, women's general position in relation to men of the same social stratum declines. Yet, a woman also belongs to particular social stratum, determined by the standing of her family, and a woman from an elite family is the social superior of a man from a lower background.[53] Gender might determine hierarchy within a particular stratum but stratum overrides gender in apportioning the relative status of people in different strata.

The political development of society also reorganized gender relations. When a society faces a major crisis such as overpopulation, drought, or warfare, it must empower strong leaders to solve pressing problems, intensifying inequality.[54] Highly unequal societies emerged in China during the Longshan phase of the late Neolithic era, giving rise to patriarchy. Rising social inequality had a mixed impact on women's status. It institutionalized the general subordination of women but also eventually gave rise to complex institutions of rulership that included queens and empresses, potentially giving a handful of women opportunities to dominate the state.[55]

The advantages of social inequality are obvious. Stable leadership can direct society's resources and coordinate labor, allowing people to undertake large-scale projects.[56] However, it is not immediately clear why inequality should have given rise to patriarchy. Why did men end up dominating women instead of the other way around? Early theories of patriarchy tended to emphasize the physical differences between the sexes. On average, men are about 7 percent taller than women in every human population.[57] And in contemporary human populations the average ratio of female to male weight is 0.84.[58] Moreover, women are generally about two-thirds to four-fifths as strong as men depending on the group of muscles.[59] Some scholars hold that men are not only larger and have more musculature than women but they are also more aggressive due to testosterone.[60]

In the 1960s, some theorists seized on these biological differences to infer that most prehistoric hunters were male so men monopolized the most important source of food.[61] Male hunters also mastered the use of weapons that they could use against disobedient women. As societies became more complex, hunters became warriors.[62] In almost every society studied by anthropologists, most of the weapons used in war and hunting belong to men. While women sometimes fight, there is no society in which women are the primary fighters. To the contrary, many societies prohibit women from participating in war. Dominance of warfare obviously gave men a major edge over women. Even when their society was at peace, they could use their weapons to seize the most important positions of authority.

Although biological determinism might seem like a persuasive explanation of patriarchy, in recent years many scholars have cast doubt on this paradigm. Like men, prehistoric women also performed arduous labor, giving many of them a musculature comparable to a modern athlete.[63] Female skeletons from the late Yangshao era Duzhong site in Henan province attest to the strength of some Neolithic women. The average humerus (upper arm) bone showed signs that the women had slightly more upper body musculature than most contemporary men.[64] Domestic labor such as grinding millet and carrying water gave them muscular physiques.

A related theory holds that male dominance arose because men could intimidate women. In addition to the fear of sexual assault, women also wanted to protect their children from harm.[65] A man could exploit a woman's maternal instincts to dominate her, bullying a mother into compliance by threatening her child. According to this account, patriarchy arose as a kind of gendered blackmail.

Inequality of the sexes also had economic underpinnings. Simple societies tend to reward valued social roles with prestige instead of material goods. In complex societies, however, material rewards become paramount.⁶⁶ Initially the goal is to encourage people to engage in dangerous or unpleasant activities by providing them with material rewards.⁶⁷ But as the sexes became increasingly unequal, the rewards for undertaking male activities became far greater than the rewards for undertaking activities performed by women. As key work and social roles became gendered, women ended up with far lower economic returns than men. Friedrich Engels believed that female subordination was a consequence of male economic power, a viewpoint that has attracted many followers.⁶⁸ In the main, however, most scholars consider economic inequity either a result of general gender inequality or only a partial cause of gender hierarchy.

Regardless of how patriarchy emerged, for it to endure it had to be bolstered by ideologies, such as religion or metaphysics, that justified male domination and female submission. Ideologies made gender distinction and hierarchy into imperatives.⁶⁹ Such was the case in early China. Early intellectual systems imbued metaphysical forces such as yin-yang and heaven-earth with a gendered dimension.⁷⁰ Many societies, including China, even portrayed women as fundamentally unclean due to menstrual discharge.⁷¹ The belief that women are inherently polluted served as a powerful justification for male superiority. In some societies, the sexes even live largely apart to keep men away from alleged pollution.⁷² The rise of misogynistic gender ideologies made it difficult for Chinese women to wield power.

The emergence of the state further bolstered patriarchy. As society developed, kinship declined in importance to be replaced by social distinctions grounded in economic differences.⁷³ Hereditary political elites gained even more control over society's productive surplus through rent and taxation. Male control of key productive resources exacerbated gender inequality. Moreover, warfare became increasingly important, empowering male leaders even more.

In state societies, people began to reconceptualize the family as a kind of miniature kingdom with the father assuming the role of absolute monarch.⁷⁴ Although the rise of states saw the decline of many female roles, patrimonialism allowed the wives of some rulers to become queens, giving them new ways to exercise authority. This stage of social

INTRODUCTION

development is particularly important in the history of Chinese women. During the Shang and Zhou dynasties, kings and nobles ruled vast domains. Their wives enjoyed high status and sometimes power as well. At this time elite women began to participate in politics. Because power was hereditary and patrilineal, a woman usually gained political influence due to her close association with a father, husband, or son. The private lives of monarchs became politicized, allowing the women closest to male leaders to claim prestige and authority by association.[75]

An extraordinary woman who lived in unusual times could sometimes gain power due to skill or charisma. Most often, however, women obtained power from being a daughter, wife, or mother. The link between kinship and power was not exclusively female. Until recently, patrilineal monarchy, with power passing down the male line of descent, was the most common system of government. This arrangement excluded women from the succession. Even so, a woman might still gain power from a kinship link to a ruler.

The role of queen differed in each time and place but few of them had formal authority.[76] The extent of a queen's powers depended on the nature of the political system as well as her own proclivities, skills, relationships, and resources. Even when a woman gained the ostensible right to exercise power, important men would often refuse to obey her because they did not like taking orders from a woman.[77] Because women found it difficult to rule directly, they usually had to pursue their goals obliquely, most often by influencing powerful men.[78]

Like kings, most queens and empresses were ordinary people who lacked special skills. Even if a queen had exceptional personal attributes such as intelligence, education, eloquence, beauty, or charisma, she could only use these advantages if conditions allowed her to do so.[79] Women had more opportunities to use their talents in the informal political systems of simple societies.[80] In ancient Japan, nobles in the nascent polity of Yamatai chose the female shaman Himiko as their ruler because of her skill in the "way of demons" (*guidao*).[81] Cherokee women participated in council meetings where important matters were decided.[82] Decision making among the Hazda, nomadic hunters and gatherers in northern Tanzania, is even more informal.[83] They do not have any clear leader or undertake systematic discussions. Instead, major actions emerge as the result of a series of ad hoc individual decisions. These sorts of informal systems allow competent women to exercise leadership.

In a complex state, a woman sometimes gained power when the system fell into chaos. Dynastic decline could thus facilitate a woman's rise to prominence. When institutions decayed, many people would support any competent leader, male or female, who could rescue the failing system. Ancient Egypt provides several examples of this sort of female power. During the nineteenth dynasty, King Seti II was succeeded by a sickly child, and his widow Tawoset became regent.[84] When the young pharaoh died, instead of putting a puppet on the throne and continuing her regency, Tawoset proclaimed herself king. Because the dynasty's institutions had fallen into decay, it was possible for her to rule in her own name.

Similarly in the Silla kingdom of ancient Korea, three women became rulers during periods of institutional weakness.[85] Each time a woman reigned as queen, it was because no man had the qualifications necessary to become the ruler. Silla had unusually strict rules governing the genealogical background of a rightful king. Occasionally no man had proper qualifications to ascend the throne so a woman assumed the position by default. Women attained power in this system due to institutional flaws. As bureaucracy developed in Korea, experienced professionals took over the government and they corrected these shortcomings. A stable political system gave women few openings to take control of the state.[86]

Some women became powerful by inheriting power from their fathers. Among men the right to rule usually passed from father to son. As people became accustomed to hereditary monarchy, they sometimes accepted a female ruler who inherited authority from her father.[87] Such was the case in seventeenth century Aceh when four sultanas reigned over the kingdom in succession.[88] All of them had the right bloodline and were deemed sufficiently talented for the role. However, elite men usually opposed putting a daughter on the throne as they did not want to weaken patrilineal succession.[89] Even if a woman inherited power, she usually had to marry as soon as possible as some essential activities could usually only be undertaken by a man. Most importantly, a female ruler usually needed a husband to go to war on her behalf and defend her lands. Yet, the subjects of a female ruler often opposed her marriage plans as they feared that her husband would usurp the male line of succession that she had temporarily interrupted.

Women sometimes gained power through marriage. However, powerful royal consorts were uncommon in world history as queens lacked high status in most cultures. Queens usually had very limited duties, and most were politically inactive. The king's spouse in ancient Egypt was typical. No more was expected of her than being a loyal wife and bearing a male heir to the throne.[90] In polygynous systems, royal wives usually had particularly low status.[91] But even if a monarch had only one wife, she rarely had any political authority.

When a king's wife had a hand in governance, it was often because she was married to an incompetent spouse. Such was the case with Caroline of Ansbach, wife of King George II of Great Britain.[92] George was foolish and mercurial while Caroline distinguished herself as intelligent, well-read, and observant. Unlike the king, she always carried herself regally in public. Caroline was so much more talented than her husband that she managed to commandeer some of his powers. However, this sort of situation was relatively rare.

A queen often came from a lofty family background so support from blood kinsmen could bolster her position. Kings in many places chose a queen from an exalted family to ally themselves with her father or brothers. In some cultures, a man could demand aid from the relatives of his mother or wife and they were morally obligated to honor this request.[93] At times this commitment was so strong that it came to be seen as a burden. In some African societies, the daughters of kings were not allowed to marry as the ruler feared that in-laws would make onerous demands. In each of China's dynasties, emperors chose spouses from different sorts of backgrounds. A wife with powerful kinsmen gave the ruler useful allies while an empress with modest parentage would usually not have family capable of threatening dynastic stability. Whatever the marriage strategy, Chinese emperors assumed that consort kinsmen might be a powerful political force, and they calculated their marriage links with this in mind.

A woman might also gain power for being the king's mother. Motherhood was usually a queen's most prestigious role, and it often overshadowed her identity as a monarch's wife. The tenth-century Byzantine empress Theodora exemplifies the royal consort who elevated herself within a theocratic system through her maternal role.[94] Theodora presented herself as not just an ideal mother but as an almost holy figure in the image of the Virgin Mary. She deployed Christian symbolism to imply that motherhood had sanctified her. Theodora realized that in the Byzantine system, the path to power lay not in being the wife of an emperor but rather in being the mother of one.

The influence of a royal mother varied according to the nature of the system and her specific circumstances. If the succession was ambiguous or contested, a queen could gain influence by placing her son on the throne. Agrippina, wife of the first-century Roman emperor Claudius, typifies the ambitious royal mother.[95] She convinced her husband to adopt Nero, her son from a prior marriage, thereby giving Nero a claim to the throne. Initially, Agrippina's strategy worked. As Nero became more prominent, her standing rose in tandem. And when Nero became emperor, everyone recognized his mother's hand in his ascent so initially she had a high profile. At first, Nero emphasized his association with his mother. As wife of the previous emperor, she provided the kinship link that legitimized his reign. But as Nero gained confidence, he felt that he no longer needed his mother and relations between the two became acrimonious. Eventually, Nero had his mother assassinated. As this case shows, if a ruler was an adult when he ascended the throne, he saw his mother as a potential rival and usually tried to limit her power.

In most monarchies, a mother gained power because her son was underage, allowing her to serve as regent. This practice is extremely ancient. In Egypt's First Dynasty, Queen Meritneith served as regent for her young son King Den during his minority.[96] It seems that she ruled as a de facto king as her tomb is the same size and style as those of the kings interred nearby. Women served as regents in many subsequent monarchies. In the Islamic world in particular, motherhood was the prime avenue for women to exercise power as the wives of Muslim rulers were rarely politically significant.[97] However, few female regents dared to depose the titular male ruler and take his place. A female usurper was bound to encounter strong resistance and would have to contend with an air of illegitimacy and a poor public image so few women dared to take this drastic step.

Some women excelled in war, and they used martial endeavors to gain prestige and authority. Historians have always been fascinated by warrior women. Cleopatra, Zenobia, and Boudicca all became legendary because of their fierceness.[98] Notably, however, all three of these warrior queens ultimately failed. In fact, failure was probably the key to their fame. Had they succeeded, traditional historians would have resented their transgressions and condemned them. Their ultimate destruction allowed male historians to safely praise their early victories.

Women usually fought not for glory but out of necessity. Dowager queens often had no choice but to become warriors to defend their rights and those of their underaged sons against potential usurpers.[99] Such was the case with Zenobia, third-century queen of Palmyra, who fought against Rome on behalf of her young son.[100] Sometimes a woman used warfare to achieve political goals. If successful, she could gain a reputation as a potent adversary, elevating herself in the eyes of those around her. Eleanor of Aquitaine participated in a crusade led by her husband King Louis VII.[101] She had wealthy and populous domains so a large portion of the French crusading army consisted of her vassals. Eleanor also provided much of the funds and supplies for this venture. Although the crusade failed, she won admiration as a devoted Christian. Likewise the wars of Queen Isabella of Castile against Muslims allowed her to portray herself as the sword of the Church.[102]

Sometimes a consort gained power because of her financial resources. In the African kingdom of Buganda, the ruler's mother and sisters had estates akin to fiefs.[103] Not only did these domains provide substantial income, but chiefs residing within these territories were subordinate to the women who possessed them. Similarly some European queens entered a royal marriage with their own hereditary title and domain giving them an identity, power base, and income independent of their spouse. Although wealth did not automatically bring political power, it could bolster a consort's influence. Queens often controlled a large income—sometimes the most important benefit of their position.

Wealth could be especially useful when a woman was cloistered. Such was usually the case with Muslim royal ladies. Although Queen Noor Jahan was the twentieth wife of the seventeenth-century Mughal emperor Jahangir, she became extraordinarily wealthy, making her unusually influential.[104] Noor Jahan owned a fleet of ships that conducted commerce with ports across the Middle East and East Africa. Dealers in her employ also traded with Portuguese, Dutch, and English merchants. Noor Jahan surrounded herself with luxuries and entertained on a grand scale. Yet, in spite of this affluence, when her husband died she immediately lost her position at court, left the capital, and lived a quiet and secluded life. The sudden end of her influence shows the limits of using wealth as a foundation for female power.

Sometimes an ambitious woman manipulated her public image to gain power. Queens often deliberately dressed opulently to flaunt their high position.[105] An intimidating appearance could astonish credulous onlookers, intimidate rivals, and gain the attention of powerful men. Particularly when a royal consort lacked a clearly defined political role, she might use a sumptuous appearance to gain power.

Queens could also participate in court ceremonies that emphasized their high position, charisma, or perhaps their sanctity.[106] Ceremonies were often what made a woman seem like a true queen. Weddings, coronations, and rituals of motherhood were often directed toward constructing the image of an ideal queen.[107] As the administration of European kingdoms became increasingly bureaucratic, women became politically marginalized. In response, queenship became increasingly ceremonial.[108] Processions and festivities kept the queen in the public eye and confirmed her as an important personage.

Another way for a consort to increase her influence was to portray herself as exceptionally virtuous. This tactic was especially useful in systems that forbade women from exercising authority publicly. Livia, the wife of Augustus, Rome's first emperor, employed this method to good effect.[109] Roman women customarily had few public roles, and any woman who promoted herself too conspicuously faced a backlash. Livia had many detractors who feared that she would use her husband's position to aggrandize herself. To circumvent their hostility, Livia presented herself as an embodiment of female virtue. Although wealthy, she spun thread and wove simple wool garments to prove her dedication to domestic virtue. She wore her hair in a homely style and avoided ostentatious clothing, jewels, and cosmetics. Propagandists working on her behalf also emphasized her fidelity and piety. Livia realized that in politics, appearance can be more important than reality. She assumed the role of an old-fashioned Roman matron and took care not to infringe on male prerogatives, influencing affairs in a low-key manner. Her strategy of self-effacement was highly effective and she became more important than any woman had been during the Roman Republic.

Religion could be particularly useful for ambitious women. Men usually regarded religion as an unthreatening realm of activity so they often allowed women to take the lead in pious endeavors. Demonstrations of religiosity provided women with opportunities to burnish their reputations and gain useful contacts. Female religious roles varied in each culture. The rise of Christianity significantly altered perceptions of queenship in the Mediterranean region.[110] Although people expected pagan Roman empresses to be pious, Christian queens took religiousness further and portrayed themselves as saintly figures. In the early fourth century, Helena, the mother of Emperor Constantine, set an example by making a pilgrimage to the Holy Land and enthusiastically promoting religion, setting down the template for the ideal Christian royal woman.[111] Henceforth, Christians expected queens to embody the ideals of their faith. Christian queens often cultivated an image similar to that of the Virgin Mary. A queen knew that if she seemed too secular, her subjects might dismiss her as insufficiently royal.

Religion allowed royal women to overcome some restrictions. The Muslim theologian al-Attar wrote, "When a woman becomes a 'man' in the Path to God, she is a man and one cannot any more call her a woman."[112] Many female rulers deliberately stressed religious activities more than their male counterparts to overcome the limitations placed on their sex. The Egyptian queen Hatchepsut, who called herself king, legitimized her unconventional reign by reviving archaic religious symbols that portrayed her gender in ambiguous ways.[113] Her emphasis on antiquated symbols distinguished her religious practices from those of male rulers of the same dynasty. Similarly, even though the famed Egyptian queen Nefertiti had no overt political role, her husband Akhenaten sponsored an unprecedented monotheistic religion, and she became prominent by participating in this new religion.[114] Nefertiti was not only presented as a living fertility symbol, she also took on the identity of the female element of the new official god Aten, allowing her to conduct ceremonies that had previously been reserved for kings.

When queens exercised power, they often used it differently than male rulers. It was rare for a woman to control the governing apparatus as female rulers were almost always seen as somewhat illegitimate. For this reason they tended to be extremely cautious. Most female reigns were notable for their conservatism.[115] In the eighteenth century, Empress Maria Theresa of Austria used her powers very warily.[116] She inherited the sprawling, multi-ethnic Hapsburg empire, which had become an anachronism in the age of nation states. To make matters worse, her spendthrift father had left her with an empty treasury. Maria Theresa resisted fashionable Enlightenment ideas and did not try to reform her empire. Her only goal was to hold it together in the face of rapidly changing circumstances. The advantages of her conservative approach can be seen by comparing her reign with that of her son Joseph.[117] When Joseph took over the reins of government, he instituted wide-reaching social, legal, economic, and administrative reforms, most notably the abolishment of serfdom. Although these measures seem admirable in retrospect, at the time they generated considerable controversy. Joseph was never as popular as his mother, and his reformist agenda gave rise to instability.

Maria Theresa's cautious approach to government resembled that of many other powerful women. She had grown up in a palace, and her sheltered upbringing made her unworldly. Moreover, as a woman she found it difficult to engage in many activities considered the preserve of men. Because of these drawbacks, she relied heavily on male advisors. Her father had surrounded himself with sycophants and mediocrities, and Maria Theresa learned from his mistakes. She chose talented officials and gave them her full backing so that they could be effective.[118]

Maria Theresa knew that she could not always behave straightforwardly. She could be extremely devious in pursuit of a goal. Sometimes she would confuse a person by treating him with favor and politeness only to suddenly turn on him in anger.[119] This seems to have been a deliberate strategy to keep potential enemies off balance. Queen Elizabeth I of England also knew how to dissemble. She used unpredictability as a weapon. Elizabeth infuriated her advisors by procrastinating and constantly changing her mind. Although many historians have interpreted her behavior as feminine caprice, this seems to have been a calculated strategy.[120] As a woman, Elizabeth feared being dominated by the powerful men around her. Her erratic behavior kept them disoriented so that could not threaten her position. Women sometimes tried to make up for their disadvantages by pursuing strategies that men found unfamiliar and misinterpreted as feminine weakness.

Many of the strategies covered in this global overview of female power apply to Chinese empresses as well. The situations faced by Chinese empresses were not unique or unusual. The ways that they gained and used power shared similarities with their counterparts in many other places. As elsewhere, kinship ties usually determined political position.[121] A woman's power did not derive from her personal qualities but from being the wife, mother, or daughter of an emperor—a man who held legitimate authority. The role of daughter connected a woman to a powerful family line through blood.

A princess usually did not inherit authority from her father because it passed down the male line of descent.[122] Instead, princesses were seen as tokens of the imperial house to be married off to outsiders. The marriage partners of princesses varied in each era. Occasionally an emperor married a daughter to a foreign ally. Native Chinese emperors detested marrying their daughters to foreigners, whom they viewed as cultural inferiors. Nevertheless, some married a daughter to a powerful khan to stabilize the borderlands. These sorts of marriages usually occurred when an emperor felt vulnerable.¹²³ Yet, because Chinese emperors disliked sending off a daughter to live among nomads, many so-called princesses were in fact not the daughters of emperors. A ruler often granted the title of princess to a female relative of the right age and married her off to a foreign leader to seal an alliance.¹²⁴

Most of these women had little influence with their husband's people. An exception was Princess Qianjin (d. 593), a cousin of a Northern Zhou emperor. After she married a Turkic quaghan, she involved herself in the politics of her new homeland.¹²⁵ This turned out to be a fatal mistake. When the Sui dynasty overthrew the Northern Zhou, Qianjin encouraged the Türks to fight against China. The Sui emperor sent her husband a message saying that he wanted her dead, and he dutifully killed his troublesome wife to placate China's new ruler.

More often emperors married off their daughters to domestic allies. The Liao dynasty, established by Khitan conquerors, had perhaps the most unusual marriage system of all the ruling houses.¹²⁶ The imperial line, surnamed Yelü, intermarried generation after generation with the Xiao, their consort kin. Due to repeated intermarriage between these two groups, a Liao emperor would marry one of his maternal relatives. He then married off his daughters to important men in the Xiao line, usually high officials. The Liao system linked status, marriage, and office more closely than any other dynasty. The Khitan seem to have developed this unusual system to reduce the power of the emperor's male relatives and prevent them from challenging him. As a side effect, daughters of the emperors ended up removed from positions where they might exercise authority. Although wealthy and privileged, they had no political power.¹²⁷

In most dynasties, emperors married their daughters to men from elite families. Medieval emperors usually selected sons-in-law from families with official and military backgrounds.¹²⁸ Princess marriage became particularly important during the Tang. Emperors of that dynasty married some princesses to foreign leaders to stabilize border regions.¹²⁹ They also used princess marriage to elevate the prestige of the ruling house.¹³⁰ The Shandong aristocracy looked down on the Tang emperors as parvenus and resisted marrying with the imperial line. In response to this snub, the emperors tried to create a new elite to replace the haughty Shandong families. They repeatedly married their daughters to men from elite families in the Guanlong region, elevating their marriage partners through displays of imperial favor. During the late Tang, the central government lost control over many regions so emperors used princess marriage to firm up ties between the center and periphery. As the imperial house weakened, they married off many princesses to local warlords.[131] Yet, in spite of having imperial parentage and important husbands, these women did not exert any notable authority. They merely served as symbols of the imperial house.

The early Tang era marked the height of princess power in China. At the beginning of the dynasty, princesses enjoyed immense privileges.[132] The palace dowered them with cash and luxury goods and they also received a regular income in coin, grain, and cloth, making them extremely wealthy. A princess did not deign to live in the same home with her husband, whom she considered a social inferior. Instead she resided in a mansion of her own built nearby. Prestige and wealth brought self-assurance. Early Tang princesses had a reputation for arrogance and independence, and some of them became involved in politics.

A few princesses gained power during a period of disorder brought on by contested imperial successions in the early Tang. The dynasty's founding emperor received valuable assistance from his daughter, the Pingyang princess. Pingyang was exceptionally competent and helped her father organize his campaigns. Other early Tang princesses gained power by allying with an empress to create a formidable faction. The Taiping princess supported her mother, Empress Wu, and the Anle princess was a partisan of the powerful Empress Wei. These two princesses belonged to opposing factions that battled for supremacy.[133] However, this adventure ended badly for both of them. Anle was killed and Taiping committed suicide.

After the deaths of these two princesses, Tang emperors reduced the standing of princesses, and thereafter these women had little involvement with politics. Subsequent dynasties went even further to ensure that emperors' daughters did not become politically significant. Song rulers restrained their daughters with stringent regulations.[134] Princesses also

Eighteenth-century woodblock print of the Pingyang Princess.
SOURCE: *PUBLIC DOMAIN*.

had lower social standing and much smaller incomes than before. Ming emperors took greater steps to curb the potential ambitions of princesses, marrying then to men of middling status.¹³⁵ After a princess left the palace, she did not receive any special privileges and lived an ordinary life. The Manchu emperors of the Qing dynasty married many of their daughters to frontier allies, Mongol nobility, or important figures in the Mongol and Chinese banners.¹³⁶ Although these women had important husbands, they do not seem to have had any political role. Overall, with the exception of a brief era in the early Tang, daughters of the emperors lacked power. In the Chinese political system, power did not descend from father to daughter.

As in other cultures, the role of wife sometimes empowered a woman by giving her a share of her husband's power. In China, however, even though an empress's title came from marriage, it did not imbue her with authority. The duties associated with this rank were ceremonial. The consort's attenuated role followed from society's view of marriage. During the Eastern Zhou era, marriage underwent ritualization.¹³⁷ According to the classical rites, society was to be organized as an interlocking series of hierarches, which meant a husband stood above his wife in rank.¹³⁸ The early imperial system integrated this ritual ideal and used it to justify positioning the emperor above the empress.¹³⁹

A Chinese empress rarely exercised authority while her spouse was on the throne. Some acted as advisors behind the scenes, affecting events indirectly through their counsel. If an emperor was weak or incapacitated, occasionally his empress would exercise power on his behalf. Most often, however, an empress gained power not by association with her spouse but from her blood kin.¹⁴⁰ She might work together with kinsmen to create a faction that could influence policy or even dominate the court. Consort kin were especially important during the Eastern Han dynasty. Thereafter, the relatives of empresses had influence only intermittently. The officialdom was highly conversant with history so they understood that the corruption and arrogance of Han consort kin had corrosive results. The insightful Qing dynasty historian Zhao Yi summed up this view when he noted that the inflated privileges of Han empresses and their kinsmen repeatedly led to catastrophe.[141] The officials and rulers of subsequent dynasties took this lesson to heart and instituted measures to keep consort kin in check, depriving empresses of their most important power base.

Almost all of the most powerful women in Chinese history were empresses dowager. Their power stemmed from the Chinese kinship system. A wife may have been subordinate to her husband, but a mother was superior to her son. In consequence, even when a consort's husband was still alive, she often presented herself as a mother and not a wife.[142] Chinese empresses dowager did not remarry so many of them spent much of their lives in widowhood. After an emperor's death, the link between his widow and the new emperor sometimes provided an opportunity for her to gain power.

An empress usually received the rank of empress dowager even if she was not the new ruler's mother. Sometimes the succeeding emperor was her son. Most often, however, he had been born to another woman in the harem and raised by nursemaids. Yet, according to custom, a son born to a concubine was considered the offspring of the official wife so an emperor would usually recognize the empress dowager as his mother even if he had been born to another woman.[143]

If dynastic rules did not mandate primogeniture, then after an emperor died the dowager often selected a successor from among his kinsmen. An ambitious dowager would elevate a child or weakling to the throne so that she could dominate the state. During some dynasties, if the emperor was a minor, the empress dowager could serve as formal regent.[144] Sometimes an unusually aggressive dowager managed to maintain her regency after the child emperor reached adulthood.[145]

From the fourth century onward it was usually considered immodest for an empress dowager to appear publicly at court, so a female regent would sit hidden behind a curtain positioned in back of the emperor.[146] Despite this show of reserve, regents could be very high-handed. Some bullied or even dethroned an emperor and so they had a poor reputation.[147] Over time, emperors set down dynastic rules that discouraged or prohibited female regencies.

INTRODUCTION

The identity of mother and son have always been closely intertwined in China. During the Shang dynasty, the rank of the mother had a major bearing on that of her son.[148] Shang kings often had several sons, and their mothers' relative backgrounds seem to have been important in determining the royal succession. During the subsequent Zhou era, the situation reversed. Under the Zhou ritual code, the status of the son determined that of his mother. The *Zuo Tradition* (*Zuozhuan*) and *Gongyang Tradition* (*Gongyang zhuan*) both specified that the rank of the mother accorded with that of her son.[149] This principle referred primarily to widows because a married woman shared the honor of her husband's rank.[150] Determining a widow's status by her son's rank became standard for the remainder of imperial history.[151] Because a widowed mother's rank was determined by that of her son, it was in her interest to ensure his success. Helping a son attain power was a prime strategy for a palace woman to elevate her own position.

The ritual canon set down conflicting principles regarding the relation between mother and son. Various texts describe a schema called the Three Obediences (or Thrice Following; *san cong*) which asserted that a woman should obey her father when young, her husband after getting married, and her son during widowhood.[152] This directive became integrated into Confucian discourse. During the Song dynasty, Neo-Confucians put great emphasis on these moral obligations.[153] Even so, this schema was usually wishful thinking. It was usually impossible for a widow to obey her son as he was likely still a minor when his father died. In reality, most widowed mothers expected obedience from their sons.

Because filial piety governed relations between mothers and sons, this virtue also served as a foundation of female power. Veneration of mothers was certainly not unique to imperial China. Mothers and children share a special bond in every society. However, the Chinese intensified and canonized this relationship. The mother was not just loved or respected but glorified as almost saintly, so her children were morally obligated to obey her. The amplification of filial piety bolstered the power of the maternal figure, providing a potent ideology that allowed some empress dowagers to overcome the limits of gender hierarchy.[154]

INTRODUCTION

Filial piety developed out of the ancient ancestral cult.[155] People reasoned that because they revered their ancestors, they ought to show similar respect to living elders as well. Although this ethic began as the son's obedience to his father, by the Western Zhou era it had been extended to mothers.[156] In fact, many sons demonstrated more enthusiastic devotion to mothers than fathers. Several passages in the *Classic of Poetry* (*Shijing*) express this sort of sentiment, mentioning that soldiers away on a campaign felt concern for the well-being of the mothers that they left behind.[157] Writers regularly declared that a mother ought to receive respect, obedience, and attention from her offspring, making filial piety the basic principle ordering relations between mother and son.[158] Philosophers accentuated this virtue by integrating it into larger ethical systems. Mencius repeatedly highlighted the importance of filial piety and declared it the wellspring of other virtues.[159] And the *Classic of Filial Piety* (*Xiaojing*) extended this obligation to the realm of government by comparing the bond between parent and child to that of ruler and minister.[160]

Ancient authorities usually specified that even though a child owed devotion to both parents, the father took precedence.[161] Yet, despite these injunctions, emotion led many sons to show more consideration to their mothers.[162] Mourning practices provide evidence for the intensity of bonds with each parent. Han dynasty records describe far more passionate mourning for mothers than fathers.[163] Sons seem to have mourned their father in a perfunctory way out of duty while extravagantly mourning their mother to express sincere gratitude. The raw emotionalism of mourning for mothers made it seem authentic and hence more virtuous than obligatory paternal obsequies.

During the Six Dynasties era, mourning for mothers reached an extreme, giving rise to a cult of motherhood.[164] Some mourners went far beyond the bounds of ritual propriety. They thought it necessary to exhibit extravagant grief to prove their sincerity. One man did not drink anything for six days after his mother died.[165] Another abandoned his wife and children so that he could devote himself fully to mourning his mother.[166] Although this sort of behavior seems absurd from a modern perspective, such a strong commitment to filial piety had practical functions. In an era of war, chaos, and poverty, people relied on a small number of key virtues, including filial piety, to stabilize and organize society.[167] The *Classic of Filial Piety* was widely venerated, and scholars analyzed it in detail.[168] It became a standard feature of the curricula that crown princes studied to prepare them morally to serve as monarchs.[169] Reverence for the *Classic of Filial Piety* shaped perceptions of ideal relations between mothers and sons. Up until the end of imperial history, the authors of histories and gazetteers celebrated men who undertook heavy sacrifices to serve or honor their mothers.[170]

The Tang government used the law to enforce filial behavior.[171] Tang rulers recognized the allure of filial piety as a political ideology so they promoted it to legitimize their reign and attract support.[172] The Tang state mandated stringent filial behavior. Whereas classical ritual required only a year of mourning for one's mother in contrast to three years of mourning for a father, Empress Wu Zetian extended the mourning period for mothers to match that for fathers.[173] This innovation eventually became standard. Tang law even made it mandatory for an official to leave office and undertake three years of mourning for a deceased parent.[174] The code made filial behavior a legal obligation, and people who failed to treat their parents properly could be punished.[175] A mother even gained the right to sue a disobedient child.[176] Amplification of the ideology of filial piety had an enormous impact on politics. The obedience that sons owed their mother gave Chinese empresses dowager an advantage rarely seen in other political systems.

China also stands out from most other cultures in that consorts held a formal title. Titles can be important as they not only convey rank but can also serve as tools of empowerment. In China, the title of empress dowager advertised the high status of the emperor's widow. The reigning emperor usually treated the empress dowager as his de facto mother or grandmother even if there was no blood connection, obligating him to defer to her at least in ritual.

Unlike China, most societies lacked a special title for a king's spouse or mother. Early civilizations were usually patrilineal monarchies that institutionalized authority in the king's person.[177] The king's wife usually did not receive any special designation. This inequity in nomenclature grew out of the patriarchal organization of early society. Although male identity was intertwined with organizations and activities within the larger community, women usually remained tied to family and lineage.[178] In consequence, most ancient peoples did not consider a king's spouse worthy of a title of her own. Ancient records mention surprisingly few reigning queens. Most were mythological characters. The rest usually appeared during the early stages of a state's political formation.[179] As a monarchy became more organized, power came to be passed down the male line of descent.

In most monarchies, the king's wife did not receive a title akin to *queen*. Her identity was defined according to her relationship with the king so she might be called "king's wife" or "king's mother."[180] The English word "queen" comes from the Anglo-Saxon word *cwén*, which originally just meant a woman or wife.[181] From earliest times, the wives of kings usually lacked a special title. Ancient Egyptian texts did not refer to the king's spouse as a queen but called her king's wife or god's wife.[182] However, the Egyptian king's mother had a higher position than his wife, and she received a special title, implying that she outranked her son's spouse.[183] Likewise, in the Mughal Empire the highest title did not go to the ruler's wife. Instead, one woman at a time, usually the emperor's mother or sister, might receive the title *padishah begum*, which she held for the rest of her life.[184]

Because the title or position of queen was usually not associated with rulership, women who reigned often called themselves kings rather than referring to themselves by a specific female designation. In a system where women were traditionally barred from ruling, a woman might even symbolically transform herself into a man to become eligible for leading the state. Because ancient Egyptian consorts lacked a title or specified political role, the few women who gained control of the state called themselves kings. Hatchepsut took control of the government by serving as regent then decided to rule in her own name. To do so she assumed the titles used for kings and underwent a kingly coronation ceremony.[185] Sometimes Hatchepsut even wore male clothing and a false beard as these were the standard accoutrements of Egyptian kingship. The practice of calling powerful women *kings* was not limited to antiquity.

Hatchepsut with a false beard.
SOURCE: *PUBLIC DOMAIN*.

INTRODUCTION

Hungarians only recognized the authority of kings, not queens, so Maria Theresa was crowned king of Hungary even though she was married to an emperor.[186] Likewise Christina of Sweden reigned as a king because the nobility and parliament would not accept the authority of a queen.[187]

In languages that have a term equivalent to "queen," the meaning is often ambiguous. In English, "queen" can refer to either the king's wife or a woman who rules. But Korean distinguishes these roles with different words.[188] The title of most queens emphasized their position as the king's spouse. However, the nature of the queen consort was vague compared to the king. She was identified not as an independent personage but as the king's appendage.[189] Sometimes a queen had a special title. The wives of many Roman emperors were called *augusta*, which sounded grand but did not come with any special role or powers.[190] An *augusta* was somewhat like a modern first lady, enjoying prestige but lacking authority. After the fall of the Roman Empire in the west, rulers' spouses lacked a title. Only around the year 1100 did Europeans begin to call king's wives "queens." Women who received this title underwent a coronation ceremony, and they dressed and behaved in ways calculated to distinguish them from other women.[191]

Because so few monarchies had special titles and roles for the wives of kings, it is significant that China had specific terms for queen, empress, empress dowager, and various minor spouses and concubines. Originally the consorts of the Shang kings lacked a special title, in line with ancient monarchies in other parts of the world. Subsequently the Zhou kings gave their wives the title *hou*.[192] Although the first emperor Qin Shihuang does not seem to have granted any of his consorts a special title, at the beginning of the Han dynasty Emperor Gaozu gave his wife the title *huanghou* (empress), parallel to his own title *huangdi* (emperor). Although not all subsequent rulers designated a consort as empress, more often than not the emperor's primary wife received this title. This convention became associated with orthodox institutions of government such that a historian who wanted to convey a regime's illegitimacy could refer to the ruler's wife as *furen* (lady) rather than *huanghou* (empress).[193]

As in many cultures, the mother of a Chinese emperor received a special title. The identity of these *huang taihou* (empresses dowager) varied.

Introduction

Some had been the empress of the previous emperor and the mother of the current ruler. Other dowagers had previously been empress but were not the successor's mother. The fiction that children born to concubines belonged to the official wife obligated rulers to treat their father's spouse as their true mother. Sometimes a woman who had not been empress but had given birth to the reigning emperor was declared empress dowager. An empress dowager held her title permanently, so if several emperors died in quick succession there could simultaneously be several empresses dowagers in the palace, an awkward situation that often led to conflict. The senior empress dowager, such as the ruler's grandmother, might be distinguished from lesser dowagers with the title *taihuang taihou*. Due to the unusually strong bond between mother and son and the ideology of filial piety, the title of empress dowager had imposing connotations. It institutionalized a woman's position in the upper reaches of the state and gave her a platform that she could use to legitimize claims to power.

Notes

1. Monter, *The Rise of Female Kings in Europe*, 2–4, 23.
2. The ancient English queen Boudicca exemplifies how a powerful woman could be forgotten, revived, and mythologized. For centuries Boudicca was rarely discussed then suddenly she assumed a prominent place in histories written during the Victorian era. Johnson, *Boudicca*, 109–37.
3. The *Historia Augusta* gives an idealized depiction of Queen Zenobia of Palmyra. The author of this work implicitly compared her to Emperor Gallienus to make him look incompetent in comparison. Southern, *Empress Zenobia*, 10–11.
4. Scott, "Gender: A Useful Category of Historical Analysis," 1067–69.
5. Whyte, *The Status of Women in Preindustrial Societies*, 95.
6. Schlegel, *Male Dominance and Female Authority*, 23.
7. Earle and Kristiansen, "Introduction," 8.
8. Paderni, "Between Constraints and Opportunities," 258; Erler and Kowaleski, "Introduction: A New Economy of Power Relations," 3.
9. Earenfight, "Highly Visible, Often Obscured," 89.
10. Sweely, "Introduction," 1.
11. Service, *Origins of the State and Civilization*, xiii.
12. Lenski, *Power and Privilege*, 15–17.
13. Parker and Parker, "The Myth of Male Superiority," 300.
14. Crumley, "A Dialectical Critique of Hierarchy," 157. For some definitions of power used by anthropologists see Endicott, "The Conditions of Egalitarian Male-Female

INTRODUCTION

Relationships," 1; Herdt, "Sexual Repression, Social Control, and Gender Hierarchy in Sambia Culture," 193–211; Kent, "Egalitarianism, Equality, and Equitable Power," 32.

15. Wolf, "Distinguished Lecture: Facing Power," 586, 593.
16. Erler and Kowaleski, "Introduction," in *Women and Power in the Middle Ages*, 1–2.
17. Levin and Meyer, "Women and Political Power in Early Modern Europe," 342.
18. Weber, *Economy and Society: An Outline of Interpretive Sociology*; Weber, *The Theory of Social and Economic Organization*.
19. This view has influenced gendered models of power. Schlegel, "Toward a Theory of Sexual Stratification," 8–9.
20. Fried, *The Evolution of Political Society*, 31.
21. Eisenberg, "Weberian Patrimonialism and Imperial Chinese History," 83–102.
22. Barnes, *The Nature of Power*, 6, 55, 57.
23. Earle, *How Chiefs Come to Power*, 3–4.
24. Earle, *How Chiefs Come to Power*, 7–8.
25. Earle, *How Chiefs Come to Power*, 8–10.
26. Ortner, "Gender Hegemonies," 78.
27. Mair, *Primitive Government*, 61, 65.
28. Miller, "The Anthropology of Sex and Gender Hierarchies," 7.
29. Rogers, "Female Forms of Power," 728–31, 735, 745.
30. Schlegel, "Toward a Theory of Sexual Stratification," 7–8.
31. Ortner, "Gender Hegemonies," 42.
32. Tang dynasty authorities asserted that the ruler's father is heaven and his mother is earth. Liu, *Jiu Tang shu*, 23:893.
33. Earle, *How Chiefs Come to Power*, 4, 6–7, 13.
34. Lenski, *Power and Privilege*, 46, 85.
35. Benedict, *Patterns of Culture*, 26. Walby, "Theorizing Patriarchy," 213–34, describes the basic qualities of patriarchy and summarizes the most important theories about it. Lerner, *The Creation of Patriarchy*, 37, stresses that patriarchy did not have a single cause. It arose for a variety of reasons so it was manifested somewhat differently in each place.
36. Goodenough, *Description and Comparison in Cultural Anthropology*, 18; Parker and Parker, "The Myth of Male Superiority," 291–92.
37. Blondel, *World Leaders*, 116.
38. Fried, *The Evolution of Political Society*, 27–28, 33–34; Flanagan, "Hierarchy in Simple 'Egalitarian' Societies," 245–66.
39. For some examples of highly egalitarian societies see Kent, "Egalitarianism, Equality, and Equitable Power," 38. Endicott, "The Conditions of Egalitarian Male-Female Relationships," 1–10, notes that many foraging societies are egalitarian. Cashdan, "Egalitarianism among Hunters and Gatherers," 116–20, argues that egalitarianism persists over the long term in societies facing severe economic constraints such as hunter-gatherers.
40. Erdal and Whiten, "On Human Egalitarianism," 177.
41. Endicott, "The Conditions of Egalitarian Male-Female Relationships," 1–2.
42. Service, *Origins of the State and Civilization*, 50, 53.
43. Fried, *The Evolution of Political Society*, 82–83.
44. Leacock, "Women's Status in Egalitarian Society," 228.

INTRODUCTION

45. Kent, "Sharing in an Egalitarian Kalahari Community," 488–90.
46. McDowell, "Competitive Equality in Melanesia," 181.
47. Crumley, "Three Locational Models," 141–73; Crumley, "Heterarchy and the Analysis of Complex Societies," 1–6; Brumfiel, "Heterarchy and the Analysis of Complex Societies: Comments," 125–31; Rattan, "Hierarchy and Heterarchy in the American Southwest, 325–33. Marcus and Feinman, "Introduction," 11, notes that heterarchy persisted as societies developed into states. Archaic states were both hierarchical and heterarchical. For a detailed description of a heterarchal society see Estioko-Griffin and Griffin, "Woman the Hunter: The Agta," 136, 140.
48. Trigger, *Understanding Early Civilizations*, 187.
49. Lyons and D'Andrea, "Griddles, Ovens, and Agricultural Origins," 517.
50. Levy, "Heterarchy in Bronze Age Denmark," 41–53; Levy, "Gender, Power, and Heterarchy in Middle-Level Societies," 62–78.
51. Hinsch "The Origins of Separation of the Sexes," 595–616; Hinsch, "Textiles and Female Virtue," 170–202.
52. Flanagan, "Hierarchy in Simple 'Egalitarian' Societies," 254, 257–59.
53. Kellogg, "The Woman's Room," 563.
54. Wiessner, "The Vines of Complexity," 233–34; Lenski, *Power and Privilege*, 119; Kent, "Does Sedentarization Promote Gender Inequality?" 513–36, discuss the reasons why societies become unequal.
55. Hamilton, "Patriarchy, Patrimonialism, and Filial Piety," 77–104.
56. Brunton, "The Cultural Instability of Egalitarian Societies," 673–74, 677–78; Woodburn, "Egalitarian Societies," 431–51.
57. Gray and Wolf, "Height and Sexual Dimorphism," 441–56.
58. Abbie, "Metric Characteristics of Adult Aborigines," 76–103.
59. Harris, "The Evolution of Human Gender Hierarchies," 57.
60. Goldberg, *The Inevitability of Patriarchy*.
61. Harris, "The Evolution of Human Gender Hierarchies," 57–79; Zihlman, "Sex Differences and Gender Hierarchies," 33–34.
62. Divale and Harris, "Population, Warfare, and the Male Supremacist Complex," 521, 524.
63. Macintosh, Pinhasi, and Stock, "Prehistoric Women's Manual Labor."
64. Sun, "Henan Mianchi Duzhong yizhi," 93.
65. Colarelli, Spranger, and Hechanova, "Women, Power, and Sex Composition," 173.
66. Schlegel, "Toward a Theory of Sexual Stratification," 5–7.
67. Parker and Parker, "The Myth of Male Superiority," 300.
68. Engels, *The Origin of the Family*, 67–71.
69. Schlegel, "Toward a Theory of Sexual Stratification," 32–33.
70. Hinsch, *Women in Early Imperial China*, 143–67.
71. Ahern, "The Power and Pollution of Chinese Women," 269–90; Jiang, "Nüti yu zhanzheng," 159–87. For a non-Chinese example see Perdue, *Cherokee Women*, 29–30.
72. Langness, "Sexual Antagonism in the New Guinea Highlands," 162.
73. Nash, "The Aztecs and the Ideology of Male Dominance," 349–62; McCorriston, "The Fiber Revolution," 517; Rohrlich, "State Formation in Sumer," 76–77, 83–84.

74. Fairchilds, *Women in Early Modern Europe*, 5; Trigger, *Understanding Early Civilizations*, 271.
75. Freisenbruch, *Caesar's Wives*, 41.
76. Huneycutt, "Queenship Studies Come of Age," 13. O'Callaghan, "The Many Roles of the Medieval Queen, 21–32, discusses some of the roles that queens used to exercise power.
77. The vassals of Eleanor of Aquitaine refused to take orders from a woman. Eventually, her husband King Henry had to march on Maine to punish barons who refused to obey her. Weir, *Eleanor of Aquitaine*, 165, 167.
78. St. John, *Three Medieval Queens*, 12–13.
79. Farenfight, *Queenship in Medieval Europe*, 26.
80. Trocolli, "Women Leaders in Native North American Societies," 49–61.
81. Kidder, *Himiko and Japan's Elusive Chiefdom of Yamatai*, 16, 131–32.
82. Perdue, *Cherokee Women*, 55.
83. Woodburn, "Minimal Politics," 253.
84. Tyldesley, *Chronicle of the Queens of Egypt*, 163–66.
85. Kim, *Women of Korea*, 25–26, 28.
86. Farenfight, *Queenship in Medieval Europe*, 121; St. John, *Three Medieval Queens*, 10–12.
87. Downey, *Isabella*, 1, 132, 135–37, 372–73; Gibbon, *The Decline and Fall of the Roman Empire*, 2:1030.
88. Ozay, "Women as Rulers Phenomenon in Southeast Asian Islamic Society," 142–51.
89. Monter, *The Rise of Female Kings in Europe*, 21.
90. Tyldesley, *Chronicle of the Queens of Egypt*, 9.
91. Mair, *Primitive Government*, 211.
92. Dennison, *The First Iron Lady*, 1, 99.
93. Mair, *Primitive Government*, 212–13.
94. Kotsis, "Empress Theodora," 11–36.
95. Freisenbruch, *Caesar's Wives*, 116–28.
96. Tyldesley, *Chronicle of the Queens of Egypt*, 33–34.
97. For example, under the Ottoman system sultans had only one son by each wife. Each son was sent off to a distant posting while still quite young. His mother accompanied him and acted as a kind of regent. While young, the boy was merely a figurehead and his mother managed his affairs. If she handled matters well, he might eventually become sultan when his father died. After the son became sultan, sometimes the mother continued to have a political role as a trusted advisor. For some examples of this arrangement see Freely, *Inside the Seraglio*, 56, 60, 62, 86–87, 91–92, 118–21; Mikhail, *God's Shadow*, 86. In the Mughal system, mothers sometimes played an analogous role. All of the sons of Emperor Babur, founder of the Mughal dynasty, wanted to inherit his throne. During the succession struggle, each claimant was supported by his mother. Mukhoty, *Daughters of the Sun*, 2–3, 20.
98. Southern, *Empress Zenobia*, 1.
99. Toler, *Women Warriors*, 65.

100. Southern, *Empress Zenobia*, 3–4.
101. Weir, *Eleanor of Aquitaine*, 48, 51.
102. Downey, *Isabella*, 145–46, 188.
103. Mair, *Primitive Government*, 211.
104. Mukhoty, *Daughters of the Sun*, 140–44, 152.
105. For example, Downey, *Isabella*, 298–99.
106. Farenfight, *Queenship in Medieval Europe*, 242, 253.
107. Kosior, *Becoming a Queen in Early Modern Europe*.
108. Farenfight, *Queenship in Medieval Europe*, 253; St. John, *Three Medieval Queens*, 10–12.
109. Dennison, *Livia*, 40–41, 93, 102, 184, 266, 268; Freisenbruch, *Caesar's Wives*, 24–27, 76, 90.
110. Farenfight, *Queenship in Medieval Europe*, 74–75.
111. Freisenbruch, *Caesar's Wives*, 221–23.
112. Roded, *Women in Islamic Biographical Collections*, 101.
113. Ratié, *La reine Hatchepsout*, 311–12, 314–15.
114. Tyldesley, *Nefertiti: Egypt's Sun Queen*, 3, 4, 80.
115. Salisbury, *Rome's Christian Empress*, 146.
116. Crankshaw, *Maria Theresa*.
117. Crankshaw, *Maria Theresa*, 300, 306, 318.
118. Crankshaw, *Maria Theresa*, 6, 35, 62.
119. Crankshaw, *Maria Theresa*, 67, 103.
120. Bassnett, *Elizabeth I*, 7–9, 120–21.
121. Rosenlee, *Confucianism and Women*, 47.
122. This practice dates back to high antiquity. Chen, "Cong qingtongqi mingwen," 36–38, examines bronze inscriptions that document the marriages of Zhou royal princesses to the nobles of various states.
123. Holmgren, "A Question of Strength," 31–86.
124. For an example, see Wei, *Suishu*, 4:86.
125. Wright, "A Chinese Princess Bride's Life and Activism," 39–48.
126. Shimada, *Ryōdai shakaishi kenkyū*, 182–89; Holmgren, "Marriage, Kinship and Succession," 44–91; Shi, *Liaochao houzu zhu wenti yanjiu*; Liu and Hu, "Liaodai hunyin zhuangkuang qianxi," 140–44.
127. The lavish tombs of Liao princesses attest to their wealth and privilege. Liaoning Sheng Wenwu Kaogu Yanjiusuo, "Liaoning Fuxin xian Liaodai Pingyuan Gongzhu mu," 46–65; Zhang, "Liaodai Chengguo Gongzhu fuma hezangmu," 45–49.
128. Huang, *Gongzhu zhengzhi*, 208–311.
129. Hayashi, "Nanshō ōken no kakuritsu," 57–87. The Tang emperors continued to employ a Sui dynasty strategy in this regard. Hirata, "Shū Zui kakumei to Tokketsu jōsei," 27–56.
130. Chen and Qu, "Luexi Tangdai gongzhu," 93–97; Wang, "Tangdai Jingzhao Wei-shi," 109–12.
131. Sun, "Luelun Tangdai gongzhu," 18–19.

132. Liu, *Jiu Tang shu*, 107:3266; Guo, "Tangdai gongzhu," 71–73; Li, "Tangdai gongzhu," 25–28.

133. Liu, *Jiu Tang shu*, 183:4738–39; Wang, "Lun Tangdai gongfu shezheng," 67–70.

134. Zhuang, "Songdai gongzhu quanli," 14–18.

135. Soullière, "Palace Women in the Ming Dynasty," 300; Zhang, "Mingdai gongzhu hunyin," 67–71.

136. Lü, "Man Meng lianhun yu Qingdai bianjiang," 65–73.

137. He, "Chunqiu shiqi hunyin tedian zhi tanjiu," 75. During the Tang, an emperor was supposed to follow the six rites of a proper wedding set down in the ancient ritual canon. Liu, *Jiu Tang shu*, 21:817.

138. Memorial and edicts often described this relationship in metaphysical terms. Ban, *Hanshu*, 8:251; Liu, *Jiu Tang shu*, 27:1027. It was also described in terms of Confucian ethical propriety. Van Norden, *Mengzi*, 118; Fang, *Jinshu*, 19:579; Li, *Beishi*, 2:72; Liu, *Handai hunyin zhidu*, 7.

139. Ban, *Hanshu*, 30:1710. To emphasize the idea that the relationship of emperor and empress was based on ritual propriety, aspects of the ruler's wedding ceremony often deliberately conformed with archaic classical rites. Shen, *Songshu*, 14:336–39; Liu, *Jiu Tang shu*, 21:817.

140. Wang, *Zhongguo gongting zhengzhi*, 143–64, describes the general characteristics of consort kin.

141. Zhao, *Nianer shi zhaji*, 3:40, 4:57. Linghu, *Zhoushu*, 9:149, expresses similar views.

142. Li, *Bei Qi shu*, 11:144; Ouyang, *Xin Tang shu*, 125:5718; Tuo, *Songshi*, 197:9884.

143. Under the Zhou dynasty *zongfa* kinship system, the sons of concubines were not considered offspring of the official wife and they had lower status and fewer inheritance rights than sons of the wife. Gao, "Zhoudai zongfa zhidu xia de 'mudi,'" 41–47. During the Zhou, there was a clear distinction between wife and concubines, and the sons of each had different statuses and inheritance rights. Zheng, *Shanggu Huaxia funü yu hunyin*, 162–63. After the end of the Zhou, the sons of concubines were considered the offspring of mothers in both the palace and society at large. Liu, "Wei Jin Nanbeichao shidai de qie," 22–23; Liao, *Tangdai de muzi guanxi*, 155; Ebrey, "Concubines in Song China," 44; Zhang, *Mingdai jiachan jiching*, 84. During the Qing, princes born to imperial concubines did not consider the empress their mother even though this was customary in society at large. This was probably because the statuses of imperial concubines and the empress were closer than in most dynasties. Rawski, "Ch'ing Imperial Marriage," 172–73.

144. Bielenstein, "The Six Dynasties, Volume 2," 24–28, gives an overview of female regency.

145. For example, Emperor Song Yingzong suffered from bad health and psychological problems so Empress Dowager Cao served as regent. Ji, *Politics and Conservatism in Northern Song China*, 77–78.

146. McMahon, *Women Shall Not Rule*, 147.

147. Cutter, "Sex, Politics, and Morality at the Wei (220–265) Court," 106–13, explores the case of an emperor dethroned on the authority of an empress dowager. For an example of a empress dowager bully see Fang, *Jinshu*, 2:27–28.

148. Wang, "Rank and Power among Court Ladies at Anyang," 97, 110.

149. Du and Kong, *Chunqiu zuozhuan zhengyi*, 3:51.1 (Yin year 3), 18:306.1 (Wen year 4), 19:311.2 (Wen year 5), 29:503.1 (Xiang year 4); Gongyang, *Chongkan Songben Gongyang zhushu fojiao kanji*, 1:11.2 (Yin year 1), 3:35.1 (Yin year 5).

150. The principle that the rank of a mother followed that of her adult son could become problematic when a son's rank exceeded that of his father. In such a case, his mother's rank would be higher than that of his father. For example, Mencius mourned his mother more lavishly than his father. This is because his official rank had increased after the death of his father so he conducted mourning for each parent appropriate to his rank at the time. Van Norden, *Mengzi*, 31–32. As a result of this inconsistency, some people began to argue that a father's rank should also follow that of the son. However there was never a definitive solution to this quandary. Zheng, *Qin en nan bao*, 39–41.

151. For some examples see Ban, *Hanshu*, 11:355; Shen, *Songshu*, 15:397, 15:409, 55:1543; Ouyang, *Xin Tangshu*, 24:530. Cen, *Tangdai huanmen funü yanjiu*, 235–36, discusses this concept as it was understood during the Tang dynasty.

152. Liu, *Handai hunyin zhidu*, 21, and Wu, *Handai nüxing lijiao yanjiu*, 21–22, explain the origins of this idea.

153. Diao and Wang, "Xiaodao yu wangchang de boni," 107–13.

154. Hill, "Imperial Women and the Ideology of Womanhood," 82–83, 93–94; Gao, *Zuozhuan nüxing yanjiu*, 41–44.

155. Kang, *Xian Qin xiaodao yanjiu*; Knapp, "The Ru Reinterpretation of Xiao," 200–202; Pines, *Foundations of Confucian Thought*, 187–99.

156. Cook and Goldin, *A Source Book*, 69, 141–42.

157. Waley, *The Book of Songs*, 95 (Mao 121), 134 (Mao 162), 158–59 (Mao 185); Karlgren, *The Book of Odes*, 78–79, 105, 127.

158. Zhou, *Festivals, Feasts, and Gender*, 242.

159. Van Norden, *Mengzi*, 98, 101.

160. Rosemont and Ames, *The Chinese Classic of Family Reverence*, 110.

161. Rosemont and Ames, *The Chinese Classic of Family Reverence*, 107.

162. Shimomi, *Bosei izon no shisō* explores the psychological dependence of sons upon their mothers.

163. Brown, *The Politics of Mourning in Early China*, 66, 72–75.

164. Zheng, *Qinggan yu zhidu*, 21–114; Zheng, "Zhonggu shiqi de muni guanxi," 157–63, 181–86.

165. Yao, *Liangshu*, 22:354.

166. Shen, *Songshu*, 92:2263.

167. Ochi, *Gi Shin nanchō no hito to shakai*, 41–46.

168. Zhu, "Lun Wei Jin liuchao shiqi de *Xiaojing* yanjiu," 97–101; Yoshikawa, *Liuchao jingshen shi yanjiu*, 419–35.

169. For example, Yao, *Liangshu*, 7:165; and Liu, *Jiu Tangshu*, 4:65.

170. Ouyang, *Xin Tangshu*, 195:4491, 5579–80, 5583.

171. Liu, *Jiu Tang shu*, 149:4031–32. Thinkers debated the relationship between filial piety and other virtues. Ochi, *Gi Shin Nanchō no kizoku sei*, 359–68.

172. Ji, "Shilun Tangdai de 'xiaozhi,'" 74–78.

173. Kutcher, *Mourning in Late Imperial China*, 36–37; Lu, "Chu Tang yanchang wei wangmu shouxiao qi yundong, 53–68.

174. Luo, *Tongju gongcai*, 490–502.

175. Qian, *Tang lü yanjiu*, 309–10; Jin, "Tangdai hunyin jiating jicheng falü zhidu chulun," 126–28; Liu, "Cong falü jiufen kan Songdai de fuquan jiazhangzhi, 483–556.

176. Zhang, "Tangdai de nüxing yu susong," 36–39; Yanagita, "Sōdai saiban ni okeru josei no soshō," 9–10.

177. Hallpike, *The Principles of Social Evolution*, 282; Trigger, *Understanding Early Civilizations*, 73.

178. Sullivan, "Those Men in the Mounds," 101–26; Boudreaux, "Mound Construction and Community Changes," 212.

179. Rohrlich, "State Formation in Sumer," 84.

180. Toler, *Women Warriors*, 82.

181. Stachurska, "Semantic Meanderings of Queen in Lexographic Perspective," 173.

182. Flannery and Marcus, *The Creation of Inequality*, 417.

183. Sabbahy, "The King's Mother in the Old Kingdom," 305–10.

184. Mukhoty, *Daughters of the Sun*, xix, 7.

185. Tyldesley, *Hatchepsut*, 1, 47, 98, 106, 117. The lesser-known female ruler Sobeknefru of the twelfth dynasty also reigned as a king. Tyldesley, *Chronicle of the Queens of Egypt*, 74–75, 78.

186. Crankshaw, *Maria Theresa*, 70–71.

187. Buckley, *Christina, Queen of Sweden*, 36–37.

188. Nelson, "Ancient Queens," 7.

189. Hocart, *Kings and Councilors*, 98.

190. Dennison, *Livia*, 133; Freisenbruch, *Caesar's Wives*, 72.

191. Farenfight, *Queenship in Medieval Europe*, 120.

192. During the Tang dynasty, the Zhou kings were posthumously elevated to the rank of emperor and their wives were posthumously declared empresses. Ouyang, *Xin Tangshu*, 76:3481. Liu, *Jiu Tang shu*, 126:3560, discusses the posthumous names of empresses.

193. Wu, *Zhengshi daodu*, 33.

CHAPTER I

Neolithic Beginnings

THE CHINESE NEOLITHIC ENCOMPASSED THOUSANDS OF YEARS AND many cultures, each with distinct characteristics. Society changed drastically during this long era. Immediately after the invention of agriculture, social organization was very simple and there was little hierarchy. Toward the end of this era, however, large-scale civilizations began to emerge and gendered political roles took shape. Evidence from the Chinese Neolithic thus shows how relatively egalitarian societies in East Asia first became unequal and why the women around powerful men assumed a subsidiary role.

When examining Neolithic archaeological material, it is important not to interpret it by superimposing gender norms prevalent in later eras.[1] The status of women in the distant past differed significantly from their situations in historical times. So when interpreting prehistoric data, both female power and male domination should be understood on their own terms and not according to subsequent standards or preconceived notions of universal gender norms.

It is extremely difficult to infer facts about social organization from material remains. Archaeologists initially assumed that mortuary treatment reflected a society's overall ranking system so they analyzed the arrangement of a grave to infer the status of the deceased.[2] More recently, however, specialists have realized that degrees of mortuary treatment do not always reflect differences in social status. Tombs might differ in size and content for a number of reasons such as stylistic variations, personal preferences, ecological conditions, rate of decay in a particular environment, availability of materials, and the range of goods provided by regional trade networks.[3] That being said, mortuary remains can nevertheless provide valuable evidence about social relationships.[4] Generally speaking, mortuary ritual becomes more directly linked to status as a society becomes more complex. Over time, funerary rites were increasingly used to express information about prestige and power. During the late Neolithic in China, differences among graves became stark, clearly reflecting mounting hierarchy.

The earliest Neolithic societies in the region were relatively egalitarian. Society had few specialized social roles and lacked hereditary leadership. Instead, kinship was paramount. A person's place in the kinship network determined social identity, and kinship groups such as lineages handled matters of common concern. Early Neolithic communities practiced different types of burial. People were usually buried singly or in groups.[5] The Jiangzhai site in Shaanxi, representative of the early Neolithic Yangshao culture, has a typical pit grave that contains the remains of sixty-six adult men and fifty-three adult women.[6] Nearby pits are filled with ashes, which were probably sacrifices burned in honor of the deceased.[7] People interred together in the same pit were likely members of the same lineage. In this stage of the early Neolithic, large kinship groups such as lineages were far more important than individuals, spousal connections, or families.[8] Notably, mortuary rituals were directed at the entire group rather than a particular person, as individuals were not distinguished from the group.

If early Neolithic society had marriage, mortuary remains suggest that it was not yet an important aspect of social identity. People still owed primary allegiance to blood kin, and the deceased were rarely interred with a spouse. It was more common to be buried alone or with a sibling, a relative of the same sex, or a group of relatives.[9] The joint burial of heterosexual couples emerged in various places at different times.[10] In the Dawenkou culture of Shandong, this practice began about 3500 BCE whereas in the Majiayao culture of Gansu it started around 2600 BCE. In many other regions, the joint burial of couples began even later.

The graves of women and men often exhibit signs of heterarchy with members of each sex respected for making vital contributions to

Stone roller and quern of the Peiligang culture.
SOURCE: *PUBLIC DOMAIN.*

the community. Different tasks were associated with each sex even at this early stage. As all gendered work roles were necessary for a society to function properly, the work of both women and men had a degree of prestige.[11] Remains of the Peiligang culture, located in Henan during the early Neolithic, exhibit signs of early gendered division of labor.[12] Men were interred with stone agricultural tools such as axes, shovels, and sickles, and women were buried with stone querns, pestles used to husk grain, pottery beakers, and bowls. These gendered remains imply that men worked in the grain fields and women performed key domestic tasks. Although the grave goods of each sex differed, those of women were generally as numerous as those of men.

As different social roles emerged, at first some women received elaborate burials, implying that they held elite status. In one Dawenkou cemetery, the most elaborate tomb belonged to a woman. Her burial was more lavish than those around her. She was interred in an elaborate coffin and surrounded by 180 funerary goods, indicating that she was a person of consequence.[13] Similarly, some women were buried with status symbols such as jade items and even stone battle axes.[14] They probably belonged to elite lineages and were honored as noblewomen.

Nevertheless, men were already acquiring more prestige than women in some places. The remains of men in many pit burials outnumber those of women.[15] Those not interred in the lineage's communal pit grave would have had their bodies disposed of less formally.[16] The unequal treatment of deceased men and women implies that some people considered men more worthy of elaborate mortuary treatment. In places where the dead were buried in individual graves, luxury and ritual goods marking status, such as jade and turtle shell, were more likely to be interred with men. Such is the case at the Banpo site in Shaanxi, where all prestige goods were placed in male graves.[17] None of these items have been found together with female remains. It seems unlikely that a woman could gain a high position on her own nor does it even seem that she could elevate herself by association with an important man.

As society stratified, leaders gained control of vital goods such as grain and then redistributed them to gain support. Some graves from that era are much larger than others and contain numerous burial items including those marking prestige, attesting to the high rank of the deceased. Almost all elite graves belonged to men.[18] Emerging leadership was male, and women were excluded from the nascent political elite. Nor did marriage to a male leader give a woman sufficient prestige to receive a lavish burial.

During the course of the Neolithic era, a monogamous kinship structure gradually emerged and the marriage bond became more prominent.[19] Eventually, monogamy became the norm for commoners while the elite sometimes had more complex marriage relations. Burial practices of the Dawenkou culture reflect the shift toward small families founded on monogamous marriage.[20] Initially, most burials were of same-sex pairs, and male-female pairs were only a small proportion of overall burials. Over time the proportion of male-female burials increased. In one Dawenkou cemetery, only 7.1 percent of early graves contained a man and woman. The number gradually increased until about half contained a heterosexual pair. The number of adults buried with children also increased over time, rising from 14.3 percent to 33.3 percent. Changing burial patterns show a growing emphasis on family ties with both spouses and children. When monogamous marriage assumed importance, men and women began to acquire status and economic position differently.[21] A man's accomplishments often determined his status while a woman's position was determined by her association with a husband or blood relatives.

Kin-based societies are usually exogamous. This marriage system reduces jealousy among men living in a group and builds alliances between different groups, reducing tension and fostering cooperation. In Neolithic China, residents of each community were often members of the same lineage so the principle of exogamy required men to bring in wives from outside the community. Women were reduced to tokens representing two kin groups and their exchange resembled gift giving. Lineages exchanging women created a reciprocal bond, giving this practice political utility.[22] For this reason political marriage remained an important practice during the historic era.

Simple kin-based societies are usually virilocal with the bride taking up residence in her husband's home. Virilocality began as a pragmatic response to labor conditions.[23] Men usually undertook tasks that had to be carried out farther from home, such as grain farming and hunting, whereas women tended to work closer to the home so that they could care for children. Hunting and primitive agriculture were cooperative activities so men needed to work together in groups to be effective. Virilocality kept male kinsmen together in the same place making it easier for men to collaborate. Likewise virilocality increased men's effectiveness in battle as blood kinsmen fought harder when they were cooperating to defend their community.

At the dawn of the historic era, virilocal residence was already the norm in China so this practice almost certainly began during the Neolithic. These early marriage patterns had a major impact on female status. Virilocality forced a bride to move to an unfamiliar community where she had no natural allies, decreasing her status and influence. A woman became ancillary to her husband's family and her status derived largely from that of her husband and his relatives.

As society developed, material inequality gave rise to extreme hierarchy marked by differing degrees of power and prestige. The emergence of hierarchy had a particularly large impact on women. As before, men assumed most tasks that required greater physical strength or had to be done far from home. Because women were sometimes physically burdened by pregnancy and subsequently tasked with childcare, their principal tasks tended to be done in the home.[24] Men moved over a far wider area, giving them opportunities to obtain valuable goods, particularly staple foods. Gendered division of labor thus gave men control of primary economic assets, further raising male status. Men increased their economic power even further by gaining control over women's labor.[25] An ambitious leader could increase his power by dominating the output of women. Likewise, men resisting the centralization of power would try to control the labor of their kinswomen. This struggle for control over women's labor degraded female status and restricted their autonomy. A wife's claim on family resources rested mainly on her role as the one who bore her husband's children and raised them.[26]

Divergent economic roles gave men control over most of society's resources, elevating their status relative to women. However, women still did essential labor, so marriage to an especially productive woman could raise a man's status by increasing his wealth. Husbands began to view wives as economic assets and sought to control their domestic output.[27] In a hierarchical society, a woman's status followed that of her father and husband, however, she did not share their privileges. Although a woman in a family of high standing had more authority and wealth than those in ordinary circumstances, they were still usually lower in status than their male kin.

Just as women's status within the family declined relative to that of men, elite men also gained authority over the community. Control over the economy gave a chief direct power over an area's residents.[28] Leaders gained power by directing patterns of production, distribution, and consumption, then used this economic power to control other aspects of people's lives. Most importantly, they demanded a share of the grain harvest. Control of the primary good in society made them wealthy, and they used their domination of the food supply to gain political power.[29]

These economic changes led to the emergence of property rights. When a society is organized around families such as small bands of hunter-gatherers, people do not divide land into bounded territories or consider it owned by a particular group. In the simplest societies, boundaries are social rather than territorial. But when a population becomes sufficiently large and dense, lineages and clans emerge. Corporate groups claim ownership of a specific piece of land, and those who participate in the group's ceremonies claim a share of this property.[30] A chief who seeks to increase his power appropriates this collective land then uses this key resource to gain even more authority.

This process is not limited to land. As society becomes increasingly unequal, many valuable items become associated with power relations. Nascent leaders accumulate rare and finely crafted objects to symbolize their authority and then distribute them to gain support.[31] In ancient China, the elites in many places viewed outstanding pottery and jade as prestige goods. As society stratified, luxury items became closely associated with powerful men, and these are rarely found in female graves. At first, people marked status by having a large quantity of valuables. Over time, prestige goods became less numerous but more distinctive and very well crafted. In a simple society, the display of prestige goods is individualistic. A so-called big man decides what to value and how to exhibit it. As the political system develops, these displays become systematized. Certain objects are recognized as standard tokens of power, and leaders handle and exhibit them in prescribed ways. The male political elite dominates, allocates, and displays valuables to establish a hereditary monarchy.

An increase in the frequency and scale of warfare also helped men gain political supremacy. With few exceptions, warfare was almost always a male pursuit. In almost every society, men monopolize war and weapons. There is no society in which the primary warriors are female. In many societies, it is even taboo for a woman to touch a weapon.[32] Because war was one of the most important activities of nascent government, male domination of war further diminished women's political importance.

In egalitarian societies, violence takes place between individuals, such as two men fighting over a woman.[33] There is no reason for the entire community to go to war. They do not see land as property nor do they have much wealth or agricultural surplus to lose. Economic simplicity means that there is little to gain from war. But as society becomes more productive and stratified, social groups accrue valuables that become sources of contention. In Mesopotamia, war began in the Uruk period (3500–3100 BCE) when early city states sought to steal resources from one another.[34] Many other early state societies, such as the Maya, were obsessed with war and made it a major activity.[35] Likewise, during the late Neolithic era in north China, Longshan settlements built large defensive walls, attesting to the rise of warfare. Some leaders conquered neighboring settlements to construct larger polities.[36]

Endemic warfare transformed the political system. When the threat of war is constant, it is expedient for one man to have the authority to mobilize a society's resources for the sake of defense. Societies that fail to centralize power are more likely to be conquered. This dynamic eventually leads to the emergence of hereditary monarchy, with the populace accepting the inherited authority of men from one family for the sake of effective defense. Although the emergence of hereditary monarchy increased the power of male leaders, it did not bolster the position of their wives.

As war became vital to a community's success and even survival, leaders emphasized its importance. In many cultures, warfare was highly ritualized with ceremonies occurring before, during, and after battle.[37] Ritualizing war grounded it in ideology and allowed the ruler to project the image of a puissant warrior. As in other places, Chinese warfare underwent ritualization as well.[38] Men used these rites and regulations to exclude women from participating in this prestigious activity.

As war became ritualized, weapons sometimes became valued as ceremonial objects. At the late Neolithic Erlitou site, weapons are present in the graves of many elite men.[39] Archaeologists have unearthed two kinds of weapons there. Some were functional and probably used by the deceased on the field of battle. Others made from jade were far too valuable and fragile to have been used as actual weapons. These luxury items were clearly tokens of status and were likely used in political rituals.

Although the consorts of Shang kings could lead armies, in subsequent native Chinese dynasties consorts rarely had any direct role in military matters, blocking a major pathway for accruing authority. In other regions, such as Europe, noblewomen sometimes learned military skills so that they could defend their property from interlopers if necessary.[40] Yet, from unification onward, China had a bureaucratic military system. Standardized and rule-based administration gave Chinese women little chance to intervene in military matters.

As political systems developed, religion served as an ideology that justified the system of government and legitimized rulers.[41] The focus of religious ceremonies shifted from the entire community to the ruler's lineage.[42] Ceremonies allowed rulers to publicly present their supremacy as part of the sacred order. They used prestige objects to materialize religious ideology, presenting abstract ideas in the form of tangible reality. Religious objects could also be owned and inherited, facilitating the orderly transfer of legitimate power. Combining military force with religious authority allowed a leader to construct a strong system capable of overcoming less-organized foes.[43]

There is copious evidence for prehistoric religion in China. As society stratified, important religious objects were more often interred with men. The grave of a leader of the Liangzhu culture exemplifies the burial of an important Neolithic leader. This grave holds the remains of a man who died at about the age of thirty as well as an impressive array of sixty burial goods. In addition, there were the remains of two human sacrifices, one male and the other female, as well as those of a human infant, a youth, a pig, and a dog.[44] Sacrificial victims were likely people whom the deceased had dominated in life such as a wife, children, officials, slaves, or captives. In an increasingly unequal society, powerful men could manipulate religious ideology and ritual to bolster their superior status even more.

As Neolithic communities became increasingly more complex, prosperous, and technologically advanced, they needed dependable and effective leadership. Initially, they invested power in what anthropologists refer to as a *big man*, someone with outstanding talent or charisma. Remains of the Majiayao culture in eastern Qinghai, dating to between 2600–2300 BCE, show signs of the sort of stratification that characterizes a big man society.[45] One cemetery has several distinct areas most likely belonging to different lineages. Most of the graves have only a few simple burial goods, and the quantity usually corresponds to the number of skeletons, implying that most people had roughly equal social status. However, three graves in the cemetery, each containing the remains of two to four people, contain finely crafted items not found in other graves, including a pottery drum and a large stone axe. These attest to high status, which was probably earned through personal achievement. These graves likely belonged to the community's big men. Significantly these men were not buried with their spouses. It seems their elevated status did not confer comparable prestige on their wives.

After the death of a big man there is often no clear successor so this arrangement is inherently unstable.[46] As society became more productive and complex, distinct strata emerged with a hereditary elite at the apex.[47] Egalitarian social organization, which lacked institutionalized leadership, gave way to hereditary chiefdoms that integrated local groups into larger political organizations.[48] Hereditary monarchy stabilized society by institutionalizing authority and clarifying succession. Rulers took control of the economy and administration, using religious ideology to justify their position and materializing it by displaying luxury goods. In chiefdoms, important men usually have titles that convey their superior position. The chief's wife might also have a title and enjoy privileges but her rank usually depends on that of her spouse.[49] If a chief dies, his wife usually doesn't retain her title.

To accrue power, early male monarchs forced their subjects to observe etiquette and conduct rites that emphasized the ruler's unique status.[50] They also demanded that their subjects provide them with luxury goods or else they traded with outsiders to obtain rare and prestigious items that they could use to show their lofty status. The ruler assembled a court consisting of followers who met in a large and conspicuous building. He also restricted access to his person to emphasize his unique position. At this crucial time in social evolution the relationship between the earliest monarchs and their spouses helped set down the relations between king and consort that served as a substrate for the imperial system that emerged much later.

Stratifying societies also developed property rights: exclusive control over land or goods.[51] The development of the state was linked to the rise of property. Elites supported the development of state institutions that could guarantee their ownership of property and arbitrate disputes over land. Initially, kin groups controlled property. Over time individuals gained ownership. It seems that early property owners in Neolithic China were mostly male. A leader used his wealth to aggrandize himself and bolster his position. The control of property thus elevated emerging monarchs even farther above their wives.

The Longshan culture of the late Neolithic exemplifies a highly stratified society immediately prior to the historic era. The Chengzi site (ca. 2500–2000 BCE) in Shandong province is representative of this type of social structure.[52] Graves contain burial goods of varying number and quality showing that people had very different social positions. Archaeologists have divided the graves into four ranks ranging from those with no accompanying items to those representing elaborate burials with numerous goods. Simple and elite graves were placed in different sections of a cemetery. Burial practices show that Longshan social structure constituted a pyramid. The higher the rank of the deceased, the fewer graves of that type. A tiny elite ruled the commoners, who constituted the bulk of the population.

While egalitarian society had been largely heterarchal with both sexes respected for carrying out necessary tasks, rising inequality caused the general status of men and women to diverge. Far more men than women received formal burial, implying that the sexes had very different social positions in life.[53] The burial goods of men generally exceeded those of women in number and quality.[54] In some late Neolithic burials, the body of a man was placed in the center of the grave with a woman to the side in a subsidiary position.[55] In other tombs, a man's remains were placed in a coffin while those of a woman rest beside the coffin, attesting to their unequal status.[56] When a man and woman were buried together, the man's body was often set down straight while the woman was flexed and positioned to face him, an arrangement that archaeologists have interpreted as a display of relative status.[57]

As populations increased, settlements became larger and more numerous. In a relatively complex prehistoric society, primary identity shifted from kin groups to territorial bonds.[58] This change allowed for the eventual emergence of states. About 4000 BCE, settlements enclosed by walls started to appear in the middle Yangtze valley.[59] Archaeologists have identified more than fifty of these sites. In the following two centuries, walled residential centers became increasingly larger and more complex. Large settlements began to have monumental features such as large gates, platforms, and facilities for conducting elaborate religious and ritual events. Eventually, settlements became large enough to be considered true cities. Some became more important than others and served as religious, administrative, or military centers.[60] Graves in important settlements often contain weapons, attesting to the importance of war to elite identity. The societies of central settlements were notably unequal. Early cities could not have carried out such complex activities without strong leadership so they were likely hereditary monarchies.

States developed gradually out of earlier arrangements and relationships.[61] The ways that rulers increased their power made monarchy a patriarchal institution. To be a ruler, a person had to have a network of clients. Rulers provided protection and stability and in return received economic resources. Over time this relationship became formalized as monarch and subject. Subjects deferred to the ruler in return for protection. The most bellicose people could thus attract the most clients. As seen from the presence of weapons in male graves, warriors were usually men. Accordingly, the rulers of nascent states were male, and they deployed patriarchal ideologies and rituals to legitimate their authority.

As the scale of government increased, not only did rulers increasingly elevate themselves above their subjects, they also became much higher than their spouses. From the beginnings of monarchy in China the wives of powerful men were relegated to a minor role and given lesser rank. The early Bronze Age Taosi site, which seems to have been an embryonic monarchy, provides a clear example of the inequality underpinning this sort of society.⁶² About 90 percent of the graves at this site are small and simple, containing the remains of male and female commoners. In addition, there are also five large tombs with wooden coffins and eighty with medium-sized coffin burials. The occupants of these elite graves are all male. In some of the large tombs, presumably those of the rulers, women are buried to the side of the coffins. These are probably the consorts of the kings of Taosi. This burial pattern implies that the ruler's wife had a much lower rank than her husband from the beginnings of monarchy in China.

Elite men also seem to have started taking secondary wives and concubines. Many tombs of the Qijia culture, an early Bronze Age society, contain one man and two women.⁶³ Men's bodies were laid out straight but the women beside them were placed in a flexed position facing the men, which seems to indicate subservience. Presumably this burial pattern is a sign of either polygyny or concubinage. A large grave at the Taosi cemetery exemplifies this sort of relationship. The elite man is buried with two women.⁶⁴ One woman was aged about thirty-five to forty at the time of her death while the other was much younger, about age twenty-five. Archaeologists assume that these women were wife and concubine.

The growing gap in the status of important men and the women around them allowed men to execute some of these women as human sacrifices. Some tombs of Liangzhu men with a rich array of funerary goods also have subsidiary female burials.⁶⁵ It is rare for several people to die at the same time so archaeologists assume that these women were sacrificed after a man's death to accompany him to the afterlife. In this society, some of the women around elite men had such a low status that people of the time looked on them as akin to luxury goods. People in many Qijia settlements also practiced human sacrifices during the funerals of important men. Most of the victims were women. One Qijia tomb contains a headless female skeleton alongside the complete remains of a man.⁶⁶ It seems that she was decapitated and then buried with him. Female remains in subsidiary burials around the tomb of an important man may also have been human sacrifices.⁶⁷ As prehistoric societies in China approached the historic era, the relations between rulers and the women around them became starkly unequal.

CHAPTER 1

NOTES

1. Whitehouse, "Gender Archaeology and Archaeology of Women," 29–30.
2. King, "Multiple Groups, Overlapping Symbols," 54.
3. Tackett, *The Origins of the Chinese Nation*, 214, 288–90.
4. Saxe, "Social Dimensions of Mortuary Practices"; Binford, "Mortuary Practices"; Tainter, "Mortuary Practices and the Study of Prehistoric Social Systems"; Sullivan and Mainfort, "Mississippian Mortuary Practices," 1–5.
5. Zhang, "Yangshao wenhua xingsheng shiqi de zangyi," 17–27; Yan, *Yangshao wenhua yanjiu*, 258, 260, 271. In the fourth and third millennia, Chinese Neolithic cultures began to have some joint burials of one adult man and one adult woman. Shang, "Dui shiqian shiqi chengnian nannü hezang mu," 50.
6. Luo, "Shilun Shangdai Yindu renkou de ziran goucheng," 346.
7. Liu, "Ancestor Worship," 137–38.
8. Gong, "Cong kaogu ziliao kan Yangshao wenhua," 32; Keightley, "At the Beginning," 16–17; Liu, "Ancestor Worship," 140–42; Gao and Lee, "A Biological Perspective on Yangshao Kinship," 289; Flannery and Marcus, *The Creation of Inequality*, 550; Leick, *Mesopotamia*, 15; Wilson et al., "Social and Spatial Dimensions," 87, 89.
9. Keightley, "Shamanism, Death, and the Ancestors," 781. For example, see Zhang, "Weishui liuyu Laoguantai wenhua," 173.
10. Shang, "Dui shiqian shiqi chengnian nannü hezang mu," 50, 52–53.
11. For examples of heterarchy in labor roles in other regions see Fagan, *Fishing*, 9; Silverblatt, *Moon, Sun, and Witches*, 14, 20, 31–32, 38.
12. Zhang and Yao, "Shilun Peiligang wenhua shiqi de shehui jieduan," 43–44; Wang, "Peiligang wenhua zangsu qianyi," 78, 80; Sun, "Lun zhongyuan xin shiqi shidai," 52. Many other Neolithic cultures show signs of similar gendered division of labor. For an example from a later period, see Wang, "Shilun Dawenkou wenhua de hezangmu," 5, 7.
13. Jiao, "Gender Studies in Chinese Neolithic Archaeology," 56.
14. Zhejiang Sheng Wenwu Kaogu Yanjiusuo, "Zhejiang Yukeng Xingqiao Houtoushan Liangzhu wenhua mudi," 48; Zhang, "Liangzhu wenhua mudi," 408, 412.
15. Luo, "Shilun Shangdai Yindu renkou de ziran goucheng," 346–47; Zhang and Yao, "Shilun Peiligang wenhua shiqi de shehui jieduan," 39–46; Liu, "Ancestor Worship," 142–43.
16. Leick, *Mesopotamia*, 13, points out that many of the ways for disposing of dead bodies leave no trace. A body may have been exposed in an uninhabited place, cremated, or placed in a marsh or river.
17. Sun, "Baopo wenhua zai yanjiu," 435.
18. Luan, "Shilun Yangshao shiqi zhongqi de shehui fenceng," 52–53.
19. Shang, "Dui shiqian shiqi chengnian nannü hezang mu," 53. Earle and Kristiansen, "Introduction," 16–17, note that monogamous marriage emerged at different types in each part of the world.
20. He and Sun, "Shilun Lunan Subei diqu de Dawenkou wenhua," 24, 28; Wang, "Shilun Dawenkou wenhua de hezangmu," 4–5.
21. Wu, "The Late Neolithic Cemetery at Dadianzi," 82, 85–86.

22. Service, *Primitive Social Organization*, 42–47.
23. Service, *Primitive Social Organization*, 48–49.
24. Murdock and Provost, "Factors in the Division of Labor by Sex," 211.
25. Joyce, *Gender and Power in Prehispanic Mesoamerica*, 88.
26. Bledsoe, "The Politics of Polygyny," 174.
27. Nelson, "Ancient Queens," 3.
28. Earle, *How Chiefs Come to Power*, 67–70.
29. Hamilakis, "Food Technologies/Technologies of the Body," 39–41.
30. Earle, *Bronze Age Economics*, 326–37.

31. Earle, *Bronze Age Economics*, 37–38. The particular significance of an item varied according to the cultural context and thus the meanings imputed to certain types of items probably changed over time. Appadurai, "Introduction."

32. Divale and Harris, "Population, Warfare, and the Male Supremacist Complex," 524–26.

33. Knauft, "Violence and Sociality in Human Evolution," 399–400.
34. Scott, *Against the Grain*, 137, 154.
35. Coe and Houston, *The Maya*, 236.

36. Lenski, *Power and Privilege*, 196–97; Earle, *How Chiefs Come to Power*, 105, 109, 132, 140.

37. Webster, "Warfare and Status Rivalry," 311, 337, 339.
38. Yates, "Making War and Making Peace in Early China," 34–52.
39. Guo, "Erlitou wenhua bingqi chulun," 230, 232.
40. Toler, *Women Warriors*, 140–41.
41. Earle, *How Chiefs Come to Power*, 143–44, 149, 151, 154–55.
42. Liu, "Ancestor Worship," 129.
43. Flannery and Marcus, *The Creation of Inequality*, 243.
44. Zhao, "Liangzhu wenwu renxun renji xianxiang shixi," 34.
45. Liu, "Ancestor Worship," 145–51.
46. Mair, *Primitive Government*, 205–6.
47. Smith, *Coosa*, 11, 13–14.

48. Johnson and Earle, *The Evolution of Human Societies*, 207–8. For definitions and basic characteristics of the chiefdom see Service, *Primitive Social Organization*, 143–71; Carneiro, "The Chiefdom," 37–79; Yoffee, *Myths of the Archaic State*, 29; Earle, *Bronze Age Economics*, 43–44, 53–65; Earle, "Chiefdoms in Archaeological and Ethnohistorical Perspective."

49. Keating, "Moments of Hierarchy," 306.
50. Mair, *Primitive Government*, 140, 160, 190.
51. Earle, "Archaeology, Property, and Prehistory," 40, 42, 46.
52. Liu, "Ancestor Worship," 151.
53. Keightley, "At the Beginning," 62.

54. Debaine-Francfort, *Du Néolithique à l'âge du bronze*, 263; Zhengzhou Shi Wenwu Gongzuodui, "Zhengzhou Dahecun yizhi 1983, 1987 nian fajue baogao," 111; Keightley, "At the Beginning," 21–24; Zhu, "Xin Zhongguo diyibu xin shiqi shidai mudi fajue," 1–7; Ma, "Anhui Weichisi Dawenkou wenhua," 25.

CHAPTER 1

55. He and Niu, "Zaozhuang Jianxin Dawenkou wenhua muzang fenxi," 23–34.
56. Wang, "Shilun Longshan wenhua shidai de renxun he renji," 25–26.
57. He and Niu, "Dawenkou Yilongshan wenhua quzhi zangsu tanxi," 79–84, 33; He and Niu, "Zaozhuang Jianxin Dawenkou wenhua muzang fenxi," 23–34.
58. Chen, "Compromises and Conflicts," 291.
59. Yan, "Wenming de shuguang," 99, 103.
60. Wang, "Zhongxin juluo xingtai, yuanshi zongyi yu qiubang shehui," 7–12.
61. Mair, *Primitive Government*, 166–69, 172; Jones and Krautz, "Issues in the Study of New World State Formation," 5–6.
62. Keightley, "At the Beginning," 27; Shanxi Sheng Linfen Xingshu Wenhuaju, "Shanxi Linfen Xiajincun Taosi wenhua mudi," 459–86; Jia and Mu, "Taosi leixing shehui xingzhi," 127–28.
63. Qian, Zhou, Mao, and Xie, "Gansu Lintan Mogo Qijia wenhua mudi," 9; Yi, "Cong Qijia dao Erlitou," 140.
64. Gao, Gao, and Zhang, "Guanyu Taosi mudi de jige wenti," 533.
65. Shanghaishi Wenwu Baoguan Weiyuanhui, "Fuquanshan yizhi disanci fajue," 51; Zhang, "Suzhou de Liangzhu yicun ji gudai wenming," 112, 115.
66. Jiao, "Gender Studies in Chinese Neolithic Archaeology," 57.
67. Gansu Sheng Wenwu Kaogu Yanjiusuo, "Gansu Lintan Mogou mudi Qijia wenhua muzang," 12–13, 16–17.

CHAPTER 2

Ancient Consorts

ALTHOUGH FEMALE RULERS WERE RARE IN COMPLEX POLITICAL SYStems, the flexible institutions of embryonic states sometimes allowed women to accrue power. The Silla kingdom in southeast Korea exemplified an emerging kingdom in which women wielded power.[1] Three queens reigned over Silla. Two never wed and the third was married to a man ineligible to become king. All of them were shamans believed to be capable of influencing the spirit world. They relied on their religious abilities as their prime source of legitimacy. Because most shamans in Silla were female, women there could sometimes use their mastery of sacred rites to gain supreme power. As institutions developed, however, men took control of the most important religious practices, depriving women of the means to serve as rulers.

Two conditions underpinned the establishment of monarchy.[2] The ruler of an emerging kingdom had to gain support by secular means, usually by controlling important goods and redistributing them to attract followers. In addition, he also asserted supernatural sanction, claiming descent from a god or performing holy rites on behalf of the community. In ancient societies, people saw religious ceremonies as benefiting the entire community not just the ruler. Religious specialists codified complex symbolic systems, promoted them as sacred, and made them concrete by performing rites and manipulating holy objects. Religion expressed and maintained fundamental collective values and customs, enforcing social solidarity and allowing a ruler to bolster social cohesion without actively exerting control.

CHAPTER 2

During the prehistoric era, complex polities grounded in the centralized control of key goods and religious beliefs emerged in China. The most complex Neolithic communities had already developed into states ruled by powerful monarchs. These rulers were male, and their consorts were relegated to a subsidiary role. Political power in the Chinese region had already become patriarchal.

The dawn of the historic era saw the emergence of Shang, an early Bronze Age monarchy. The Shang dynasty marks the formal beginning of the history of Chinese consorts as divination records attest that some royal spouses enjoyed prestige, wealth, and authority.[3] The Han dynasty historian Ban Gu even implied that consorts of the Shang kings deserved a share of the credit for the dynasty's success.[4] Nevertheless, the institutions of this archaic state differed considerably from those of subsequent dynasties, so the powers of Shang women did not set lasting precedents.

The titles of the highest-ranking Shang women differed from those of later eras, and these distinctive appellations convey clues about their identities and roles. The fact that Shang consorts had titles is itself significant as the wives of kings in most societies lack this distinction. For women close to the monarch, to be awarded prestigious designations singled them out as persons of consequence. However, the names and terms of address of elite women were not yet fixed. A woman had various appellations that marked her social position and relationships with the people around her. These terms shifted through the course of her life in response to changing circumstances.

Wives of the Shang kings had the title *fu*.[5] The modern version of this character is written with a female radical and simply means "woman" or "married woman." In the archaic Shang script, the character is written either with or without the female component, and the denotation differs from the modern reading.[6] The social categories in early states were often ambiguous, and such was the case with people called *fu*.[7] Various inscriptions mention more than sixty *fu*, and they seem to have had a range of identities.[8] Some were undoubtedly the king's wives or concubines.[9] However, women other than the king's partners sometimes had this title as well.[10]

Kings conducted divinations to express concern for the well-being of some *fu*, showing that they had a close relationship.[11] But in other inscriptions a king inquires if he should love the child of a certain *fu* like his own offspring.[12] These women were clearly married to other men. It seems that all *fu* were female, married, and associated with men of high status. Scholars have proposed that a *fu* may have been the wife of a king's brother or son, the wife of a king's sister, the wife of a Shang high official or noble, or the wife of a foreign ruler.[13] Some were significant personages because of the importance of their natal families, and sometimes a *fu* served as an intermediary between the king and her own lineage or the foreign kingdom of her birth.[14]

Sometimes an important woman is identified by a single character denoting a personal name.[15] The character *fu* also appears by itself to label a particular woman. And *fu* appears in combination with up to five other characters as a way of identifying an individual more distinctly.[16] Most commonly, *fu* is paired with another character to form the two-character appellation *fu*-x. The second character often has a female radical added to feminize it.[17] In some cases, the second character seems to refer to a clan or lineage.[18] Although most scholars assume that this identified a woman's natal clan, some suggest that it might have been her husband's clan marker.[19] In other cases, the second character seems to have designated a place name.[20] About a quarter of these are foreign places, suggesting that these women were the daughters of foreign leaders who married into the Shang elite to cement political ties. Other places were probably noble domains within the Shang realm where these women were born.

Inscriptions on many bronze vessels identify a woman with an archaic graph that later diverged to become two different characters: *mu* and *nü*. Later these characters came to mean "mother" and "unmarried woman" (or just "woman") respectively, but during the Shang era they were written the same way and used interchangeably.[21] Many dowry vessels are inscribed with this character so it seems that *mu* or *nü* often designated an unmarried woman. There are far fewer inscriptions with *mu* or *nü* than *fu* so it seems that this term was not as common. Most likely a woman was called *mu* or *nü* until she wed after which time she became *fu*. There were also women called *chen* who were mentioned together with *mu* and *fu* as being in proximity to the king.²² The identity of *chen* women remains unclear.

After her death a royal consort was called *hou* instead of *fu*.²³ For example, one of the consorts of King Wu Ding was called *Fu Hao* when she was alive and *Hou Mu Xin* after her death.²⁴ In this case, *hou* identifies her as a high-ranking deceased lady, *mu* is a conventional polite term designating a woman, and *xin* was one of the ten stems marking a day of the ten-day Shang week. This was likely the day when her spirit received regular sacrifices. Other records identify the same woman as *Bi Xin*, with *bi* meaning ancestress.²⁵ A deceased woman was sometimes referred to by a two-character appellation consisting of *fu* together with a character from the ten stems calendrical system.²⁶

Putting all of this evidence together, it seems that people addressed a consort differently depending on her phase of life and the nature of their relationship with her. A young woman was called *nü* or *mu*. If she married a king, people referred to her as *fu*, a polite term of address that emphasized her wifely status. After she died, her children called her *hou* or *bi* while her former husband continued to call her *fu*. In sum, Shang consorts lacked a fixed title equivalent to "queen" or "empress." Their names and titles were built around relational kinship terms, and these changed as a daughter became a wife, then mother, and finally an ancestress.

Royal marriage practices fluctuated over the course of the Shang, affecting the status and identity of the king's spouses. Documents regarding ancestral sacrifices provide most of the information about the activities of royal women in this period. Female ancestors in the royal line received regular sacrifices in the ancestral temple. However, many consorts were not included in this ceremonial system or else they had a modest position within it.²⁷ A woman only gained a place in the sacrificial calendar if her son was enthroned as king because a king sacrificed to his mother but not to his father's other consorts. For most of the dynasty the throne passed down through the brothers of one generation before descending to the next generation. If two brothers served as king in succession, only the spouse of one of them appeared in the official genealogy for that generation. Moreover, many consorts likely never bore sons or else their sons did not become kings. These conventions guaranteed that many royal partners would not be recorded in ancestral records so it is impossible to know how many consorts most kings had.[28]

The consorts of the earliest Shang rulers were not recorded. Once sacrificial cult records began to record the identities of royal ancestresses, they listed one consort per ruler. Some scholars have concluded that these kings were monogamous.[29] There are also tombs of noblemen from the era accompanied by just one woman, implying that they had a single spouse.[30] However, monarchs may have had other partners in addition to those included in sacrificial records, so this evidence does not conclusively prove that early Shang kings were monogamous.

Although monogamy was the norm for the common people, the tombs of some noblemen include subsidiary burials of two or more women.[31] Some Shang kings seem to have been polygynous.[32] Monarchs in many cultures have multiple wives and concubines as polygyny has many uses. A king might take multiple partners to produce an heir, guarantee access to numerous sexual partners, display status, or bind him to important clans and foreign rulers.[33]

Three Shang kings had two consorts each in the sacrificial cycle, and King Zu Ding had four. King Wu Ding is believed to have had between fifty-eight and sixty-three *fu* women, and his brothers seem to have had at least ten women each. Not all of these *fu* were necessarily wives or concubines. Some may have been akin to servants or palace administrators. Of King Wu Ding's *fu*, only three were definitely comparable to wives as their descendants offered them sacrifices. The evidence regarding consorts suggests that either the Shang royal marriage system was usually monogamous but went through a phase of royal polygyny, or many kings were polygynous but most of their consorts were not recorded and soon forgotten.[34] If a king had more than one consort, these women might have held different degrees of status.[35]

For Shang kings, the choice of marriage partners seems to have had political significance as they married women from other clans for political gain.[36] Shang was the largest state ever to emerge in East Asia up to that time. Institutions were still rudimentary so rulers relied on a dense web of kinship relations to hold the state together. The royal clan used marriage to maintain links with the nobles representing major clans as well as the rulers of neighboring settlements and tribes.[37]

Later historians alleged that the legendary rulers of high antiquity before the Shang used marriage to achieve political ends.[38] During the late Neolithic era, the rulers of emerging states likely relied on marriage to bind together different groups and construct nascent states. The Shang relied heavily on political marriage. The names of many elite Shang women refer to various kinship groups and foreign places.[39] Oracle inscriptions also imply that the rulers of foreign states and peoples (*fang*) sent women as a kind of tribute to pay homage to the Shang king and bind themselves to him.[40] Some of the *fu* ladies around the king may have come into the palace from neighboring regions as human tribute. Kings also married off their daughters to powerful nobles.[41] Although they favored the birth of sons, the Shang kings also needed daughters to expand their network of kinship connections.

Elite Shang women were akin to nobles and had their own domains (*yi*).[42] The *fu* who married kings controlled productive agricultural land and had authority over the people residing there, making them significant personages in their own right. Consorts went back and forth between the royal capital and their domains as they had important matters to attend to in each place. Some *fu* received independent income from their domains, and it seems that this income was sometimes considerable. They had sufficient resources to engage in activities valued by the Shang elite including gift giving, the presentation of tribute, and making religious sacrifices.

Wide-ranging exogamy at the top of Shang society influenced the status of elite men. For a man to qualify as a king or noble, bloodline was paramount. Although nobles were patrilineal, because some were polygynous, an important man could have several sons by different mothers. As a result, a son's maternal background seems to have affected his relative rank. Some oracle texts identify a man as the son of a particular woman so maternal background was clearly important.[43] Sons of minor wives and concubines likely had a lower status in the family.

The posthumous treatment of royal consorts provides additional clues regarding their social identity. In every culture, children and parents are united by an intimate bond. In China, however, this relationship continued after the parents' death.[44] People believed that the spirit of the deceased continued to exist in supernatural form so children still owed them care and deference. The royal clan practiced an elaborate system of ancestral sacrifices. These complex rites required considerable time and resources, but people believed that venerating their ancestors earned tangible rewards while ignoring them might bring harm to the living.[45]

After death, a major consort had a tomb furnished with jade, bronze vessels, and other luxurious items connoting high status.[46] The large tomb of one important woman was more than ten square meters (107 square feet) in size and contained five sacrificial victims as well as more than ninety burial items including twenty-four prestigious bronze vessels.[47] Although this was impressive compared to ordinary burials, consort's tombs were much smaller than those of kings.[48] Moreover, unlike kings, consorts were not buried in a dedicated cemetery. They were interred in various places around the royal city.[49] One woman's tomb was even damaged in antiquity by subsequent construction showing that its location had been forgotten. Only the most important consorts received an individual burial. Less important partners would be buried in or beside the king's tomb. Whether or not they had a coffin depended on their status.[50]

The Shang kings and other members of the royal clan sacrificed to forebears of both sexes. However, female ancestors were far less important than the spirits of men. In one group of Shang ritual vessels, 93.29 percent were dedicated for use in sacrifices to deceased men and only 6.71 were for venerating female ancestors.[51] Also, people prayed to male ancestors regarding the most important matters such as rain and harvests.[52] Sacrifices to deceased women had more limited goals so they were less frequent and not nearly as important. These rites showed respect for the dead and appeased the spirits to keep them from causing harm. Children in the royal clan sacrificed to each parent on a different day of the week.[53] Female ancestors received sacrifices on days considered less auspicious than those for sacrificing to male ancestors.[54]

Once every ten-day week both male and female ancestors received a routine sacrifice. In addition, they could receive special sacrifices.[55] The *yu* sacrifice was intended to propitiate the deceased and keep her spirit from harming the living. People also sometimes performed the *bin* sacrifice to ancestors from the distant past. A female ancestor with the posthumous name Bi Geng is recorded as having received fifteen different kinds of sacrifices.[56] During these sacrifices, she received twenty-four kinds of offerings including slaves, pigs, cattle, sheep, dogs, and weapons. These rites were undertaken for various reasons such as in response to a dream, sickness, or bad mood or to implore blessings.

The Shang believed that a woman could remarry after death. This idea implies that a deceased woman had a somewhat independent identity and was not just an extension of her husband or family. Some divinatory texts ask if a male ancestor should marry an unnamed, deceased *fu* or a particular dead woman.[57] One inquires whether the deceased royal consort Fu Hao should marry Di, an important Shang god. Another asked if she should marry Tang, the first king of Shang.[58] The Shang even conducted weddings between deceased people, which seems to have been modeled after regular wedding ceremonies.[59] The Shang custom of posthumous weddings (*minghun*) endured long after the dynasty had ended and continued to be practiced to the end of imperial history with its popularity fluctuating in each era.[60]

A Shang consort's most important duty was to bear the ruler's children. Kings often divined about the pregnancy and childbirth of *fu*.[61] They also asked about the sex of unborn children and whether the infant would live or die. According to divination records, kings considered the birth of a son "good" and that of a daughter "not good." Although daughters could be married off to form alliances, sons were far more useful as they could take on the most important duties. The Shang believed that female ancestors could grant fertility so kings offered them prayers and sacrifices to entreat for progeny.[62] They seem to have considered the bestowal of fertility the most important power of female ancestors. Frequent divinations regarding fertility and childbirth may even have been rituals intended to induce fertility and ensure a safe delivery.[63]

Fu were deeply enmeshed in the network of exchanges that distributed luxuries and resources in a society that had neither currency nor systematic commerce. The nobility frequently exchanged gifts with one another to form and maintain social bonds. These goods served as tangible symbols of their relationships. Presenting someone with a gift brought prestige to the giver and required the recipient to reciprocate.[64] Some of the jade and bronze items found in the tomb of Fu Hao, consort of King Wu Ding, had the names of other people on them.[65] Most likely she received these valuables as gifts and the person's name reminded her of the giver. The tomb also included items of royal tribute likely given to Fu Hao by the king as a sign of favor.

Fu ladies frequently sent tribute to the king.[66] Those with a domain had sufficient resources to obtain tribute items themselves. *Fu* from foreign states may have served as conduits for the presentation of tribute to the Shang king on behalf of their people.[67] *Fu* were also involved in collecting, preparing, and consecrating the bones and turtle shells used in divination rites.[68] Turtle carapaces had to be brought from distant coastlands so *fu* acquired carapaces from coastal peoples and had them transported to the Shang capital. In an age of primitive communication and transportation, this would not have been a simple matter.

Tribute was both an obligation and a privilege for *fu*. Noblewomen with a domain were apparently obligated to present items of value to the king, and he used these gifts to perform the numerous sacrifices necessitated by the religious ideology of the Shang state. Kings also relied on conspicuous consumption to assert their status and power.[69] Presenting tribute thus allowed consorts to participate in a vital aspect of Shang politics.

Women were excluded from the most important sacrifices.[70] Nevertheless, they participated in numerous religious rites.[71] They implored for rain, begged spirits to stop epidemics, and sacrificed to the god of heaven and nature deities. They also conducted rites to male and female ancestors according to the regular calendar of sacrifices or as an additional propitiatory ritual.

CHAPTER 2

Consorts sometimes participated in aspects of government administration although their roles do not seem to have been clearly defined.[72] Kings sometimes ordered them to carry out certain tasks on an ad hoc basis. Early states such as the Shang were patrimonial and rulers made little distinction between the government and their household. This informal arrangement sometimes gave a king's consort the opportunity to participate in matters of public concern.[73] Sometimes a king told one of his consorts to handle a specific task on his behalf. Women reported unusual occurrences to the monarch, helping to keep him informed of potentially important matters. Consorts also oversaw fields in the royal domain, the source of much of the king's income.

Some royal consorts participated in warfare. In this respect, Shang gender conventions differed strikingly from those of subsequent dynasties. From the Zhou dynasty onward, women were almost always kept away from military matters.[74] War was a central activity of the Shang state so participation in martial activities elevated a woman's status.[75] Female involvement in warfare was possible due to the way that the Shang organized the military. When the king decided to launch a campaign, nobles raised troops from their domains and led them into battle. Some female nobles had domains so they were also obligated to levy and lead warriors if the king commanded them to do so.[76] Women led troops to defend the realm against invading enemies.[77] In some cases, a husband and wife guarded a border region together.[78] The king's consorts led campaigns against the Shang's enemies.[79] Women also went hunting, an exercise often used to practice the skills used in war.[80]

Fu Hao took part in almost every major campaign during the reign of her spouse, King Wu Ding. At one point she led an army of thirteen thousand soldiers, the largest force mentioned in Shang records.[81] Weapons were placed in the tombs of some women to symbolize their high status or participation in warfare.[82] Numerous bronze weapons, some extremely large and elaborately decorated, were found in the tomb of Fu Hao, including battle axes, knives, halberds, and arrowheads.[83]

Very little is known about most Shang consorts. Most women are mentioned in only a few brief divinatory inscriptions. However, there is more information about a few important *fu*. Fu Jing, senior consort of King Wu Ding, was extremely prominent as evidenced by her grand tomb.[84] Her tomb was given a place of honor near the royal cemetery.[85] Although far smaller than the tombs of nearby kings, Fu Jing's tomb is extremely large compared to those of commoners, minor nobility, and other consorts. The tomb has a long ramp leading down to the bottom of the burial pit. It held the skeletons of thirty-eight human victims and eleven skulls with an additional twenty-two skulls on the ramp. The large number of human sacrifices attests to her high standing. Her tomb also contains the largest bronze ritual vessel ever unearthed from the site of Anyang, the Shang capital. Although the tomb was plundered, this enormous rectangular tripod was too large and heavy for the looters to remove so they had no choice but to leave it behind. They also left 251 bone arrowheads.[86] These weapons suggest that Fu Jing led troops into war even though surviving records do not mention her taking part in military campaigns. Subsequent generations conducted sacrifices to the spirit of Fu Jing after her death.

Of all the *fu*, King Wu Ding's consort Fu Hao is by far the best understood. Not only is she mentioned in numerous divinatory inscriptions, but hers is the only Shang royal tomb that escaped looting. Fu Hao died from illness soon after returning from one of her many military campaigns. Unlike Fu Jing she was not buried near the royal cemetery but across a river at a distance from her spouse suggesting that Wu Ding did not consider his relationship with her paramount. This mode of burial presents an image of Fu Hao as having a strong identity of her own rather than just being an appendage of her powerful husband.

Fu Hao's tomb is smaller than that of Fu Jing and lacks an entry ramp. Nevertheless, it was lavishly furnished with 468 ritual bronzes, 755 jade items, more than five hundred carved hairpins, twenty-nine bone arrowheads, and various objects made from ivory, shell, stone, and pottery.[87] The tomb also contains the sacrificial remains of sixteen humans and six dogs.[88] Fu Hao's body was placed inside two coffins, the inner coffin fitting inside the outer one. Originally there was an ancestral shrine atop the tomb that was used to conduct sacrifices to the deceased. The assembly of bronzes and other items in this tomb does not seem to have been unique or exceptional. Her burial follows standard mortuary

Tomb of Fu Hao.
SOURCE: PUBLIC DOMAIN.

conventions of the time and honors her according to her rank as a secondary wife of a major king.[89]

Inscriptional evidence shows that Fu Hao participated in every activity expected of royal consorts. She conducted a wide array of sacrifices to the gods and ancestors, led armies into battle, presented tribute to the king, and received valuable gifts from other nobles and foreign peoples. Her tomb includes two ritual battle axes of the type often interred with leaders, symbolizing her power.[90] Although her authority was far less than that of her spouse, she was an important person intimately involved in important affairs of state. The achievements of Fu Hao illustrate the possibilities open to royal consorts under the patrimonial political system of the Shang dynasty.

The Zhou people conquered Shang in 1046 BCE, initiating a new dynasty. The Zhou came from a region far to the west of the Shang heartland, a buffer zone between the agricultural peoples of the Central Plains and steppe nomads. As their culture developed, they dealt with both sides and received influences from each. In consequence, many aspects of Zhou religion, ritual, kinship, and administration differed from Shang norms.

Zhou royal and noble women employed a new system of names and titles.[91] A woman had several names and designations that varied depending on her relationship with the person addressing her and the particular situation. A woman was often referred to by the surname of her father or husband. Due to the custom of surname exogamy, a woman's surname differed from that of her husband's family so it could be used to identify her.

The Zhou continued to observe the Shang custom of calling a woman *fu* plus a surname. However, the term *fu* had lost its former ambiguity and usually referred specifically to a wife. Alternatively a style name (*zi*) could be added to a woman's surname to identify her. The style name often consisted of a character that conveyed birth order. Because Zhou nobles sometimes married two or more sisters, it was convenient to identify them by their order of birth. A woman's name might also include the name of her natal state. Another naming method combined the woman's personal name (*ming*) with her surname. Deceased women were often referred to by a posthumous name and surname. In addition, family members and more-distant relatives called women by relational kinship terms. The same woman might be addressed as mother (*mu*), mother-in-law (*gu*), or ancestress (*bi*) depending on a person's tie to the deceased.[92]

A royal woman might also be called by one or more formal titles or honorifics.[93] Terms of address had yet to become standardized. A king's wife might have the prefix "great" (*da*) or "honorable" (*zi*) added to her name to mark high status. The ruler's primary wife was called *qi* and secondary mates were *fei*. A prefix to *fei* such as *yuan* (primary) or *ci* (secondary) conveyed a woman's rank within the harem. The character *wang* (king) was also sometimes placed in front of other terms to mark a woman's link to the monarch. A consort might thus be called *wangqi* (king's wife). *Wang* might also be combined with a woman's natal surname to identify a particular royal consort. Similarly, the wife of a high noble might prefix the title *gong* (duke) to her natal surname. Consorts were also called by vague honorific titles that were also used to refer to important men such as *hou* and *jun*. Eventually, women appropriated the title *hou* and it came to refer exclusively to the queen.

Although commoners were monogamous, aristocrats were often polygynous.[94] Western Zhou polygyny diminished the status of harem women. In a monarchal system, polygyny tends to degrade each woman's status as she lacks a unique relationship with the ruler. The formal wife may have enjoyed a higher status in relation to other harem women but this superiority was only relative. Most importantly, polygyny emphasized male supremacy.[95]

Sometimes a nobleman married several wives over the course of his life. Titled men also practiced a custom called *ying*, which anthropologists refer to as sororal polygyny or accompanying concubinage.[96] In this sort of marriage, a bride was accompanied to her husband's home by younger sisters, nieces, or other women of the same surname. In this sort of group marriage, it seems that one woman was the main wife and the others were considered minor spouses or concubines. The term *ying* originally meant "to send" or "to give," so minor spouses were sent along with the bride as a kind of dowry.

By this time, wives (*qi*) were already being distinguished from concubines (*qie*).[97] These two social roles had different positions within the *zongfa* kinship system of the Zhou nobility, with the wife clearly superior. This distinction is most clearly seen in the different statuses of sons born to wives and concubines. Although a man's sons were all considered brothers, a son's relative position within the family hierarchy depended on his mother's status. According to *zongfa*, the eldest son of the formal wife had the highest rank and would inherit the royal or noble title. Other sons of the wife ranked above those born to concubines, who could not be enfeoffed as nobles. Distinguishing the rank of each son reduced competition among siblings. The eldest son of the legitimate wife was automatically the designated heir so other sons would be less inclined to compete with him. Whenever kings and high nobles overrode this rule, chaos resulted.

Western Zhou burials show that wife and concubine had different ranks in the kinship network. At one early Western Zhou cemetery in Shanxi, the remains of some important men are accompanied by female human sacrifices.[98] Most sacrificed women lacked coffins, showing them to have been of low rank, perhaps servants. However, sometimes a higher status victim was buried in a coffin beside the deceased, perhaps a concubine sacrificed soon after her master's death. A wife was not subject to human sacrifice. Her remains were encoffined and placed in the main grave alongside those of her husband.

An aristocratic burial in Shaanxi clearly displays the different ranks of wife and concubine.[99] The site consists of a pair of adjacent tombs. One contains the nobleman's wife and the other has the man's remains in a double-layer coffin together with those of a woman who was sacrificed and placed in a simpler coffin near him. Inscriptions on burial goods identify the sacrificed woman as his favorite concubine. His wife received a respectful burial after she died a natural death while the concubine was killed to accompany her master to the grave. There were sixty-nine bronze vessels in these tombs. Of these the *ding* and *gui* vessels were considered most important as their numbers reflected the rank of the deceased. The nobleman had thirteen elaborate *ding* and *gui*, his wife had eleven simpler vessels, and the concubine had nine, symbolizing their relative ranks.

The Zhou practiced surname exogamy so people of the same surname could not wed.[100] This rule forced the nobility of different states to intermarry, binding the realm together in a dense network of marriage ties. Numerous bronze inscriptions and archaeological remains attest to political marriage among the royalty and nobility.[101] In distant antiquity, the Ji and Jiang lineages repeatedly intermarried, binding these two groups together to form the Zhou elite.[102] And before the Zhou conquest of Shang, the ruler of Zhou married the daughter of a Shang noble, tying the Zhou more closely to the Shang realm.[103] During the Western Zhou era, the wives of some important nobles were buried with objects from northern nomadic peoples.[104] These were likely foreign princesses who had married Zhou nobles as part of political alliances.

Political marriages were usually not reciprocal. Nobles often received a wife from a social inferior as they considered giving away a bride to someone of lower status disgraceful. Accordingly, the king of Zhou would give away his daughter in marriage using an aristocrat as an intermediary so that he could avoid embarrassment.[105] Likewise, when the king married the daughter of a major noble, the ruler's new in-law gained prestige from the transaction. While political marriage made noblewomen important to interstate relations, it reduced them to tokens of exchange between powerful men.

Western Zhou–era queens were not secluded in the inner palace, and they engaged in various public activities.[106] Queens went about openly, conferred with officials and nobles, presented gifts, made appointments, and issued orders. They were expected to emulate the deportment of the dynasty's earliest queens, who were allegedly paragons of virtue.[107] Jiang Yuan, the mythic ancestor of the Zhou people, served as the idealized archetype for Zhou consorts.[108] She was said to have given birth to Hou Ji, an agricultural deity considered the first Zhou leader. As the first human ancestor of the Zhou, Jiang Yuan had a high status in the state cult.[109]

Tai Ren, wife of King Ji, was frequently invoked as a queenly role model. As mother of King Wen, she was usually referred to as "Mother of Wen" (Wen Mu). Later generations seem to have celebrated Wen Mu for her maternal bond with the revered King Wen and not because of any personal accomplishments of her own. Bronze inscriptions and poetry claim that she was virtuous, respected her mother-in-law and ancestors, bore many offspring, and contributed to the success of her husband and son.[110] In other words, she was an outstanding wife and mother. Zhou women were exhorted to imitate her example, and an exceptional woman could be praised by calling her a Wen Mu.[111] This paragon was considered so saintly that women sometimes imitated her to gain divine aid and invoke fertility.[112]

Some Western Zhou queens exercised political authority directly.[113] A queen had her own staff and controlled considerable wealth.[114] She appointed an official who controlled access to her person, and audiences followed standard procedures. Queens sometimes issued orders when the king was away from the capital. Communication was slow so some kings empowered their spouse to handle routine matters in their absence.[115] For example, some queens sent officials as envoys to various domains while the king was away. Even when the ruler was present in the capital, the queen might issue orders to certain officials and craftsmen attached to the palace.[116] Nevertheless, the political importance of Western Zhou queens should not be overestimated. There is no evidence that the spouses of Zhou kings issued important orders. Activist queens may have been exceptional.

Unlike Shang consorts, Zhou queens did not lead armies. However, the presence of a woman in the army camp was still considered acceptable, and queens sometimes accompanied the ruler on military expeditions.[117] They traveled with the army in the role of king's spouse rather than as a participant and do not seem to have been involved in hostilities in any meaningful way. The Western Zhou was a pivotal time in the development of women's relationship with warfare. Before this era, some royal consorts had important military roles. Afterward, ritual restrictions and custom discouraged women from having anything to do with military matters.[118]

Perhaps the most significant activity of Western Zhou queens was their participation in the elite exchange network.[119] As before, in the absence of reliable commerce, the exchange of gifts kept valuables circulating through society. The regular presentation of gifts from the king to the nobility and officialdom also helped resolve a major flaw in the Western Zhou system. Because nobles had their own fiefs, they did not depend on the monarch so they did not necessarily have to show him respect or obey him. Moreover, the fiscal system was so primitive that officials did not receive a regular salary, making it difficult for the king to control them. Western Zhou rulers solved this problem by constantly handing out gifts to people in key positions. Gift giving created personal ties that obligated the recipients to reciprocate with a show of goodwill. By frequently presenting gifts to important people, kings managed to hold their realm together even as the nobility became increasingly stronger and more independent.

Although most gifts came from the king, queens controlled some economic resources and they also handed out gifts on a regular basis. The Western Zhou court was still patrimonial so the queen's bond to the king allowed her to act on his behalf in certain matters. It seems that a gift from the queen was seen as equivalent to a gift from the monarch himself so it also served to bind nobles and officials to the court.

Sometimes a queen distributed largesse in recompense for specific services. More often she presented a gift to a noble for no specific reason other than as a show of generosity intended to strengthen bonds between the royal court and the periphery. Common gifts included cowries, cloth and clothing, grain, horses, ornaments, bronze vessels and jade items, and precious metal.[120] Queens also handed out plots of land to the king's vassals.[121]

Queens participated in the feasting rituals that punctuated court life. Although these activities might sound trivial, banquets in fact had political significance as they symbolically bound the aristocracy to the throne. Queens held banquets to welcome visiting nobles and officials.[122] These formal meals had a ceremonial dimension and sometimes included the ritual consumption of alcohol. Feasting with important men allowed queens to take on a high-profile public role.

A queen's status did not necessarily diminish with the death of her spouse. Inscriptions record queens dowager performing politically significant activities. They ordered palace workers to carry out routine tasks, paid visits to nobles, and handed out largesse.[123] It is not clear why widowed queens maintained such a high status. It may have been because of their marriage to the previous monarch or perhaps it was their position as mother of the new king. According to the sacrificial system of the Zhou, mothers and sons shared a close bond, and this tie might have given queens dowager an elevated status.[124]

In this era, the wives of major aristocrats sometimes undertook activities akin to those of queens. Although Zhou was theoretically a unity, the greatest nobles gradually acted as de facto rulers of independent domains. Unlike the Zhou queen, the wives of nobles did not hand out precious gifts as their husbands did not have to distribute largesse to maintain the integrity of their domains.[125] However, they received gifts from the king and queen including cowries, jade and bronze objects, cinnabar, horses, silk, and food items.[126] Royal largesse shows them to have been significant personages, and they were likely seen as representatives of the domain and of the lineages of their husbands or fathers.[127] Rulers may have given these women gifts to attract the support of powerful men close to them. Although noblewomen received gifts from the throne, they received fewer than their husbands.[128] Men not only received far more gifts but were also given items of far greater value. Women were more likely to receive small articles that were largely symbolic.

A noblewoman occasionally undertook important affairs. She participated in the institutions overseeing her husband's domains and occasionally acted on his behalf in matters such as managing agricultural land.[129] But unlike royal consorts, there is little evidence that the wives of the high nobility routinely handled administrative matters on their own. Most frequently they are mentioned carrying out supporting roles in ancestral rituals conducted by their husbands.[130] This duty was so important that when a noblewoman married, her father sometimes dowered her with bronze vessels to be used in ancestral sacrifices, and she might also receive them from others as gifts.[131] Women were responsible for preparing food for the banquets associated with these sacrifices.[132] Ancestral rites featured ecstatic dancing in the ancestral temple. It was up to women to perform a ritualistic dance that pantomimed the virtuous behavior of King Wen's mother (Wen Mu). These dances emphasized swaying movements and stylized facial expressions.[133] Participating in the ancestral rites constituted a major aspect of elite female identity. By sacrificing to her husband's ancestors, a woman officially gained membership in his family.[134]

After a noblewoman's death, her progeny venerated her as an ancestral spirit. Archaeologists have recovered many bronze vessels used in sacrifices to specific female ancestors.[135] Other deceased women received sacrifices as an appendage of the sacrificial cult of their husbands.[136] Overall, female ancestors received far less ritual attention than men. In one survey of Zhou-inscribed bronze vessels, 93 percent were used in sacrifices to a male ancestor and only 7 percent for deceased women.[137] Nevertheless, female ancestors were respected as moral paragons and lauded as inspirations to the living.[138] One man credited his deceased mother with giving him the strength to lead an army into battle and prevail over his enemies.[139] A deceased woman's children were obligated to show her not just respect but also continued obedience.[140] A filial son inscribed two vessels with the vow that he would continue submitting to his deceased father and mother and carry out the commands they had given him.[141]

Over time the status of both queens and noblewomen declined. When the Zhou dynasty began, the system was initially in flux, allowing women to arrogate power and symbols of status.[142] However, as the ritual system matured, kinship and social roles became clearly defined. Under this body of rules, women had a far lower position than the men close to them. Symbolizing this regression, fewer ancestresses received sacrifices individually, and women were increasingly subsumed into rites dedicated primarily to their husbands.[143] According to a survey of bronze inscriptions, 64 percent of Western Zhou noblewomen received individual sacrifices and 36 percent received sacrifices along with their husband. During the Eastern Zhou, only 16 percent had individual sacrifices. The remainder had been subsumed into a husband's sacrificial cult. Married couples were buried together more often, showing the integration of the wife's ritual identity with that of the husband.[144] The tombs of noblewomen also gradually declined relative to those of their husband. They were buried with fewer prestigious bronze goods, chariot fittings, bells and chime stones, and even ceramic vessels.[145] Changing mortuary treatment shows that noblewomen steadily lost an independent identity. At the beginning of the dynasty, they were often known by their own name, but as they lost importance they were increasingly referred to as the "wife of" their spouse.[146]

During the Eastern Zhou era, society and politics changed considerably, giving rise to new opportunities and constraints. At this time elite culture became far more homogeneous, and it became common for the Chinese to contrast their civilization with the alleged barbarism of neighboring peoples.[147] This mindset made the standards of female behavior a component of Chinese identity. Concurrently the aristocracy tried to cope with rising chaos by embracing a canon of norms and rituals. These rules restricted women's actions and gave them far fewer chances to use their talents. The thinker Xunzi summed up this new view of ideal womanhood.[148]

> "May I inquire about the proper way to be a person's wife?" I say: If your husband follows the dictates of ritual, then compliantly obey him and wait upon him attentively. If your husband does not follow the dictates of ritual, then be apprehensive but keep yourself respectful.

As the rites constrained female autonomy, women increasingly became valued not for their personal attributes but as representatives of their natal family. Moreover kings declined into insignificance, pulling down their spouses with them. Due to these changes, Eastern Zhou queens were ciphers. Historians usually did not even bother to mention their names, and they are not recorded engaging in any significant public activities. These queens seem to have lived quiet lives in the palace, attending to family duties and conducting court rituals. As the influence of kings diminished, the high nobility assumed their powers. Dukes began to call themselves kings, and their domains became independent countries in all but name. Nobles used their daughters as tokens to forge alliances with the lords of other states.

As the Zhou political system fragmented, naming customs for women became more diverse.[149] A woman had a given name but it was considered disrespectful to say this to her face. An elite woman's proper name incorporated her natal surname as her father's family remained an important aspect of her identity even after marriage. In some inscriptions, a woman is referred to by her natal surname alone. A woman was often called by the ancient honorific *fu* together with her family's surname. She could also be identified by a combination of her given name together with her natal surname. In bronze inscriptions, a woman is often identified by her father's surname, natal state, and position in the kinship hierarchy. And after death a woman was known by the combination of her natal surname and a posthumous name. Sometimes her children would refer to her posthumously as *mu* (mother). As before, the primary wife of a king was titled *wanghou* (queen). The wife of a deceased king or mother of the current king was titled *taihou* (queen dowager).[150] The wife of a king might also have the term *da* (great) affixed to her name to mark her superior status.[151] Other terms marked the inferior status of lesser harem women. After her death, a high-ranking noblewoman might be called by the posthumous title *jun* (lady).[152]

Political marriage was an important factor in interstate relations. Sometimes ruling families intermarried repeatedly to maintain an important link. For example, children of the rulers of Qin and Jin married one another for generations, often wedding their cousins. Two ruling lines could become so intertwined that the ruling elites of the two states effectively merged into a single kin group.[153] The kings of Chu took the opposite approach, deliberately marrying with a wide range of partners to increase the scope of their influence.[154] At first the Chu kings married their daughters to the ruling families of small neighboring states to dominate them. Later they used political marriage to forge alliances with large states.

In theory, a wife joined her husband's family. Yet, in reality, she still owed primary loyalty to blood kin. Sometimes the states of a woman's husband and of her father fell into acrimony or even went to war. When forced to choose between father and husband, women chose the former.[155] In fact, it was expected that a wife would use her position to pursue her father's interests. A ruler's wife sometimes even represented the interests of her father's state at the court of her husband.[156] In later periods, powerful women often continued to side with their father over their husband or sons. Under the imperial system, many empresses promoted their father and brothers even if this meant going against the interests of husband and sons. The practice of favoring natal relatives, which had a major impact on the history of the Eastern Han and other eras, grew out of the ancient kinship system.

Surname exogamy affected relations between the Zhou realms. Rulers of the various states had about twenty different surnames.[157] Because of the taboo against marrying a spouse of the same surname, they had to wed counterparts from other states.[158] This intermixing had profound results, binding various regions together politically and culturally. The rulers of states even addressed one another by kinship terms. Sometimes these designated actual kinship relations, but they also treated non-relatives this way to cultivate a sense of intimacy and bring the two sides closer together.[159]

Sororate marriage became increasingly common, and it was not unusual for a ruler to marry several sisters at the same time.[160] When a primary wife died, one of the women who had accompanied her into marriage might be promoted to take her place. When a ruler had more than one spouse, he distinguished them according to rank.[161] The primary wife was called lady (*furen*). Lesser spouses (*fei*) had titles that specified their relative status in the harem, such as "second" (*er*) and "lower" (*xia*). In this era, the nobility also practiced levirate marriage (*zheng*).[162] When a man died, his son might marry the father's wives as a way of keeping them in the family. It seems that the husband having paid a bride price, these women were seen as belonging to the husband's family even after his death.

The duties of Eastern Zhou noblewomen were mostly ceremonial. They were expected to know how to properly conduct ancestral rituals, and fathers dowered brides with the bronze vessels used to perform these rites.[163] The ruler's wife also helped administer the rear palace and keep the establishment running smoothly.[164] Women occasionally claimed expertise in divination, and powerful men sometimes believed them.[165] Female diviners employed a variety of techniques, making use of turtle shells, yarrow stalks, and dream interpretation, and they used the resulting prophecies to further their political goals.

Unlike elite women in the Shang and Western Zhou, Eastern Zhou queens could not legitimately exercise authority on their own. They had to manipulate powerful men to get what they wanted, so harem women sometimes became involved in schemes and intrigues. For this reason men began to see female power as a source of confusion. Because it was so difficult for a woman to engage in politics, she usually did so only to benefit herself and those close to her.[166] A concubine might scheme to have herself promoted to wife or to have her son made heir apparent. Women also became involved in intrigues to help a paramour or cover up their adultery.

Historical works depict discussions of political matters taking place in the inner palace among family members.[167] The informality of patrimonial power sometimes allowed a woman to influence a man making key decisions. However, the oral nature of political discourse put women at a disadvantage. In later periods when administration had become more bureaucratic, discourse about important matters was largely written.[168] At this time, however, arguments were still presented orally before an audience of decision makers so the aristocracy held eloquence in high regard. A person making a speech was expected to be able to quote relevant passages from the canon of ancient poetry and other classical texts to support assertions.[169] Occasionally a woman appeared before men at a banquet and made an eloquent speech, gaining admiration for citing poems deemed appropriate. However, it was difficult for women to show off rhetorical skill as men usually excluded them from the important meetings where speeches were made.

On a few unusual occasions an Eastern Zhou consort managed to gain a role in administration. Toward the end of his reign Duke Ling of Wei lost interest in his duties and turned over responsibility for running the state to his wife Lady Nanzi.[170] Historians have had mixed judgments of Nanzi's stewardship. Some describe her as an intelligent and moral woman who tried to raise the ethical tenor of the state while other accounts portray Duke Ling as a weak, dissipated alcoholic and criticize

Nanzi for transgressing political norms. Overall, posterity took a negative view of this unusual era of Eastern Zhou female leadership.

Even as noblewomen lost power, the role of mother still presented them with opportunities to influence policy. Although the kinship structure was patrilineal, a man's bond with his mother was often stronger than that with his father.[171] Eastern Zhou authors praised the filial man who relied on his mother for guidance and deferred to her advice.[172] The ideology of filial piety eventually allowed some widowed consorts to declare a regency over young rulers. The first recorded female regency occurred in the state of Qin. In 306 BCE, Zhaoxiang ascended the throne as king of Qin. Although he was an adult, he was apparently not very capable so his mother, Queen Dowager Xuan, stepped forward and declared a regency.[173] However, she did not handle matters by herself. Instead, she made the fateful decision to bring in her younger brother Wei Ran to oversee the Qin government. Although some historians have criticized Wei Ran, in fact it seems that he was extremely successful. He handled domestic matters deftly and continued to expand the state through conquest, helping to put in place the conditions that allowed Qin to eventually unify China.

The unprecedented rule by Queen Dowager Xuan and Wei Ran was possible due to alterations in the fundamental fabric of Zhou society. Shifts in the kinship system brought mothers and sons much closer, and this intense bond seems to have provided Queen Xuan with a justification for defying precedent and declaring a regency for the first time. Moreover, flaws in the Qin system of government allowed the rise of consort kin.[174] At this time, Qin had a weak king and many high officials were mediocre and untrustworthy, making rule by consort kin seem efficient in comparison. The fact that Wei Ran managed the state so deftly drew the attention of subsequent generations. In later centuries, consort kinsmen gained opprobrium for arrogance and corruption. During this episode, however, rule by a talented consort kinsman seemed like a pragmatic strategy to overcome administrative shortcomings. Although the powers of Queen Dowager Xuan and Wei Ran were anomalous in the context of Eastern Zhou history, their collaboration set down a model of governance that later consorts would emulate.

Chapter 2

Notes

1. Nelson, "The Queens of Silla," 77–78, 83, 89.
2. Mair, *Primitive Government*, 108, 214, 227; Yoffee, *Myths of the Archaic State*, 33; Trigger, *Understanding Early Civilizations*, 145; Coe, "Religion and the Rise of Mesoamerican States," 157, 159; Keatinge, "The Nature and Role of Religious Diffusion in the Early Stages of Stage Formation," 172–73, 183, 185; Freidel, "Civilization as a State of Mind," 188–90, 224.
3. Qi, "Cong Yinxu jiaguwen kan Shangdai funü" gives a general introduction to the circumstances of Shang women.
4. Ban, *Hanshu*, 22:1071.
5. For the orthography of these characters, see Chen, *Shang Zhou xingshi zhidu yanjiu*, 50–54; Qi, "'Fu' zi benyi shitan," 149–54; Shima, *Inkyo bokuji kenkyū*, 94. Also Wang, *Wu diguo*, 144–46. Although this book is extremely speculative overall, some discussions of orthography have merit. Hu, *Jiaguxue Shangshi luncong*, 1:93–97, provides some of the most important sources regarding women titled *fu*.
6. Thorp, *China in the Early Bronze Age*, 209. The character *fu* is inscribed by itself at least fifty-five times. Considering the brevity of Shang bronze inscriptions, a single character inscription was not usual. There are several possible meanings for a character appearing in this sort of context. It may refer to the person who commissioned the item or the person who received it as a gift from someone else, in which case it indicated possession. Alternatively, it might refer to a deceased person who received sacrifices using this vessel. Cao, *Jinwen yu Yin Zhou nüxing wenhua*, 24.
7. Yoffee, *Myths of the Archaic State*, 115.
8. Keightley, "At the Beginning, 29–30; Chen, *Shang Zhou xingshi zhidu yanjiu*, 59.
9. Cao, *Jinwen yu Yin Zhou nüxing wenhua*, 26–27.
10. Chang, "A Brief Discussion of Fu Tzu," 113.
11. Keightley, "At the Beginning," 31–32; Qi, "Cong Yinxu jiaguwen kan Shangdai funü shehui diwei," 128–29; Wang, Zhang, and Yang, "Shilun Yinxu wuhao mu de Fu Hao," 14–16.
12. Zhao, "Zhufu tansuo," 102–3.
13. Chou, "Fu-x Ladies of the Shang Dynasty," 356–60; Cao, *Jinwen yu Yin Zhou nüxing wenhua*, 26–27.
14. Vandermeersch, *Wangdao ou la Voie Royale*, 275–76.
15. For example, Mei 媚, Huang 煌, and Xun 妎. Cao, *Jinwen yu Yin Zhou nüxing wenhua*, 39–40.
16. Cao, *Jinwen yu Yin Zhou nüxing wenhua*, 23; Chen, *Shang Zhou xingshi zhidu yanjiu*, 79–89, 112–14.
17. Chang, "A Brief Discussion of Fu Tzu," 104; Cao, *Jinwen yu Yin Zhou nüxing wenhua*, 22; Zhao, *Zhongguo zaoqi xingshi zhidu yanjiu*, 126–27. Not all two-character women's names include the character *fu*. Sometimes a character giving the country of a woman's birth, her lineage marker, or kinship relationship would come first, followed by her given name. In other cases, the woman's given name came first followed by a lineage marker. Cao, *Jinwen yu Yin Zhou nüxing wenhua*, 40–41.

18. Yang, "The Shang Dynasty Cemetery System," 57; Cao, *Yinxu Fu Hao mu mingwen yanjiu*, 77–84; Cao, "'Fuhao' nai 'Zifang' zhi nü," 381; Chang, "A Brief Discussion of Fu Tzu," 119; Li and Guo, "Yin Shang wenhua de fanrong," 57. These characters denoting kinship units were not surnames. True surnames did not emerge until the Zhou dynasty. Pulleyblank, "Ji and Jiang," 12; Chun, "Conceptions of Kinship and Kingship," 26.

19. Cao, *Jinwen yu Yin Zhou nüxing wenhua*, 22–23.

20. Cao, "'Fuhao' nai 'Zifang' zhi nü," 383; Cao, *Jinwen yu Yin Zhou nüxing wenhua*, 30.

21. Cheng, "A Study of the Bronzes," 83, 96–97, 99, 101–2; Zheng, *Shanggu Huaxia funü yu hunyin*, 118; Cao, "Jinwen 'nü,' 'mu' de xingyi shixi," 128–31; Chen, "Shangdai jinwen zhong zhi 'nüzi' mingci shuolue," 105–6; Wang, *Wu diguo*, 142; Chen, *Yinxu buci zongshu*, 447; Cao, *Jinwen yu Yin Zhou nüxing wenhua*, 32–37; Wang, "Rank and Power," 103; Zhao, *Jiaguwen yu Shangdai wenhua*, 126–27. Shima Kunio argues that the Shang pronounced the character *fu* the same way as *mu*. Shima, *Inkyo bokuji kenkyū*, 455. Shima also argues that the term *mu* was used in the early Shang. Later in the dynasty they used an archaic character equivalent to the modern character *he* to refer to the consorts of kings. Shima, *Inkyo bokuji kenkyū*, 93.

22. Zhao, "Zhufu tansuo," 105; Chang, "A Brief Discussion of Fu Tzu," 109–10; Zheng, *Shanggu Huaxia funü yu hunyin*, 136.

23. This character is often misread as *si*, the inverted form. *Hou* seems to be the correct reading. Yin, "'Di si' yu 'si mu' kao," 431; Song, *Xia Shang shehui shenghuo shi*, 154; Cao, *Jinwen yu Yin Zhou nüxing wenhua*, 19.

24. Cheng, "A Study of the Bronzes with the 'Ssu T'u Mu' Inscriptions," 101–2; Yin, "'Di si' yu 'si mu' kao," 433, 436; Song, *Xia Shang shehui shenghuo shi*, 153; Keightley, "At the Beginning," 40; Cao, *Jinwen yu Yin Zhou nüxing wenhua*, 15. For a dissenting opinion see Rao, "Fu Hao mu tongqi, yuqi," 299.

25. Cheng, "A Study of the Bronzes with the 'Ssu T'u Mu' Inscriptions," 82–83; Chang, *Early Chinese Civilization*, 81, 83; Cao, *Jinwen yu Yin Zhou nüxing wenhua*, 15, 106; Deng, "Shangdai Wu Ding shi guizu," 3–4. Guo, "Shi zubi," 1–60, examines the terms for female and male ancestors in detail.

26. Cao, *Jinwen yu Yin Zhou nüxing wenhua*, 23.

27. Chang, *Early Chinese Civilization*, 82–83; Keightley, "The Religious Commitment," 217; Keightley, "At the Beginning," 38; Zheng, *Shanggu Huaxia funü yu hunyin*, 117; Wang, "Rank and Power," 108–9; Chen, "Shixi Shangdai de zongmiao zhidu," 24. If a royal consort was not qualified to receive sacrifices in the ancestral shrine of the Shang kings, her children and other descendants would sacrifice to her at a small shrine built atop her tomb. Chen, "Shixi Shangdai de zongmiao zhidu," 24; Hu, "Tengzhou Qianzhang da Shangdai muzang dimian jianzhu jianxi," 146–51. There is the foundation for an offering hall on top of M5, the tomb of Fu Hao. The foundation was 6.5 x 5 meters wide. On top of the foundation were columns arranged in two bays. It was probably a sizeable roofed structure without walls that was used only for sacrifices to the spirit of the deceased. Thorp, *China in the Early Bronze Age*, 186–87. Fu Hao was exceptionally important, and few *fu* women had a sacrificial shrine on top of their tomb. Keightley, "At the Beginning," 44. In most cases, a woman probably received posthumous sacrifices as a subsidiary member of her husband's sacrificial cult.

28. For lists of names of the known Shang royal consorts see Hinsch, *Women in Ancient China*, 42; Li, "Yindai shehui shenghuo," 418–19; Shima, *Inkyo bokuji kenkyū*, 96–98; Chang, *Shang Civilization*, 167–68; Chen, *Yinxu buci zongshu*, 383–84.

29. Li, "Yindai shehui shenghuo," 419; Hu, *Jiaguxue Shangshi luncong*, vol. 1, 82–85. The Shang referred to women as *qi* and *qie*, which later meant wife and concubine respectively. These characters had yet to develop separate meanings, and both still referred to a female spouse. Zheng, *Shanggu Huaxia funü yu hunyin*, 143.

30. Song, *Xia Shang shehui shenghuo shi*, 141–43.

31. Song, *Xia Shang shehui shenghuo shi*, 145; Keightley, "At the Beginning," 29–31. For the monogamy of commoners see Geng, "Yinxuzu mudi zhong de 'fufu hezang mu,'" 35–39; Gao, *Zhoudai hunyin xingtai yanjiu*, 8–10; Qiao, "Lun Yinxu 'yi xue he zang' mu de tezhi," 149–50.

32. Li, "Yindai shehui shenghuo," 420; Zheng, *Shanggu Huaxia funü yu hunyin*, 117–18; Wang, "Rank and Power," 109–11; Fan, "Cong Wang Hai 'bin yu you yi,'" 71; Cao, *Jinwen yu Yin Zhou nüxing wenhua*, 11.

33. Knauft, "Violence and Sociality," 399.

34. Zheng, "Shangzu de hunyin zhidu," 9–10; Ge, "Zhouji buci zhong de zhixi xianbi," 121–28; Cao, *Jinwen yu Yin Zhou nüxing wenhua*, 31.

35. Gao, *Zhoudai hunyin xingtai yanjiu*, 10; Keightley, "At the Beginning," 35–40; Wang, "Rank and Power," 97, 100–101, 107.

36. Fan, "Cong Wang Hai 'bin yu you yi,'" 70; Zhao, "Shangdai neihun," 132–34. Vandermeersch, *Wangdao ou la Voie Royale*, 274–75, 288–92, argues to the contrary that the Shang elite were probably endogamous. This viewpoint used to be popular, but recently opinions have shifted and most scholars now believe that the Shang were largely exogamous.

37. Chang, "Urbanism and the King in Ancient China," 8.

38. Cui, *Xian Qin zhengzhi hunyin shi*, 37–49.

39. Vandermeersch, *Wangdao ou la Voie Royale*, 297; Cao, *Jinwen yu Yin Zhou nüxing wenhua*, 182; Cui, *Xian Qin zhengzhi hunyin shi*, 49–55.

40. Song, *Xia Shang shehui shenghuo shi*, 160.

41. Keightley, "At the Beginning," 43.

42. Zheng, *Shanggu Huaxia funü yu hunyin*, 130–31; Yang, "Jiaguwen zhong suojian Shangdai de gongna zhidu," 31; Wang, Zhang, and Yang, "Shilun Yinxu wuhao mu de Fu Hao," 5–7; Qi, "Cong Yinxu jiaguwen" 130; Wang, "Cong 'pinji zhi chen' xianxiang," 23.

43. Zheng, *Shanggu Huaxia funü yu hunyin*, 128; Wang, "Rank and Power," 97, 110.

44. Baker, *Chinese Family and Kinship*, 71–74.

45. Keightley, "At the Beginning," 41.

46. Zheng, *Shanggu Huaxia funü yu hunyin*, 129; Mumford, "Death Do Us Unite," 10.

47. Yang, "The Shang Dynasty Cemetery System," 55.

48. Keightley, "At the Beginning," 44–45.

49. Yang, "The Shang Dynasty Cemetery System," 55.

50. Linduff, "Women's Lives Memorialized in Burial," 263.

51. Cao, *Jinwen yu Yin Zhou nüxing wenhua*, 45. Divinations concerning prayers to a deceased woman were also sometimes performed in the ancestral temple of her husband,

reducing her to a subsidiary member of her husband's sacrificial cult. Keightley, "At the Beginning," 43.

52. Keightley, "At the Beginning," 41, 43.

53. Chang, *Shangdai zhouji zhidu*, 86, 105; Chang, *Shang Civilization*, 171. People sometimes sacrificed to a deceased married couple together but this practice was not used in sacrifices to kings and their consorts. Cao, *Jinwen yu Yin Zhou nüxing wenhua*, 46–49.

54. Keightley, "At the Beginning," 43. Chang, *Shangdai zhouji zhidu*, 108–9; and Chen, *Yinxu buci zongshu*, 386–88, each have lists of which ancestors and ancestresses received sacrifices on each day of the ten-day weekly cycle. A deceased consort might also receive sacrifices at a shrine on top of her tomb. Chen, "Shixi Shangdai de zongmiao zhidu," 24.

55. Chang, "A Brief Discussion of Fu Tzu," 115; Xu, "Shangdai zhufu de zongjiao diwei," 456–57; Zhao, *Jiaguwen yu Shangdai wenhua*, 145–46; Liu, "Shangdai houqi jizu yishi leixing," 80–94; Lian, "Shangdai de baiji yu yuji," 26, 53.

56. Deng, "Shangdai Wu Ding shi guizu 'zi,'" 5.

57. Song, *Xia Shang shehui shenghuo shi*, 178; Zhao, *Jiaguwen yu Shangdai wenhua*, 146–49.

58. Wang, Zhang, and Yang, "Shilun Yinxu wuhao mu de Fu Hao," 19–20.

59. Xu, "Shangdai zhufu de zongjiao diwei," 456–57.

60. For example, Li, "Tangdai minghun fengsu xinyi," 286–93.

61. Vandermeersch, *Wangdao ou la Voie Royale*, 264–70; Hu, "Shangdai 'yuzi' lei buci," 46; Keightley, "At the Beginning," 33–34; Hu, *Jiaguxue Shangshi luncong*, 1:114–24; Cao, *Jinwen yu Yin Zhou nüxing wenhua*, 12, 18; Qi, "Cong Yinxu jiaguwen," 131–32.

62. Keightley, "At the Beginning," 42.

63. Song, *Xia Shang shehui shenghuo shi*, 171–77.

64. Mullis, "Toward a Confucian Ethic of the Gift," 178–81.

65. Yang, "Jiaguwen zhong suojian Shangdai de gongna zhidu," 28–30; Cao, *Jinwen yu Yin Zhou nüxing wenhua*, 13–14.

66. Chou, "Fu-x Ladies of the Shang Dynasty," 365; Yang, "Jiaguwen zhong suojian Shangdai de gongna zhidu," 31; Qi, "Cong Yinxu jiaguwen kan Shangdai funü shehui diwei," 129.

67. Chou, "Fu-x Ladies of the Shang Dynasty," 361.

68. Zheng, *Shanggu Huaxia funü yu hunyin*, 135–36; Cao, *Jinwen yu Yin Zhou nüxing wenhua*, 10, 17, 29; Xu, "Shangdai zhufu de zongjiao diwei," 450; Zhao, *Jiaguwen yu Shangdai wenhua*, 141.

69. Douglas and Isherwood, *The World of Goods*; Brumfiel, "Consumption and Politics at Aztec Huexotla," 676.

70. Herdt, "Sexual Repression, Social Control, and Gender Hierarchy," 195.

71. Wang, Zhang, and Yang, "Shilun Yinxu wuhao mu de Fu Hao," 7–10; Chou, "Fu-x Ladies of the Shang Dynasty," 365; Zheng, *Shanggu Huaxia funü yu hunyin*, 135–36; Keightley, "At the Beginning," 31–33; Cao, *Jinwen yu Yin Zhou nüxing wenhua*, 5–6, 12, 27–28; Xu, "Shangdai zhufu de zongjiao diwei," 452–55; Yang, "Qianyi jiaguwen suo fanying de Shangdai funü diwei," 371–73.

72. Chou, "Fu-x Ladies of the Shang Dynasty," 371–74; Zhao, "Zhufu tansuo," 104–5; Zhao, *Jiaguwen yu Shangdai wenhua*, 143; Cao, *Jinwen yu Yin Zhou nüxing wenhua*, 16–17.

CHAPTER 2

73. Wheatley, *The Pivot of the Four Quarters*, 56; Rohrlich, "State Formation in Sumer," 87.
74. For example, Li, *Beishi*, 79:2651.
75. Divale and Harris, "Population, Warfare, and the Male Supremacist Complex," 521.
76. Wang, Zhang, and Yang, "Shilun Yinxu wuhao mu de Fu Hao," 2–5; Wang, "Cong 'pinji zhi chen,'" 22–23; Yang, "Qianyi jiaguwen suo fanying de Shangdai funü diwei," 373–74; Zhao, *Jiaguwen yu Shangdai wenhua*, 139; Qi, "Cong Yinxu jiaguwen kan Shangdai funü shehui diwei," 129–30. There was a common link between women's lordship over a fief and female participation in warfare. Toler, *Women Warriors*, 140–41.
77. Zhao, *Jiaguwen yu Shangdai wenhua*, 140.
78. Cao, *Jinwen yu Yin Zhou nüxing wenhua*, 28.
79. Chou, "Fu-x Ladies of the Shang Dynasty," 368–71; Chang, "A Brief Description of the Fu Hao Oracle Bone Inscriptions," 136; Keightley, "At the Beginning," 31–33; Zhao, *Jiaguwen yu Shangdai wenhua*, 140; Cao, *Jinwen yu Yin Zhou nüxing wenhua*, 7–9, 16; Wang, *Wu diguo*, 291–95.
80. Zheng, *Shanggu Huaxia funü yu hunyin*, 134.
81. Cao, *Jinwen yu Yin Zhou nüxing wenhua*, 8.
82. Thorp, *China in the Early Bronze Age*, 104.
83. Cao, *Jinwen yu Yin Zhou nüxing wenhua*, 9.
84. Cao, *Jinwen yu Yin Zhou nüxing wenhua*, 19–20.
85. Linduff, "Women's Lives Memorialized," 263–65.
86. Wang, "Rank and Power," 102.
87. Hao, "Yinxu Xiaotun M5 zai tantao," 20–26; Wang, "Rank and Power," 101–2; Li, "Yinxu Fu Hao mu xieshi dongwuxing yuqi," 120–21; Cao, *Jinwen yu Yin Zhou nüxing wenhua*, 11, 13.
88. Tang, "The Burial Ritual of the Shang Dynasty," 176.
89. Xu and He, "Xin shiji Yinxu kaogu de zhongda faxian," 70.
90. Wang, "Rank and Power," 103.
91. Wang, "Nü zi shuo," 163–66; Zhang, "Zhoudai nüzi de xingshi zhidu," 67–68; Cao, "Zhoudai jinwen," 79–80; Mu, "Zhoudai jinwen zhong de fuming," 54–55, 15; Cao, *Jinwen yu Yin Zhou nüxing wenhua*, 106, 113–17.
92. Cao, *Jinwen yu Yin Zhou nüxing wenhua*, 199.
93. Chen, "Cong qingtongqi mingwen," 254–64; Mu, "Zhoudai jinwen zhong de fuming," 15; Cao, *Jinwen yu Yin Zhou nüxing wenhua*, 64, 78, 86–87.
94. Li, "Zhouzu de shizu zhidu yu Tuobazu de qianfengjian zhi," 244; Zheng, *Shanggu Huaxia funü yu hunyin*, 211–12; Xie, *Zhoudai jiating xingtai*, 50–54. The poem Mao 101 ("Southern Hill") demands that commoners practice monogamy. Waley, *The Book of Songs*, 80; Karlgren, *The Book of Odes*, 65–66.
95. Schlegel, *Male Dominance and Female Authority*, 98; White and Burton, "Causes of Polygyny," 872.
96. Granet, *La polygynie sororale et le sororat dans la Chine féodale*; Cao, "Cong jinwen kan Zhoudai yingnü hunzhi," 101–4; Cao, *Jinwen yu Yin Zhou nüxing wenhua*, 151–56, 171–75; Cao, "Chunqiu shiqi yinghun yanjiu," 105–6; Cai, "Chunqiu shiqi guizu shixing yingqie," 111–17.

97. Zheng, *Shanggu Huaxia funü yu hunyin*, 138–39, 162–66; Gao, "Zhoudai zongfa zhidu xia de 'mudi,'" 41–47. Chen, *Chunqiu hunyin lisu yu shehui lilun*, 8, argues to the contrary that the distinction between wife and concubine did not become apparent until the Chunqiu era.

98. Mumford, "Death Do Us Unite," 10.

99. Yu, "Ritual Practice, Status, and Gender Identity," 119, 123–24, 127.

100. Li, "Zhouzu de shizu zhidu yu Tuobazu de qianfengjian zhi," 239; Kurihara, *Kodai Chūgoku koninsei no rei rinen to keitai*, 383–455; Cui, *Xian Qin zhengzhi hunyin shi*, 1–23; Cao, *Jinwen yu Yin Zhou nüxing wenhua*, 144–49; Liu, "'Shijing' zhong suojian de Zhoudai tongxing bu hun lisu," 92.

101. Cao, *Jinwen yu Yin Zhou nüxing wenhua*, 182–88.

102. Some scholars theorize that every other generation, the king of Zhou had to marry a woman surnamed Jiang due to the *zhaomu* system. Chen, "Cong qingtongqi mingwen," 39–45.

103. Mao 236 ("Major Bright"). Waley, *The Book of Songs*, 229; Karlgren, *The Book of Odes*, 187–88.

104. Ying, "Gender, Status, Ritual Regulations," 194–95.

105. Chang, *Early Chinese Civilization*, 90.

106. Chen, "Cong qingtongqi mingwen," 18–34; Liu, "Xi Zhou jinwen zhong suojian de Zhou wang houfei," 85–90.

107. Yang, "Zhoudai shengmu songge tanxi," 277–78.

108. Mao 245 ("Birth to the People") and Mao 300 ("The Closed Temple"). Waley, *The Book of Songs*, 244–47, 313–17; Karlgren, *The Book of Odes*, 199–202, 257–61. Under the imperial system she was still assumed to have been an archetypal royal mother. For example, see Shen, *Songshu*, 27:764–66.

109. Liu, *Jiu Tang shu*, 21:839, 23:891.

110. Pang, "The Consorts of King Wu and King Wen," 124–35; Ban, *Hanshu*, 22:1071; Wei, *Weishu*, 108C:2786–87; Cook, *Death in Ancient China*, 74; Goldin, *The Culture of Sex in Ancient China*, 53–54.

111. Cook and Goldin, *A Source Book of Ancient Chinese Bronze Inscriptions*, 277; Liu, *Jiu Tang shu*, 62:2390.

112. Cook, "Ancestor Worship during the Eastern Zhou," 260–61.

113. Goldin, *The Culture of Sex in Ancient China*, 57–58, describes the controversy over the identity and role of a female adviser at the court of King Wu.

114. Creel, *The Origins of Statecraft in China*, 394–95; Li, *Bureaucracy and the State in Early China*, 69.

115. Cao, *Jinwen yu Yin Zhou nüxing wenhua*, 67–69.

116. Cook and Goldin, *A Source Book of Ancient Chinese Bronze Inscriptions*, 51; Xie, "Jinwen zhong suojian Xi Zhou wanghou shiji kao," 149.

117. Xie, "Jinwen zhong suojian Xi Zhou wanghou shiji kao," 146–47.

118. Wang and Sun, "Zhanguo Qin Han shiqi de nüjun," 113–14, 116. During the Eastern Zhou era, queens had no role in warfare. Female commoners sometimes performed supporting roles, such as building fortifications and mending soldiers' clothing. Weapons were also generally absent from female tombs, whereas they were common in

the tombs of male nobles. Yu, "Ritual Practice, Status, and Gender Identity," 133; Huang, "Gender Differentiation in Jin State Jade Regulations," 146; Jiang, "Zhanguo shiqi gu Shu shehui de bianqian," 341.

119. Xie, "Jinwen zhong suojian Xi Zhou wanghou shiji kao," 143–44.

120. Pang, "The Consorts of King Wu and King Wen," 129–30; Xie, "Jinwen zhong suojian Xi Zhou wanghou shiji kao," 143–45, 147–49; Cao, *Jinwen yu Yin Zhou nüxing wenhua*, 64–68.

121. Cao, *Jinwen yu Yin Zhou nüxing wenhua*, 70; Cook and Goldin, *A Source Book*, 49.

122. Xie, "Jinwen zhong suojian Xi Zhou wanghou shiji kao," 144–45; Cao, *Jinwen yu Yin Zhou nüxing wenhua*, 64–67.

123. Xie, "Jinwen zhong suojian Xi Zhou wanghou shiji kao," 148; Cao, *Jinwen yu Yin Zhou nüxing wenhua*, 83–84.

124. According to the *zhaomu* system of the state of Lu, which preserved the ancient rites most completely during the Eastern Zhou era, the ancestral tablet of a father was placed in a different row from those of his sons but the mother's tablet was placed in the same row as her sons. Li and Yu, "Lu guo zhaomu zhidu lice," 44.

125. Nevertheless, female nobles did hand out some gifts, as the exchange of gifts was an important practice that helped maintain the Zhou social and political networks. Cao, *Jinwen yu Yin Zhou nüxing wenhua*, 84.

126. Creel, *The Origins of Statecraft in China*, 394–95; Cao, *Jinwen yu Yin Zhou nüxing wenhua*, 78–81, 83–84; Cook and Goldin, *A Source Book*, 40, 91, 128.

127. Cao, *Jinwen yu Yin Zhou nüxing wenhua*, 81.

128. Cao, *Jinwen yu Yin Zhou nüxing wenhua*, 99.

129. Cao, *Jinwen yu Yin Zhou nüxing wenhua*, 82; Cook and Goldin, *A Source Book*, 253–54.

130. Baker, *Chinese Family and Kinship*, 82–91; Geng, "Zhoudai jiazu jisi yu liangxing guanxi lunlüe," 9–22; Cook, "Education and the Way of the Former Kings," 315; Cao, *Jinwen yu Yin Zhou nüxing wenhua*, 212–14.

131. Cook and Goldin, *A Source Book*, 276.

132. Mao 209 ("Thick Star-Thistle"), Waley, *The Book of Songs*, 194–96; Karlgren, *The Book of Odes*, 161–64.

133. Cook, "Moonshine and Millet," 15; Cook, "Ancestor Worship during the Eastern Zhou," 254, 260–61.

134. Shiga, *Chūgoku kazokuhō no genri*, 459–66; Li, *The Readability of the Past*, 150.

135. Cao, "San Bo Che Fu qi yu Xi Zhou hunyin zhidu," 63–65; Cao, *Jinwen yu Yin Zhou nüxing wenhua*, 85, 111–12; Cook and Goldin, *A Source Book*, 73; Zhou, *Festivals, Feasts, and Gender Relations*, 201–2.

136. Feng, "Wo fangding mingwen yu Xi Zhou sangdianli," 185–212; Cao, *Jinwen yu Yin Zhou nüxing wenhua*, 201–6, 260–67; Cook and Goldin, *A Source Book*, 8–9, 65–66, 261.

137. Cao, "Jinwen zhong de nüxing xiangjizhe ji qi shehui diwei," 80.

138. Yang, "Zhoudai shengmu songge tanxi," 277–78; Cao, *Jinwen yu Yin Zhou nüxing wenhua*, 109.

139. Cao, *Jinwen yu Yin Zhou nüxing wenhua*, 107–9; Zhou, *Festivals, Feasts, and Gender Relations*, 202–3; Cook and Goldin, *A Source Book*, 69.
140. Hamilton, "Patriarchy, Patrimonialism, and Filial Piety," 77–104.
141. Cook and Goldin, *A Source Book*, 141–42.
142. Ying, "Gender, Status, Ritual Regulations, and Mortuary Practice," 182.
143. Cao, "Jinwen zhong de nüxing xiangjizhe ji qi shehui diwei," 84.
144. Mumford, "Death Do Us Unite," 11–12.
145. Ying, "Gender, Status, Ritual Regulations, and Mortuary Practice," 174–75, 179, 184, 196–97; Huang, "Gender Differentiation in Jin State Jade Regulations," 142–45.
146. Ying, "Gender, Status, Ritual Regulations, and Mortuary Practice," 161–62.
147. Tackett, *The Origins of the Chinese Nation*, 147–48.
148. Hutton, *Xunzi*, 120.
149. Mu, "Zhoudai jinwen zhong de fuming," 54–55; Liu, "Handai funü de mingzi," 35–36; Zhang, "Zhoudai nüzi de xingshi zhidu," 67–68; Cao, *Jinwen yu Yin Zhou nüxing wenhua*, 241–46. Besides the types of names mentioned here, many other honorifics and terms of address were in use as well. Cao, *Jinwen yu Yin Zhou nüxing wenhua*, 258–59; Mu, "Zhoudai jinwen zhong de fuming," 15. In Chu, elite women were addressed differently. Cao, *Jinwen yu Yin Zhou nüxing wenhua*, 247–50; Luo, "Chuguo de taizi zhidu yanjiu," 71.
150. Cao, *Jinwen yu Yin Zhou nüxing wenhua*, 252–57; Gao, "Qin guo hunyin zhidu yanjiu," 90; Xu, *Qin huiyao dingbu*, 1:12–15.
151. Mu, "Zhoudai jinwen zhong de fuming," 15.
152. Huang, "Chuguo sanggui zhidu yanjiu," 64–67, 58.
153. Zhang, *Hunyin yu shehui*, 46. Baştuğ, "Kinship, Marriage and Descent in Early China," 149–187, argues that the Zhou nobility had a Dravidian-style kinship system centered on cross-cousin marriage.
154. Zhang, "Dong Zhou Chu guo lianhun kaoshu," 52–57.
155. Thatcher, "Marriages of the Ruling Elite," 44; Geng, "Dong Zhou zhengzhi waijiao hunzhong de xingbie chayi," 135–36; Li, *The Readability of the Past*, 150–51.
156. Yao, *Chunqiu huiyao*, 1:44–50. Qing dynasty scholars used transmitted sources to compile a list of the known consorts of major nobles from the Chunqiu period. Bai, "Xian Qin nüxing yanjiu," 166–83, provides a comprehensive table of Zhou dynasty political marriages, organized according to state. Thatcher, "Marriages of the Ruling Elite in the Spring and Autumn Period," 25–57, records 150 noble marriages from the Chunqiu era. Also see Cao, "Cong jinwen kan liang Zhou hunyin guanxi," 108–14; Cao, *Jinwen yu Yin Zhou nüxing wenhua*, 216–25; Zhao, "Jin guo furen kao," 313–14.
157. Wang, "Shilun 'Zuo zhuan' zhong de hunyinguan," 116.
158. Yang, "Chunqiu shidai zhi nannü fengji," 21; Cao, *Jinwen yu Yin Zhou nüxing wenhua*, 210. For exceptions to surname exogamy see Wang, "Shilun 'Zuo zhuan' zhong de hunyinguan," 117; Zheng, *Shanggu Huaxia funü yu hunyin*, 236–38; Yang, "Chunqiu shidai zhi nannü fengji," 21–22. The Shang remnants in the state of Song had unique marriage customs. Sometimes the ruling family married with counterparts from other states, but they also married with the families of Song officials. This practice seems to have

been a holdover from Shang dynasty marriage practices. Cai, "Chunqiu shiqi Song 'nei hunzhi' kaocha," 117–18.

159. Hsu, "Development of State-Society Relationship in Early China," 5.

160. Xu, *Qin huiyao dingbu*, 7:92–94; Cao, "Cong jinwen kan Zhoudai yingnü hunzhi," 100–7; Chen, "Chunqiu shiqi de ying jiahun ji qizhong de nüxing," 22–25; Zhang and Li, "Lun Zhoudai de ying hun zhidu," 170–72; Wu, "Zhoudai 'ying' de diwei," 137–38; Zhu, Huang, and Shen, "Shilun Chunqiu shiqi ying hunzhi," 73–76; Deng, "Yizhong huangdan de hunzhi," 90–94; Cao, "Chunqiu shiqi yinghun yanjiu," 105–9. Cai, "Chunqiu shiqi guizu shixing yingqie, zhidi hunzhi ma?," 111–17, believes that sororate was a kind of monogamy.

161. Li, "Zhouzu de shizu zhidu yu Tuobazu," 244; Thatcher, "Marriages of the Ruling Elite in the Spring and Autumn Period," 29, 31. Chen, "Chunqiu hunyin lisu yu shehui lilun," 8. The kings of Chu did not clearly distinguish among the ranks of harem women. Zheng, *Shanggu Huaxia funü yu hunyin*, 232–36.

162. Qian, *Zhoudai zongfa zhidu yanjiu*, 53–60; Huang, "Gudai Xila yu Zhongguo Zhouchao jichengzhi de bijiao," 438–47; Liu and Zhang, "Lun Chunqiu shiqi 'zheng' hunzhi de he 'li' xing," 169–71.

163. Cao, *Jinwen yu Yin Zhou nüxing wenhua*, 216–18; Cook, "Education and the Way of the Former Kings," 321.

164. Cao, *Jinwen yu Yin Zhou nüxing wenhua*, 238–41.

165. Zhen, "Shanggu Jiang shi buzu minsu yicun," 77–80; Kalinowski, "Diviners and Astrologers," 351, 359; Li, *The Readability of the Past*, 233–48.

166. Geng and Liu, "Chunqiu shiqi guizu funü de canzheng yu liangxing guanxi," 97–101; Zhao and Lu, "Chunqiu shiqi Qi guo guifu 'luanzheng' tanxi," 120–21; Wang and Zhang, *Zhongguo funü tongshi: Xian Qin juan*, 190–97; Guo, "Cong Li Ji sha Shen Sheng shuoqi," 84–86.

167. Gao, *Zuozhuan nüxing yanjiu*, 151.

168. Cook, "Education and the Way of the Former Kings," 307.

169. Zhou, "Virtue and Talent," 1–3, 12–13, 19–20; Cook, "Education and the Way of the Former Kings," 334.

170. Milburn, "Gender, Sexuality and Power in Early China," 1–29.

171. Van Norden, *Mengzi*, 31–32 (1B16.1). Mencius's mourning rituals for his mother were famously more lavish than those for his father. This is because his official rank was higher when his mother died than when his father died. In each case, he conducted mourning in a manner appropriate to his official rank.

172. Shimomi, *Kō to bosei no mekanizumu*; Shimomi, *Bosei izon no shisō*. For example, Cao, *Jinwen yu Yin Zhou nüxing wenhua*, 110–11.

173. Takigawa, *Shiki kaichū kōshō*, 5:64–69; Xu, *Qin huiyao dingbu*, 1:16; McMahon, "Women Rulers in Imperial China," 193.

174. Wang, "Zhanguo houqi Qin guo waiqi yanjiu," 108, 110.

CHAPTER 3

The Imperial System

After Qin Shihuang unified China in 221 BCE, he established a new system of government intended to hold together and effectively administer the largest country the world had ever seen. Central to this restructuring, he created a new form of monarchy that discarded the rites and traditions of the previous dynasty. He deemed the title "king" insufficiently grand and styled himself *huangdi* (emperor). The Qin dynasty may have been brief, but because it established the basic components of the imperial system, it served as an important point of transition between the aristocratic Zhou and Han dynasty monarchy.

During the late Eastern Zhou era, the state of Qin had a typical consort system. Specific titles designated queens, queens dowager, lesser consorts, and the wives of princes.[1] Qin kings sometimes practiced sororal polygyny, but only one spouse received the title *wanghou* (queen).[2] Qin Shihuang did not consider it necessary to name an empress as a counterpart to the emperor. In fact, he does not seem to have envisioned any role for women in the new imperial system.[3]

It is impossible to know the precise number of women in the palace in any era of Chinese history, and the reign of the first emperor was no exception.[4] Qin Shihuang likely had thousands of concubines, many of them captured from the palaces of defeated monarchs. He kept a huge harem to project a grandiose image for his new dynasty. Various concubines bore the emperor about fifty children.[5] These women had a low position. When Qin Shihuang died, all of the childless concubines in the palace were reportedly sacrificed and buried in his massive tomb to accompany him to the afterlife.⁶ Although archaeologists have yet to unearth that section of his mausoleum, it probably houses the remains of hundreds or even thousands of women.

Qin Shihuang did not allow his mother to participate in the government. She allegedly disgraced herself by committing adultery with a man who died during an attempted coup against the emperor. As punishment she was confined to a marginal palace for the remainder of her life.⁷ Even so, the emperor honored his mother with the novel title empress dowager (*di taihou*). Perhaps Qin Shihuang considered this title proper because she had been called queen dowager (*wang taihou*) after her husband's death under the old system of royal ranks.

After the collapse of the short-lived Qin, the rebel Liu Bang reunited the realm and established the Han dynasty in 202 BCE. He revived the Qin dynasty title emperor (*huangdi*) and is known to posterity as Emperor Han Gaozu. However, unlike Qin Shihuang, Gaozu granted his wife the corresponding title empress (*huanghou*).⁸ As married women of the time were called by their natal surname, Han dynasty empresses were designated by their father's surname together with their title.⁹

Although the Chinese have long been accustomed to the titles of emperor and empress and understand what these roles entailed, at the beginning of the Han dynasty these were strange-sounding neologisms. No one was certain what an empress was, what powers she had, and how she ought to conduct herself. The first empress, Gaozu's wife Lü Zhi, exploited this ambiguity to take control of the government after her husband's death. By initially defining the empress as having an active and important role, she had a decisive impact on the history of the institution.

Han empresses could accrue power in several ways. Many were extremely wealthy. The Han fiscal system included units of taxation called benefices (*yi*). Taxes paid by the residents of these districts went to the empress and other high-ranking people as stipends.¹⁰ Wealth from a large benefice gave the empress an independent income. An ambitious empress could also use her access to the ruler, bonds with her sons, and the prestige of her lofty status to accrue power. Moreover, because dynastic regulations prohibited princes from serving in the central government,

Han emperors often appointed their in-laws to sensitive posts, allowing many of the family members of empresses to accrue immense power.

The Han dynasty stands out as the most important era in the evolution of the institution of the empress, as this was the time when the role of the Chinese empress was created and defined. As people had yet to form clear ideas of what an empress should do and how she should behave, there was initially considerable flux. Under each reign, consorts and their kinsmen had somewhat different relationships with the emperor and officialdom. Han empresses sometimes enjoyed considerable power and prestige, and officials assumed that they might be important political actors. However, this outcome was not predetermined. If Han emperors and officials had acted differently, the dynasty's empresses might have ended up hidden from sight and insulated from politics, as was the case in most monarchies in other regions of the world. Yet, due to a complex series of events, imperial consorts often became important figures at the Han court and sometimes even seized control of the government. To understand how the empress became so important at this time it is necessary to examine in detail the key events that affected women's roles in the evolving imperial system.

Unlike Qin Shihuang, who does not seem to have had a designated wife, Emperor Gaozu established monogamy as a standard for his new dynasty. Monogamy had long been the norm for ordinary people during the Zhou era.[11] Because the founder of the Han had been born a commoner, he readily embraced monogamous marriage. Monogamy simplified the palace structure and helped emperors avoid some of the scandals and intrigues that plague polygynous systems. Gaozu also seems to have promoted the conjugal bond to stabilize a society that had been wrecked by lengthy warfare.[12] Moreover, the monogamous relationship of emperor and empress made the palace seem like a morally pure space, helping to legitimize the new political system.[13]

Emperor Gaozu's decision to name an empress and practice monogamous marriage had immense ramifications. From the Han dynasty onward, law and custom enforced monogamy as the norm for both rulers and subjects. Henceforth, most Chinese emperors had one official wife, who was labeled *huanghou* (empress). Other women in the harem were lesser consorts. Most were concubines with low standing but some were dignified with various titles. Later, conquering nomads who ruled over north China during the Six Dynasties practiced alien marriage customs. However, Tang dynasty emperors revived many Han dynasty practices and regulations, making Han views of imperial marriage and the empress standard features of Chinese government.

Monogamous marriage intensified the bond between the emperor and empress. Emperors declared that the married couple constitutes a single unit and justified marriage as a practice rooted in natural human predispositions.[14] As emperor and empress were husband and wife, it was assumed that they ought to have a close relationship. Accordingly, just as commoner couples of the time were buried together, the empress was usually interred next to her spouse albeit each in a separate tomb as befitted their high status.[15] Although both spouses were supposed to treasure marriage and strive to make it work well, moralists taught that the burden fell mostly on the wife. For a marriage to flourish, the wife had to conduct herself in an exemplary manner. This assumption led moralists to advocate female reclusion, so empresses and minor consorts were usually confined to the palace.

Early historians described empresses in different ways.[16] The two earliest major histories of the imperial era, *Memoirs of the Historian* (*Shiji*) and *Records of the Han* (*Hanshu*), mention most empresses only in passing.[17] In contrast, *Records of the Latter Han* (*Hou Hanshu*) has a separate section dedicated to the biographies of empresses, and some authors of subsequent official dynastic histories followed this format.[18] Giving empresses such a prominent place in the standard history of the Eastern Han recognized the political importance of consorts and their families at that time.

Classical studies conditioned scholars to assume that figures from the past should be subject to moral judgment. In this way, history became suitable material for ethical instruction.[19] As a result, descriptions of empresses were often overtly judgmental and moralistic. Some biographies exaggerated a woman's virtues, while others blamed women for the political chaos that eventually brought down a dynasty.[20]

Lü Zhi, the first empress of the Han dynasty, had the greatest role in shaping this embryonic institution, making her perhaps the most important woman in Chinese history.[21] Lü used her position as empress dowager to seize control of the government after her husband's death, setting an important precedent. Henceforth, everyone assumed that under the right circumstances, an empress might become politically important.

The new Han system of government allowed Lü Zhi to obtain considerable power. Under the Zhou, status had been largely hereditary. A complex body of kinship regulations known as *zongfa* largely determined a person's position, making it almost impossible for a woman to take control of the state. Qin Shihuang swept away that rigid system when he unified China, unleashing unprecedented social mobility. Unlike the Zhou, which limited social mobility with a system of fixed ranks, status became highly variable under the imperial system. With power and legitimacy concentrated in the ruler, a person's relationship with the throne now became the most important factor determining status and power. Someone close to the emperor could be instantly catapulted to the highest levels of society and government. This arrangement gave the emperor's spouse and mother privileged positions that they could use to aggrandize themselves.

Han Gaozu reigned as emperor for only seven years, so when he died the new dynasty as yet lacked comprehensive and stable institutions. The roles of emperor and empress and the mechanics of succession remained uncertain. This ambiguity gave Lü Zhi, now Empress Dowager Lü, the opportunity to establish procedures that maximized her own authority. The precedent of Queen Dowager Xuan of Qin, who had acted as regent and managed the government together with her brother, allowed Lü to justify taking control of the state after her husband's death.

Lü gave birth to one son, and Gaozu's concubines bore him seven more boys. Some of them were far more talented than the empress's mediocre offspring, and the emperor liked them more. Even so, Gaozu designated the son of his wife, the empress, as his heir. It seems that he gave precedence to his empress's son to avoid infighting and to guarantee a smooth transfer of power in spite of the boy's shortcomings. The accession of the son of the official wife had also been customary under the Zhou dynasty. Due to these preparations, Gaozu was succeeded by fifteen-year-old Emperor Hui, son of Empress Lü. Yet, in reality, this feeble boy never really reigned. He was merely a figurehead who sat on the throne while his strong-willed mother exercised power.

Emperor Hui's insignificance set another important precedent with far-reaching consequences. Henceforth, people not only accepted the possibility that an empress dowager might take control of the government, but they also assumed that the titular emperor might be an inconsequential puppet. Many subsequent Han emperors were young and passive so their powers were appropriated by those around them: empresses dowager, consort kinsmen, high officials, generals, and eunuchs.

Empress Dowager Lü did not run the government by herself. Instead, she followed the example of Queen Dowager Xuan and put her kinsmen in key offices. Unification had made it convenient for the ruler's in-laws to participate in government. Under the Zhou, due to strict surname exogamy, queens came to their husbands' domain from a different state so they lived apart from their relations. After unification, the family of the ruler's spouse lived in the capital, putting them in a position to accumulate power and prestige. Empress Dowager Lü enfeoffed many of her kinsmen as kings and marquises and gave them important civil and military posts. The nascent Han bureaucracy was unable to oppose the sudden rise of these interlopers.[22]

The empress dowager had a large family so her kinsmen could simultaneously occupy numerous important positions. The Lü clique dominated the government so thoroughly that the historian Sima Qian did not even consider Emperor Hui to have reigned, much less ruled. Sima bowed to pragmatism by admitting Empress Dowager Lü's supremacy and putting the imperial annals for that period under her name. Of course Emperor Gaozu did not intend for any of this to happen. But when he died the new imperial system still lacked clear guidelines, and the first empress dowager exploited the atmosphere of uncertainty to empower herself and her family.

Although some subsequent historians were critical of Empress Lü's rule, she helped hold the fissile new dynasty together and allowed effective institutions to coalesce. She avoided taking risks and pursued a relatively passive style of governance.[23] The dowager also prioritized military matters, completing the pacification of the realm and ordering the construction of an immense wall around the capital Chang'an.[24] This was a major undertaking as each side of the wall was five to six kilometers long, sixteen meters thick at the base, and eight meters high. These defenses served the dynasty well and helped ensure its survival. Lü made another fateful decision by choosing to remain a widow. Although she received a marriage proposal from a Xiongnu khan, she decided not to remarry even though widow remarriage was common at the time.[25] Her decision set down an important principle. Future empresses dowager followed her example and remained widows for the remainder of their lives.

Despite her achievements, Empress Lü is remembered largely for her cruelty. She murdered four of her husband's sons born to other women and had his favorite concubine grotesquely mutilated and tortured. Historians have struggled to account for her extravagant brutality. Some suspect these stories are libelous hyperbole. History was written by officials and gentry, the natural rivals of empress dowagers. Perhaps Sima Qian exaggerated Empress Lü's cruelty to imply that women could not be trusted to hold power. However, this interpretation is hard to justify. While Sima does not portray Lü in a favorable light, neither does he vilify her.[26] In fact, he seems to suggest that her despotic actions had justifiable motivations as she was acting to protect herself and her family in a hostile political environment. Moreover, Sima Qian does not suggest that Empress Dowager Lü intended to usurp the dynasty. Only after her death did her family take up arms against the imperial family out of fear that they would be executed.

Lü Zhi's low birth might have affected her values, giving her a propensity for brutality. Because she had been born a commoner, she had not been taught the principle of moderation fundamental to the aristocratic code of ritual. When Qin Shihuang extinguished the Zhou dynasty nobility, their ethical system became obsolete, leaving the new ruling house bereft of a clear moral compass. Lü seems to have felt that she could do as she wished. Without traditional rites to restrain her, anything seemed permissible.

Perhaps Empress Dowager Lü behaved viciously as a pragmatic strategy, as she lacked better options. The formal institutions of government were entirely male. Lü had usurped the ruler's prerogative, and she lacked legitimacy within the patriarchal system. Unable to employ the regular mechanics of administration, she used terror to dominate the bureaucracy. By frightening the men who surrounded her, she impelled their cooperation. This despotic mode of rule worked. Overall, Lü was a competent ruler who was effective in implementing her plans.

Exaggerated or not, tales of Empress Lü's cruelty cast a pall over her posthumous reputation. Sima Qian may have portrayed her in fairly neutral terms, but Ban Gu depicted her as unduly harsh.[27] Perhaps Ban criticized Lü to express his disapproval of powerful empresses dowager in general. Ban lived during the Eastern Han, a time when empresses and consort kin had seized control of the dynasty. Whatever his rationale, Ban Gu's negative portrait of Empress Dowager Lü became the mainstream assessment and was generally accepted by subsequent historians.[28] She was also blamed for enabling consort kin to gain power, which ultimately had disastrous consequences. The perceptive Qing dynasty historian, Zhao Yi, declared that from the beginning of the Han dynasty, powerful consort kin were a disaster for the dynasty.[29]

Empress Lü also stands out for her loyalty to blood kin. In other cultures, powerful women often worked to further the interests of their husbands and sons as they considered their own fate bound together with that of the members of their conjugal family. In contrast, Chinese empresses often put the interests of their natal family first. Due to the nature of the kinship system at the time, a married woman still considered herself a member of the family of her birth so it made sense for her to pursue the interests of her father, brothers, and even uncles over those of her son.[30] Empress Dowager Lü exemplifies this way of thinking. Even though the emperor was her son, she deliberately diminished him. She was interested only in promoting her blood kinsmen. Many subsequent empresses behaved in the same manner. Only during the Tang dynasty, when links between women and their natal families began to weaken, did empresses became less likely to promote blood kin.[31] Thereafter, they tended to act on their own and kept their relatives in the background.

The Imperial System

Emperor Hui suffered from a sickly constitution and died without issue at the age of twenty-two. With no clear heir to the throne, Lü stepped forward and selected the next two emperors, setting another important precedent. The empress dowager had the authority to select the emperor due to the patrimonial nature of the Han imperial system. The *zongfa* system of the Zhou specified that the eldest son of the senior wife would automatically inherit the royal title. But because Qin Shihuang had swept away the Zhou nobility and their kinship system, succession lacked clear rules. It was up to the empress dowager to set down the standards for choosing an emperor.

Everyone agreed that an emperor had to be a lineal descendant of Gaozu, the dynastic founder. The senior male member of the imperial Liu clan thus became emperor of China. The hereditary nature of imperial status made succession primarily a matter of kinship not politics, giving the empress dowager control over the process. When an emperor died, the imperial line temporarily lacked an elder. This arrangement allowed the wife or mother of a previous emperor to step in and choose the next head of the imperial clan, who also assumed the position of emperor. Under the Han system, the eldest son did not necessarily inherit the throne. In fact, the dynasty's emperors were rarely the eldest son of the previous monarch. All male descendants of previous emperors were qualified to serve as emperor. Many emperors died without progeny so more distant kinsman of previous rulers often became clan head, hence emperor.

Empress Dowager Lü could have selected one of her deceased husband's adult sons as Hui's successor. However, she knew that these men resented her and her family, and she would find it difficult to bend an adult emperor to her will. To maximize her power, Lü chose the youngest possible candidate: a baby. After three years this infant died, and Lü appointed another baby emperor. Sima Qian did not consider these infants real monarchs since Lü used them as patent figureheads. Empress Dowager Lü stamped her own seal on official documents, signaling that she was reigning in her own name. Authority to oversee the imperial succession turned the empress dowager into a kingmaker. And by selecting an infant as emperor, an empress dowager could be ruler in all but name.

Chapter 3

Empress Dowager Lü maintained a firm grip on the government until her death in 180 BC.

The death of the empress dowager instantly severed the kinship link between the Lü family and the imperial line, and they lost any pretensions to legitimacy. The Lü had made many powerful enemies who were eager for vengeance. Three kings descended from Emperor Gaozu raised troops and marched on the capital to restore the supremacy of the Liu. Even though the Lü controlled many high civil and military offices, they had little support. The restorationists easily captured Chang'an, massacred the Lü and their supporters, and regained control of the state.

The violent fall of the Lü clique marked the beginning of another important pattern in Han dynasty history. Repeatedly through the course of the Han, ambitious consort kin ascended to the heights of power. Emperors knew that their in-laws might become powerful so they often selected a wife with the intention of using her family to counterbalance other factions at court.[32] However, consort kinsmen usually abused their privileges and gained a reputation for arrogance and corruption, earning the hatred of officialdom and gentry. After a key member of the consort kinsmen died, severing the link with the imperial line, a backlash ensued, and a rival faction massacred the consort clique. This pattern of the rise and fall of consort kin was repeated through the course of the Han.

After the extermination of the Lü, a new emperor had to be chosen. Government ministers demanded an adult emperor who could restore order, establish a coherent system of government, and stabilize the imperial institution. There was no empress dowager to appoint a monarch so a conclave of officials took on the responsibility.[33] Because the imperial system was so new, the features of a good emperor remained a matter of conjecture. Officials reasoned that he should be a capable adult descended from the dynasty's founding emperor and have suitable character. In addition, officials paid close attention to the relatives of the mother and wife of each candidate as they assumed that these women's families would be politically significant. The behavior of the Lü had already created the expectation that empress dowagers and their kinsmen would be important personages, a principle that endured for the remainder of the dynasty.

The king of Qi, one of Gaozu's grandsons, had led the rebellion that overthrew the Lü. Even so, the most important ministers did not want him to assume the throne. Although he had demonstrated competence and leadership, his mother had a domineering personality and officials feared that she would be like Empress Dowager Lü. So instead of choosing the obvious candidate, they enthroned the son of one of Gaozu's minor concubines as Emperor Wen.[34] The new monarch's most important qualification seems to have been the benign character of his relations. His maternal kin and in-laws seemed like reasonable people, and they earned the trust of suspicious courtiers.

Emperor Wen had a long and successful reign during which he managed to stabilize the dynasty. His in-laws indeed stayed in the background, which allowed him to institute a workable system of government. Nevertheless, a revealing incident showed that people continued to assume that the emperor's mother outranked her son.[35] When Emperor Wen announced his determination to conquer the Xiongnu nomads, his officials tried to dissuade him but failed. They finally enlisted aid of the ruler's mother, Empress Dowager Bo. When she insisted that he abandon this dangerous plan, he complied. Yet, even though the empress dowager had the power to overrule the emperor, she showed no interest in politics and stayed in the background.

Although the empress dowager and consort kinsmen did not cause problems in this era, Emperor Wen's spouse Empress Dou expressed strong opinions about the proper ideology of government.[36] She detested Confucianism and forced her son, the future Emperor Jing, to study a Daoist curriculum. Partly due to her backing, Daoism and Huanglao were the main strains of political thought in this era. However, it seems that Dou had little impact on specific policies.[37]

Instead of pursuing power, Dou cultivated a reputation for virtue. She put great stress on sericulture and oversaw the manufacture of the silk robes worn by the emperor during important ceremonies.[38] Dou saw a devotion to spinning and weaving as a way to demonstrate seriousness and diligence.[39] Many subsequent empresses followed Empress Dou's example and tried to prove themselves moral paragons by undertaking

Terracotta figure of a servant from the tomb of Empress Dou.
SOURCE: *PUBLIC DOMAIN.*

symbolic acts of virtue. Lady Shen, a minor consort, similarly gained a reputation for integrity by wearing unusually simple clothing.[40]

During the Han dynasty, filial piety became a mainstay of education for both women and men, conditioning attitudes toward the relationship between mothers and sons. The *Classic of Filial Piety* (*Xiaojing*) compared parents to rulers, implicitly demanding not just their children's respect but also loyalty and obedience.[41] The palace library had various versions of this text, together with related books and commentaries, attesting to the topic's political significance.[42] Over time the education of empresses and other consorts, as well as emperors and princes, increasingly stressed filial piety.[43]

The focus of filiality gradually shifted to mothers. During the Western Zhou era, filial piety originally involved relations between fathers and sons. Yet, by the Han dynasty, accounts of mourning show that people put greater emphasis on the funerals of mothers than fathers even though the classical rites demanded the opposite.[44] People considered extensive mourning for fathers a ritual duty, but mourning obligations for mothers were far less onerous. Passionate mourning for a mother thus seemed a much more authentic display of filial devotion. As mothers became more important to filial discourse, sons felt a stronger duty to revere and obey them, further bolstering the authority of Han dynasty empresses dowager.

Emperor Wen believed that his own behavior and lifestyle would have a direct impact on the entire realm. He did not consider this influence merely symbolic or exemplary but direct and tangible. This belief grew out of the philosophical teaching that the cosmos is akin to an organism with each part exerting a sympathetic resonance on all the other parts.[45] The imperial palace was seen as the center of the realm so the emperor's actions sent out ripples of influence that affected his subjects. This cosmological model affected the treatment of palace women. People came to assume that excessive female power in the locus of the realm, or even the presence of too many women there, would radiate negative waves outward and unbalance society.[46] The government responded to a crisis by manipulating the emperor's lifestyle, including his relationship with women. Officials often remonstrated with the ruler, demanding a reduction in the number of palace women, so when disaster struck, emperors frequently reacted by expelling women from the palace.[47]

When Emperor Wen died in 157 BC, his son succeeded him as Emperor Jing. His reign was marked by the Rebellion of the Seven Kingdoms, the largest uprising of the Western Han. This catastrophe resulted from a dangerous flaw in the dynasty's framework. When Emperor Gaozu founded the Han, he enfeoffed important generals and warlords as kings to reward his most powerful backers. When Emperor Jing attempted to sideline them and centralize power, seven kings rebelled simultaneously. They almost toppled the dynasty but loyalist forces managed to quell the rebellion. Strangely, even though the dangers of the kingdom system were undeniable, Jing kept it in place, enfeoffing fourteen of his sons as new kings. It seems that he still considered kings potentially useful as they had previously shown their value. When the relatives of Empress Dowager Lü threatened to overthrow the ruling house, kings led the army that defeated the Lü and saved the dynasty. A fear of empresses and their kinsmen thus dictated the Han dynasty's unusual political structure.

After the death of Jingdi in 141 BC, his tenth son ascended the throne as Emperor Wu.[48] Wu became emperor when he was only fifteen years old and died at the age of sixty-nine. At fifty-four years, he had the longest reign prior to the Qing dynasty. Generally speaking, the longer an emperor's reign the greater his influence, so the extraordinary length of Wu's reign made him a major figure in Chinese history. Wu had decades to transform the imperial system and ideology, and his innovations had a lasting impact.

When Wu became emperor he was too young to rule so his grandmother Empress Dowager Dou served as regent. In declaring a regency, Dou followed the precedent set by Empress Dowager Lü and the court readily acquiesced. Because Dou was an enthusiastic Daoist, her government was relatively passive.[49] But this approach failed to address pressing problems. A year into his reign, Emperor Wu wanted to abandon Daoist passivity and implement more activist policies along Confucian lines. Empress Dowager Dou steadfastly opposed these measures as she detested Confucianism. Perhaps the low position of women in the ideal Confucian social hierarchy prejudiced her against this rival philosophy. When the young emperor promoted reform, Dou and her faction began to see him as a troublemaker. Some believed that they should depose him and enthrone one of his brothers as a Daoist emperor.

Sensing that he was in danger, Emperor Wu withdrew his proposals and became extremely docile. He attended to minor routine matters and let his grandmother rule. Because the emperor no longer threatened Dou, she allowed him to remain on the throne. This interlude allowed Emperor Wu to quietly begin reshaping the government behind the scenes. As regent, the empress dowager controlled the regular bureaucracy, known as the outer court (*waichao*). However, the emperor could still select officials for the inner court (*neichao*), the palace bureaucracy. Whereas the outer bureaucracy followed elaborate procedures, the emperor could simply issue orders to the inner court and have them immediately implemented. For the remainder of his reign, Wu preferred to govern directly via the inner court. Emperor Wu's power struggle with Empress Dowager Dou thus led him to implement an authoritarian power structure, a momentous shift that repeatedly gave rise to myriad problems for the remainder of the dynasty. Much of the chaos of subsequent periods can be attributed to Emperor Wu's transfer of power to the inner court, which allowed him to circumvent regular bureaucratic procedures and rule as a dictator. Later empresses, consort kin, eunuchs, and generals imitated him and used the inner court to seize control of the government, repeatedly plunging China into crisis.

In 135 BC, Empress Dowager Dou died. Emperor Wu's mother was still alive but Dou seems to have blocked her from accruing power and she did not participate in official matters.[50] When Emperor Wu assumed full authority, he abandoned passive Daoist ideology and initiated a major military campaign. Wu was infuriated by the frequent raids of Xiongnu nomads into China so he launched a major offensive to secure the northern border. He chose four generals to lead attacks on the Xiongnu. Three of them failed but Wei Qing succeeded. This was the first time that Chinese troops managed to defeat a Xiongnu army.

Wei Qing was the brother of Lady Wei, one of the emperor's minor consorts. Because a general controlled a large military force that could potentially attack the capital, emperors took care when choosing these powerful officers. Significantly, Wu selected the kinsman of one of his palace ladies for this sensitive post. Despite the catastrophe wrought by the Lü, Emperor Wu still believed that consort kinsmen could be trustworthy allies. Some of Wu's other generals and high officials were also family members of various consort factions. The power exercised by consort kin during Emperor Wu's long reign reinforced the practice of empowering imperial affines. Wu was an unusually strong ruler so his in-laws did not cause any major problems. But in later eras when the dynasty endured a long succession of weak rulers, consort kin repeatedly seized control of the government. Even under Emperor Wu, consort kin formed rival factions that constantly struggled for power. Sometimes these tussles broke out into the open.

The rise of Wei Qing exemplifies the unusual degree of social mobility that characterized the Western Han. After Emperor Qin Shihuang destroyed the Zhou aristocratic system, status became much more fluid. Instead of genealogy, connections with the imperial institution now became the most important factor determining high position. People with ties to the emperor rose rapidly in the social hierarchy regardless of their background. Wei Qing exemplified this new social dynamism. His mother was originally a slave (*binü*), and historians do not even mention his father's identity. Maybe Wei Qing did not know his paternity. Nevertheless, Wei Qing became an important general and was enfeoffed as a marquis. Before the Han it would have been unimaginable for someone from such a low background to become so powerful. But because Wei Qing's sister had entered the imperial harem and gained the ruler's favor, the fatherless son of a slave could rise to the highest rungs of society.

This era is also notable for another development that ultimately had immense consequences. At the beginning of the Han, students preparing for government service studied texts from various intellectual traditions, so they came to their posts with different mindsets and values. Daoism and Huanglao served as important political ideologies. However, Emperor Wu favored Confucianism and made it the intellectual foundation of government. He patronized Confucian education and scholarship and promoted officials who had studied the Five Classics or exhibited stereotypical Confucian virtues. Wu had great success altering the dynasty's intellectual foundation. Thereafter, Han emperors and officials usually employed Confucian ideas and vocabulary to discuss policy. Two millennia later, Confucianism remained the dominant mode of political discourse. This ideological shift had profound consequences for imperial consorts. Henceforth, palace women who wanted to gain power had to do so within a Confucian ideological context.[51] They often spoke and acted in ways that conformed with Confucian ideals even as they pursued their ambitions.

Emperor Wu was exceedingly superstitious. He was fascinated by tales of magic and immortality, and he surrounded himself with mystical charlatans. At that time, it was not uncommon for women to use magic spells and charms to seek blessings for themselves and to curse their enemies.[52] The emperor's fear of black magic gave rise to widespread hysteria. Rivals of Empress Chen accused her of using magic to curse Lady Wei, a favored concubine.[53] The empress had already lost Wu's favor so he deposed her and executed her supporters. Once it became clear that Wu would give credence to slanders about magic spells and potions, many people came forward to accuse their enemies of witchcraft. Wu usually believed these allegations and executed numerous important personages for black magic, together with their families and followers. Untold thousands died during these pogroms.

When Emperor Wu fell ill in old age, he realized that he had to choose an heir to ensure a smooth transition. Wu had killed the previous heir apparent and had not designated a new successor as he did not trust his sons. Although Wu could have selected a mature candidate as heir, instead he chose a six-year-old boy who would not pose a threat to him during his declining years.

Upon Wu's death this child ascended the throne as Emperor Zhao. When Wu selected his successor, he executed Lady Zhao, the boy's mother, and appointed three officials to serve as a committee of regents.[54] Wu killed the boy's mother because he feared that if she became empress dowager and had a long regency, she and her kinsmen might follow the example of Empress Lü's family and try to usurp the dynasty. Other Han dynasty emperors were not so cruel and they declined to execute the mothers of their heirs. Much later, however, Wu's action would eventually have a significant impact. Rulers of the Northern Wei dynasty revived this practice and routinely killed the mothers of their heirs to prevent the emergence of consort kin. Some historians even praised these murders as they helped avoid the disorder created by arrogant and greedy consort kin.[55]

When the child emperor's reign began, a triumvirate of officials ran the government. However, one of the regents died and the other was executed, allowing Huo Guang to become a de facto dictator. Emperor Zhao died in 74 BC at the age of twenty. According to precedent, the empress dowager had the final say in the succession. Empress Dowager Shangguan was Huo Guang's granddaughter so he could use her to enthrone the candidate of his choice. One of Emperor Wu's sons was still alive but Huo Guang did not trust him and suspected that he would want to rule on his own. Instead Huo chose one of Wu's grandsons, Liu He, as emperor. This mysterious figure is known to history as the King of Changyi.[56]

Given the unusual circumstances surrounding Liu He's brief reign, his true personality and actions cannot be known with certainty. Later historians cast him in a negative light and did not consider him a legitimate emperor. Soon after his ascending the throne, Huo Guang expressed disappointment with the new ruler and had him accused of 1,127 mistakes. Most likely Liu He refused to be a puppet so Huo removed him. The empress dowager, Huo Guang's granddaughter, issued an order deposing the emperor, who stepped down after a reign of less than a month. Liu He's subordinates were executed, and the disgraced emperor retired to a quiet life in the countryside.

This incident demonstrates the immense power of the empress dowager in the Han dynasty system. She even had the power to overthrow a sitting emperor. The unusual authority of the empress dowager's position resulted from a kinship hierarchy that put her above the emperor. Although Chinese kinship was patriarchal, the doctrine of filial piety obligated a man to respect and even obey his mother and grandmother. This moral principle explains why an empress dowager could dethrone an emperor. Although he reigned as sovereign, the empress dowager was his superior within the framework of Confucian ethics.

Huo Guang chose a great-grandson of Emperor Wu to reign as Emperor Xuan.[57] The new emperor already had a wife but Huo Guang wanted his own daughter to be empress as this would renew his kinship link with the ruling line. Huo Guang's wife poisoned Xuan's wife, and they forced him to marry Huo's daughter. When Huo Guang died six years into Xuan's reign, the emperor immediately took control of the government and sidelined the Huo family. The Huo clique plotted to depose the emperor but their scheme was discovered and they were all executed. Xuan detested his empress, who had been foisted upon him, so he sent her into ignominious exile. The fall of the Huo repeated the pattern set by the Lü. Powerful consort kin were usually domineering and haughty, so they attracted numerous enemies. Once a key member died, their opponents took the opportunity to destroy them.

The next era when consorts and their kinsmen affected government occurred during the reign of Emperor Cheng.[58] His twenty-six-year reign saw the irrevocable decline of the Western Han. Consort kin increasingly dominated affairs of state, and society descended into chaos. This inept ruler had no interest in the tedious mechanics of government so he allowed the relatives of Empress Dowager Wang to handle matters on his behalf. She had numerous kinsmen, and they dominated the government though sheer numbers. Not only did the Wang attain high office but several became generals, and the emperor ennobled seven of them as marquises. Overall, the Wang were more competent and less corrupt than previous consort kin, earning the support of their peers in officialdom.

The dangerous combination of a feeble emperor and strong consort kin threatened the dynasty's stability. To make matters worse, Emperor Cheng empowered two low-born concubines. The sisters Zhao Feiyan and Zhao Hede were born into the lowest rungs of society and entered the palace as dancers.[59] Beautiful, talented, and fiercely ambitious, they caught the emperor's eye. He was smitten and catered to their whims. The Zhao sisters were jealous of the empress, their main rival, and accused her of witchcraft. The credulous emperor deposed his wife and elevated Zhao Feiyan to the rank of empress. Emperor Cheng's reckless behavior scandalized the court. Officials were appalled by the sight of a ruler in thrall to such low-born women. In later centuries, stories about the infamous Zhao sisters became increasingly exaggerated, and they have come to exemplify the archetypal evil consort.[60]

After Emperor Cheng's death his nephew ascended the throne as Emperor Ai.[61] There were four empresses dowager at the time, each with her own faction, and their struggles for supremacy destabilized the court.

Chapter 3

Qing dynasty woodblock illustration of Zhao Feiyan.
SOURCE: PUBLIC DOMAIN.

The sickly Ai died after a short reign and his young cousin took his place as Emperor Ping. At this time, the Wang faction of consort kin rose to supremacy once again. The Wang differed from previous consort kin in a key respect. Up to this time powerful consort kinsmen first became in-laws of the emperor then used this link to attain high office. The Wang reversed this pattern. They served as high officials first then married into the imperial line and became consort kinsmen. This was the beginning of a new model of consort kin power. Henceforth, most empresses and consort kin would come from elevated backgrounds, and they dominated the Han for most of the remainder of its history.

Emperor Ping was still a child and needed a regent. Empress Dowager Wang gave the post to her nephew Wang Mang. The regent married his daughter to the young ruler, making her empress. Wang Mang then

The Imperial System

executed rival consort kin and decimated their factions, emerging from the bloodbath in control of the state. Wang Mang eventually poisoned the figurehead ruler, toppled the Han dynasty, and declared himself the emperor of a short-lived new dynasty called Xin.

Although both Western Han and Eastern Han were nominally the same dynasty, the institutions and underlying circumstances for each period differed substantially. After Emperor Guangwu restored the Han dynasty, he instituted a system of administration designed to address the challenges that he faced. When the Western Han began, Emperor Gaozu felt confident, so he put in place a resilient system. In contrast, Guangwu was comparatively weak so he created a highly flawed scheme that devolved into endemic chaos.

To reunite the realm, Guangwu had to fight for almost two decades against rebel groups, warlords, and bandit chieftains. Xiongnu nomads took advantage of China's internal chaos and raided the northern regions so Guangwu had to battle external foes as well. An interminable series of crises made Guangwu insecure. He did not trust the regular bureaucracy to handle such difficult challenges so he took charge of important matters himself. To do so he revived Emperor Wu's administrative framework and ruled through the inner palace bureaucracy. Subsequent emperors maintained this arrangement. In the long run, this turned out to be a catastrophic error. Emperors Wu and Guangwu were strong-willed adults so they were able to keep control of this authoritarian system. However, with a few exceptions, Eastern Han emperors were either minors or incompetents. By disempowering officials in the regular external bureaucracy and concentrating authority in the palace, Guangwu unwittingly established a system that later empresses dowager and their relatives could use to repeatedly commandeer the government.

Whereas Western Han empresses came from relatively modest backgrounds, their Eastern Han counterparts were selected to represent powerful factions so they came from the most important families in the realm. Emperor Guangwu began this practice when he selected his spouse, Empress Guanglie. She came from a prominent northern family, and he married her to consolidate his hold on that key region. Guanglie had a meek personality and was married to a strong-willed husband so she did not have much influence on affairs of state. Nevertheless, in choosing an empress from such a high background, Emperor Guangwu set a fateful precedent. For the remainder of the dynasty, the ruler's wife usually came from a powerful family at the core of a political faction. Consort kin had plagued the state during only a few eras of the Western Han but they dominated the government for most of the Eastern Han. Due to the institutions and practices instituted by Emperor Guangwu, factional struggles became increasingly intense and violent.

Guangwu ignored the wisdom of his ancestor Gaozu in another way as well. Gaozu learned from the mistakes of the Qin dynasty and prudently separated the treasuries of the government from the emperor's personal funds. These independent fiscal systems were managed by different officials. They received revenue from different sources and disbursed it through different government organizations. Separating funds for the emperor's personal use from those of the government prevented a spendthrift ruler from squandering government revenue on useless luxuries. Guangwu united these two fiscal systems, giving the emperor direct control over all tax revenue. Because consort kin controlled the government for most of the Eastern Han, they could abuse this unified fiscal system to embezzle immense sums. In many eras, they stole so much revenue that the government could not pay for essential services. This rampant pilfering doomed the state to a long and irreversible decline.

Guangwu left behind a contradictory legacy. He distinguished himself as a capable general and effective ruler who performed his duties well. Decades of warfare had plunged many people into poverty and hardship so he led a relatively simple and thrifty life. Guangwu was hardworking, intelligent, benevolent, and a good judge of character. But although capable in his own right, he brought disaster to future generations by instituting a deeply flawed system of government. Most dangerously, he empowered empresses dowagers and their families and provided them with the means to dominate the state and plunder its riches. Subsequently, long periods of consort kin misrule weakened the dynasty and fostered chaos. Largely due to Emperor Guangwu's flawed system of administration, the Eastern Han never cohered. The history of the era is a story of protracted decline.[62]

Although the first three emperors of the restored dynasty were capable adults, subsequent monarchs were mostly children or mediocrities who had little role in policy. After the first three reigns, Eastern Han political history consists of struggles among competing factions. Most cliques centered on the empress and her kinsmen, so the marriages or divorces of emperors usually determined the balance of power within the government.

Guangwu's son ascended the throne as Emperor Ming.[63] Like his father, Ming chose his wife, Empress Ma, with political considerations in mind.[64] He wed the daughter of a leading general to gain useful allies. After Ming's death, Emperor Zhang ascended the throne. Conflicts between various consort kin factions marred his reign, presaging the chaos yet to come. The faction of Empress Dowager Ma clashed with that of Emperor Zhang's wife, Empress Dou, who also came from a powerful family.[65] This conflict lasted until Empress Ma's death severed her faction's kinship connection with the emperor. The Ma faction immediately declined and the Dou became preeminent.

Empress Dou did not bear a son so when Emperor Zhang died she had to select a successor from among the sons of his other consorts. Instead of an adult she chose a child, Emperor He, so that she could declare a regency.[66] The Dou were extravagantly corrupt, autocratic, and arrogant, setting a dismal standard of behavior for future consort kinsmen. Empress Dowager Dou did not rule by herself but relied heavily on her brother Dou Xian, a successful general. She appointed him grand marshal (*da sima*), thereby giving him control over the entire army.[67] The elevation of Dou Xian marks the beginning of another consequential Eastern Han practice. The Dou circumvented the civilian bureaucracy by using a military office to rule China. Thereafter, seven grand marshals served as regents during the remainder of the dynasty, shifting power from the civilian bureaucracy to the military.

Dou Xian was not only arrogant but also violent. He assassinated prominent rivals, raising resentment against himself and the Dou regime. Even his sister the empress dowager began to detest him. In the year 91, Emperor He conducted a ceremony to celebrate his majority. As an adult, he could rule by himself so he no longer needed a regent. The emperor hated the Dou so he cooperated with eunuchs to accuse Dou Xian of plotting to murder him. They used this excuse to kill and exile the Dou and their adherents.

Although Emperor He destroyed the detested Dou faction, he did so with support of palace eunuchs. Thereafter, he continued to view the eunuchs as his core supporters and relied on them to rule. He even enfeoffed a eunuch as marquis, the first time a castrated man had been ennobled. Later, many more eunuchs became marquises, and they adopted sons to pass down their title. From this time forward, eunuchs were a key faction in Eastern Han politics as emperors sometimes used them to counterbalance the factions of empresses and consort kin. This practice had a corrosive effect. Not only were eunuchs infamous for selfishness and corruption but their prominence revolted the gentry, the most important group in society whose support was vital for the dynasty's survival. The rise of the eunuchs thereby threatened the underpinnings of the Han.

Before this era, Eastern Han rulers had chosen their empresses from powerful northwestern families. Emperor He broke with tradition and selected consorts from powerful factions centered in other regions. His first spouse, Empress Yin, was unusually jealous and bullied the emperor's favorite consort until she committed suicide. Yin's ferocious demeanor attracted many enemies, who accused her of using black magic to harm her rivals. The ruler used this excuse to depose his unloved wife, and her family members suffered execution or exile. His new wife, Empress Deng, deliberately kept a low profile and ensured her family's survival by refusing to allow them to accrue power or honors.[68]

When Emperor He died, Empress Dowager Deng had the right to name a successor. As usual, she chose the youngest candidate so that she would have the longest possible regency. This baby soon died and Deng had to choose another ruler from among the descendants of Emperor Zhang. Some of these candidates were adults so she could have selected a mature monarch who might have stabilized the realm. Instead, she selfishly selected another child, a twelve-year old who ascended the throne as Emperor An.[69] Although Empress Deng declared a regency, unlike most Eastern Han empresses dowager she did not empower her family members.⁷⁰ She employed her brothers in official roles but made key decisions herself. Even after Emperor An became an adult, Empress Deng continued to rule despite intense hostility from officialdom. Emperor An knew that he might be murdered or deposed if he caused problems for the regent so he kept a low profile. But as soon as the empress dowager died in 121, An removed her relatives from official positions and sentenced them to exile. Many committed suicide.

Emperor An's spouse, Empress Yan, was unusual in that she did not come from an important family.⁷¹ Yet, despite her modest background, everyone at the time assumed that an empress would have a major political role so she immediately gained power. Emperor An declared one of his sons the heir apparent but Empress Yan and her faction opposed this move. She wanted the chance to eventually name his successor so that she could choose a puppet child ruler and have a long regency. The pliable emperor backed down and demoted the heir apparent. This incident highlights the destructive impact of ambitious empresses.

When Emperor An died, Empress Dowager Yan selected a child as successor. He died a few months later, and historians did not even bother to record his name. The empress dowager wanted to put another infant on the throne but this time she faced strong opposition. The court had two powerful eunuch factions. One supported the Yan while the other backed the ten-year-old son of Emperor An. Competing eunuch factions fought a pitched battle in the palace, ending in the defeat of the Yan gang. The Yan suffered exile and execution, and Empress Dowager Yan died under detention. The victorious eunuchs then proclaimed one of the previous emperor's sons, Emperor Shun.⁷² Even though the new ruler had come to the throne in a disgraceful manner, having been selected by eunuchs, he nevertheless enjoyed the support of the military and civilian officials as they had detested the Yan.

When Emperor Shun ascended the throne, many people hoped that he would be a strong emperor who would reverse the dynasty's decline. However, he turned out to be lazy and incompetent. Uninterested in ruling, Shun turned over important matters to the family of his wife, Empress Liang.⁷³ Nine years older than her husband, she came from a distinguished northwestern family. Shun appointed his father-in-law regent, and his empress's kinsmen took up important positions in the government. However, Emperor Shun soon regretted his decision. He found that his confidence in the Liang had been misplaced as they were particularly despotic and corrupt.

To counterbalance his powerful in-laws, Shun elevated eunuchs to important positions. The power of eunuchs derived from their propinquity to the emperor so they steadfastly supported the ruler and defended him from enemies. Shun enfeoffed eighteen eunuchs as marquises, creating a castrated aristocracy that could serve as his personal shield. But by this time, decades of misrule had brought disarray. Administration had become so ineffective that when multiple rebellions broke out, the army was unable to quell them, so the government lost control over large swaths of territory.

Emperor Shun had a single newborn son. When Shun died in 144, this baby became Emperor Chong. With another infant on the throne, Empress Dowager Liang and her family gained control over the government. She relied heavily on her brother Grand Marshal Liang Ji, and he used his control of the army to maintain a firm grip on the government.[74] As before, the Liang were corrupt and violent, and the quality of administration continued to decline.

When the titular ruler died after just a year, Empress Dowager Liang chose a seven-year-old boy to replace him as Emperor Zhi. Although young, the boy seemed to have been unusually intelligent and strong willed, and he criticized the Liang for their arrogance. The Liang realized that this boy would be increasingly difficult to control as he grew older so they poisoned him. As a replacement, the empress dowager chose a fourteen-year-old youth who became Emperor Huan.[75] Although older than most puppet emperors, Huan was engaged to marry one of the Liangs, so the dowager assumed that she could use his empress to control him. Empress Dowager Liang served as regent, and she and her brother Liang Ji controlled the government.

The eunuchs allied with the Liang against the gentry. Both saw gentry officials serving in the regular bureaucracy as their key rivals so the Liang and eunuch factions cooperated to denounce the most important outer court officials and had them executed. Their attacks cowed officialdom, giving the Liang and their eunuch cronies free rein.

In 150, Empress Dowager Liang died. As before, the death of a key member of a consort clan severed their blood relationship with the emperor, putting them in danger. Emperor Huan was seventeen years old, hence potentially capable of reigning on his own. Nevertheless, Liang Ji remained the most important figure in the government. While his sister was alive, she had curbed his worst impulses. After her death, Liang Ji became even more high-handed. The emperor hated Liang Ji and wanted to rule the realm himself. He also detested his wife, Empress Liang, a jealous woman obsessed with luxury. Empress Liang did not bear any children so whenever a consort became pregnant, she had the woman murdered, causing Huan to abhor her even more.

Empress Liang died in 159, severing all kinship links between Liang Ji and the ruling line. Not only did Liang Ji now lack any justification for his extraordinary powers, but his brutality and haughtiness had earned the hatred of the emperor and officialdom. Liang Ji hoped to force the emperor to marry another of his female relatives but the ruler steadfastly refused. Yet, however much the emperor hated him, Liang Ji was still grand marshal. Because he controlled the army, toppling him was not a simple matter. The emperor needed the help of a powerful faction to dislodge Liang Ji from his military post. Emperor Huan turned to the eunuchs for support. Confident of their backing, the emperor denounced Liang Ji. Faced with formidable opposition, Liang admitted defeat and committed suicide. The remaining members of the Liang family and their faction were massacred. Over time they had assembled an unusually large number of supporters, and this pogrom killed off so many officials that the government almost ceased to function from lack of personnel.

As before, eunuch leaders demanded to be rewarded for their invaluable support. Emperor Huan enfeoffed five of them as marquises, and many others assumed high office. Henceforth, Huan relied heavily on eunuch support and treated them as his own faction. However, the eunuchs were even worse than Liang Ji and they brazenly looted state coffers. To head off criticism, the eunuchs executed some of their detractors and persecuted numerous students, officials, and gentry, forbidding them from holding office. This proscription was so extensive that it became difficult to recruit men of talent into the bureaucracy. Making matters even worse, the emperor began to sell offices to the highest bidder to raise funds. He even sold military positions. People who purchased a government post were only interested in exploiting it for profit so the quality of governance plummeted even further.

Emperor Huan died childless. His widow, Empress Dowager Dou, invited representatives of her consort kinsmen, officialdom, and eunuchs to choose the next emperor.[76] As usual, she did not want an adult on the throne so she selected an eleven-year-old boy who became Emperor Ling.[77] Three officials served as regents. The most powerful was Dou Wu, the empress dowager's father.[78]

Emperor Ling's reign began with a crisis. The number of eunuchs had swelled from fourteen at the beginning of the dynasty to about two thousand. During the reign of Emperor Huan, eunuchs had become accustomed to running the government. They disliked the new emperor because they had less influence over the new regime so they wanted to replace him with their own puppet. Dou Wu and his consort kin faction supported the emperor and opposed the eunuchs. The students and gentry also hated the eunuchs so Dou Wu assembled a large anti-eunuch coalition. Eventually, armies loyal to the eunuchs and Dou Wu came to blows. However, Dou's troops did not dare fight because the emperor supported the eunuch faction. Dou Wu committed suicide, his family was slaughtered, and Empress Dowager Dou was put under house arrest. Emperor Ling rewarded the victorious eunuchs with gifts, land, government posts, and marquisates.

Empress Dowager Dong had considerable influence over her young and impressionable son Emperor Ling. However, the faction of Ling's wife, Empress He, also wanted to control the government, so the two women and their kinsmen competed for supremacy.[79] Each consort faction included generals who had armies loyal to them personally. The state had decayed so much that these generals were independent warlords in all but name. The rival consort kin factions backed different candidates as heir apparent, but Emperor Ling did not dare choose sides so he refused to name a successor.

In the face of so many intractable problems, China began to disintegrate. Peasant revolts, mutinies, religious uprisings, foreign incursions, and battles between warlords tore the nation apart. When Emperor Ling died in 189, rival factions struggled for control. The mother of Emperor Ling soon died as well, allowing Empress Dowager He to select the new titular ruler. She enthroned a teenager as Emperor Shao and declared herself regent.

Everyone hated the eunuchs and agreed that they had to be destroyed. The eunuchs knew that they were in danger of being exterminated so they tried to seize the government. However, this time they lacked troops, so an army commanded by officials entered the palace and slaughtered them. During the chaos, the young emperor fled the palace. Dong Zhuo, a warlord who controlled the area around the capital, discovered the emperor and his brother cowering in terror on a mountain path. The traumatized young man was so frightened that he could not speak so his brother conveyed what had happened to them. The mute emperor made a bad impression on Dong Zhuo so the warlord deposed Emperor Shao and enthroned his younger brother as Emperor Xian, the last emperor of the Han dynasty. Dong Zhuo did not have the authority to depose or select an emperor on his own so he ordered the empress dowager to approve these measures then killed her. His murder of Empress Dowager He marked an end to the power of Han dynasty empresses and their kinsmen. Thereafter, various warlords struggled for supremacy, and the dynasty collapsed.

This panorama of four centuries of the Han dynasty history reveals why empresses and consort kinsmen gained power so often under the new imperial system. During the first half of the Western Han, rulers and officials usually contained the ambitions of consort kinsmen. But as institutions decayed at the end of the Western Han, factions headed by empresses dowager filled the power vacuum. For most of the Eastern Han era, empresses dowager and their families were far more powerful than the figurehead emperors who supposedly reigned.

CHAPTER 3

Standard histories of the era emphasize the importance of Eastern Han empresses. In *Records of the Later Han* (*Hou Hanshu*), the historian Fan Ye gives unusual prominence to the biographies of empresses, listing them immediately after the annals describing the dynasty's emperors. These biographies were intended to serve as Confucian admonitions on the consequences of female malfeasance. The life stories of empresses were used to substantiate the premise that female involvement in politics inevitably leads to chaos.[80] Imperial historians portrayed female power as a major institutional failure that eventually brought down the Han dynasty.[81] The opinion of Gao Yun, an official under the Wei dynasty, was typical. He submitted a memorial to the throne in which he discussed the reasons for the fall of Han.[82] Gao singled out the corrosive privileges of consort kin as a major reason for the dynasty's failure.

The power of empresses dowager originated in the precedent set by Queen Xuan of the state of Qin. Xuan had declared a regency over an adult king and turned the government over to her brother Wei Ran. Wei Ran proved a capable administrator. He managed domestic affairs well and enlarged the domain through conquest, putting Qin into a position to ultimately unify China. This successful episode made empress regency and consort kin rule seem like an attractive alternative to having the state managed by a mediocre monarch.

The nature of Han dynasty elite kinship also empowered that dynasty's empresses. With the Zhou aristocracy annihilated, a new elite rose up at the beginning of the Han. The new elite, wealthy landlords, were descended from commoners so they had no interest in the kinship rules of the extinct aristocracy. The values of the Han gentry originated in grassroots village society and differed significantly from those of the Zhou aristocracy. Due to this disjunction, the Han elite had a novel kinship system that affected the distribution of power. It so happened that some of these new kinship rules favored the interests of women close to the monarch.

Most importantly, intensified interpretations of filial piety, particularly the ties binding mothers and sons, governed the relationship between empresses dowager and reigning emperors. A sitting emperor was obligated to show immense respect and even obedience to his mother and the wives of previous emperors, allowing them to assemble factions of kinsmen and supporters. At times, several factions of rival empresses dowager vied for power, plunging the court into chaos.

Although Confucianism is often portrayed as inimical to female interests, this body of thought included the principle of filial piety, which bolstered the power of mothers. Not surprisingly, women were often enthusiastic proponents of Confucian education. During the Han dynasty, Confucianism became the ideology of government. Female support helped Confucianize politics, an intellectual turn that exerted a profound effect on every aspect of Chinese society up to the end of the Qing dynasty in the early twentieth century.

In antiquity, a woman was considered part of her father's family for life. Although she theoretically joined their husband's family upon marriage, the conjugal bond was still weak compared to blood ties. Under the prevailing kinship system, women were closely bound to their natal kinsmen. The intensity of this tie explains why empresses so often sought to benefit their fathers, brothers, and even nephews to the detriment of their sons. It also accounts for the rise of consort kinsmen in tandem with empresses. Empresses favored their male kin not just out of family loyalty but also because male relations could serve in military and civil posts, extending an empress dowager's reach into the bureaucracy. Consort kin could occupy important posts and work together to dominate the government.

Kinship norms also gave rise to close relationships between men and their maternal uncles.[83] People assumed that a man ought to have a close relationship with his mother's brothers as they considered them closely related. Just as filial piety intensified the mother-son bond, so the kinship system stressed the uncle-nephew tie. Consort kin exploited this peculiarity of the Han kinship structure. An empress dowager could use this convention to justify elevating her brothers, father, and other blood relations to high positions.

The organizational nature of the early imperial system also allowed consorts and their families to gain power. In aristocratic Zhou society, heredity largely determined social status. Even if a powerful noble became close to a commoner, that person's social status would probably not rise very much. The Han system operated according to very different principles. The Han emperor had a far higher status than the king of Zhou, and those around him were elevated simply by their proximity to the seat of authority.[84] Closeness to the emperor raised the status of empresses and their kinsmen, and sometimes they could use their nearness to the ruler as grounds for seizing the government.

The patrimonial Han system fused the imperial line with the government. The titular head of the Liu lineage became emperor. Because the selection of lineage head was a family matter, empresses dowager had the authority to make this decision, not government ministers. Officials usually wanted a capable adult ruler because they hoped for competent government, but empresses dowager usually selected a young boy so that they could declare a regency and rule via a puppet monarch. For this reason the prerogatives of empresses dowager weakened the institutions of government. A long succession of young emperors and grasping consort kin doomed the Eastern Han to long stretches of disastrous rule, sending the dynasty into terminal decay.

Finally, the novelty of the imperial system also favored the interests of ambitious women. Zhou dynasty traditions had included many safeguards that limited the powers of high-born women and their kinsmen. However, in unifying China, Emperor Qin Shihuang annihilated the politics, society, and aristocratic culture of the Zhou. Moreover, Han officials despised the failed Qin. Neither Zhou nor Qin provided a workable template so the ruling elite of the Han dynasty did not feel compelled to follow precedent. Emperors had no choice but to set up a very different system of government, making the Han akin to a revolutionary regime.

With the old standards gone and new protective measures yet to develop, empresses dowager had considerable freedom of action. They established precedents that subsequent empresses dowager could use to empower themselves. Empress Dowager Lü, the widow of the founding emperor of Han, had a particularly important role in this regard. After her husband's death, she claimed the authority to make key decisions and made herself the de facto ruler of the empire. The new dynasty's nascent institutions lacked rules or norms to constrain her. Empress Dowager Lü's aggressive behavior set the pattern for female power. Subsequent imperial widows followed her example, making rule by empresses dowager and their kinsmen a standard aspect of Han dynasty government. The emperors and officials of subsequent dynasties had to deal with this challenging legacy.

Notes

1. Xu, *Qin huiyao dingbu*, 1:12–15, 15:241–42, 15:244–45; Gao, "Qin guo hunyin zhidu yanjiu," 90–91.
2. Xu, *Qin huiyao dingbu*, 7:92–94.
3. Xu, *Qin huiyao dingbu*, 1:12–15, documents the various titles for women in Qin.
4. Ebrey, "Rethinking the Imperial Harem," 178.
5. Zhang, *Qin Shihuang pingzhuan*, 325–26.
6. Li, *Taiping yulan*, 560:3a; Yin, "Lun Dabaozishan Qin gong lingyuan de renxun," 80–87; Gan, "Luelun Qin de renxun wenhua," 14–17; Guo, "Qin Han shiqi de renxun xianxiang shulun," 34–35. The remaining harem women were carried off by Xiang Yu when he burned down the Qin palaces at Xianyang. Ban, *Hanshu*, 31:1808.
7. Takigawa, *Shiki kaichū kōshō*, 6:8–9, 85:6–7, 85:11–14; Shen and Xu, "Qianlun Qinren zhenjieguan de qianghua," 39–43; Wang, "Qin Shihuang zhenjie funüguan de xinli tanyin," 30–35. Bodde, *Statesman, Patriot, and General in Ancient China*, 18–21, suggests that much of this account in *Shiji* was interpolated later by another author.
8. Gu, *Handai funü shenghuo qingkuang*, 190–226, analyzes the fiefs, titles, and awards received by elite women during the Han.
9. Liu, "Handai funü de mingzi," 38. In addition to the natal surname, female commoners were called by other types of names as well. Liu, "Handai funü de mingzi," 37, 39–40, 42–43. Zhao, *Nianer shi zhaji*, 19:252–53, describes how posthumous names for empresses were constructed under different dynasties from Han to Tang.
10. Xue, "Handai tangmuyi yanjiu," 99–105; Zhu, *Han Tang shi jian*, 2:1a–2a; Xu, *Qin huiyao dingbu*, 15:241–42, 15:244–45.
11. Gao, "Qin guo hunyin zhidu yanjiu," 93; Zu, "Cong Shuihudi Qin jian," 54.
12. Ban, *Hanshu*, 22:1028; Wu, *Handai nüxing lijiao yanjiu*, 40–41.
13. Lin, *Kongjian, shenti yu lijiao guixun*, 14–32.
14. Ban, *Hanshu*, 8:251, 11:339.
15. Huang, "Chang'an's Funerary Culture," 161, 163; Lin, *Kongjian, shenti yu lijiao guixun*, 144.
16. The Qing dynasty scholar Yan Kejun brought together information about Western and Eastern Han empresses and other important consorts, providing a handy compendium of important records. Yan, *Quan Han wen*, 10:92–111; Yan, *Quan Hou Han wen*, 9:76–89.
17. Durrant, *The Cloudy Mirror*, 123–24, 143.
18. Yi, "Social Status, Gender Division and Institutions," 132–33, gives helpful tables that indicate which standard histories have sections devoted to the biographies of empresses and minor consorts, princesses, consort kin, and virtuous women.

19. Mou, *Gentlemen's Prescriptions for Women's Lives*, 13–14.
20. Yi, "Hou Hanshu de shuxie nüxing," 17–41.
21. Takigawa, *Shiki kaichū kōshō*, ch. 9; Ban, *Hanshu*, ch. 3; Raphals, *Sharing the Light*, 70–78; Wang, "Lü Zhi, Empress of Emperor Gaozu," 174–77; Loewe, *A Biographical Dictionary*, 426–29.
22. Wang, "Zhanguo houqi Qin guo waiqi yanjiu," 110.
23. Ban, *Hanshu*, 23:1097, emphasizes the deliberate passivity of government under Empress Dowager Lü.
24. Ban, *Hanshu*, 2:89, 35:1904.
25. Ban, *Hanshu*, 37:1976. Empress Lü was outraged by this proposal, which she dismissed as impertinent.
26. Van Ess, "Praise and Slander," 233.
27. Van Ess, "Praise and Slander," 252–54. For example, see Ban, *Hanshu*, 36:1960.
28. Chan, *A Precious Mirror for Governing the Peace*, 237. An interesting interpretation was written by Li Hua in the eighth century. He saw each dynasty as characterized by the contrasting forces of pattern (*wen* 文) and substance (*zhi* 質). Pattern embodies refinement but can lead to extravagance and obsequiousness. In contrast, the austerity of substance encourages coarseness and crudity. Ideally a government balances these opposing forces. Li Hua believed that the substance of the early Han system allowed the Liu ruling house to overcome threats posed by Empress Lü and her kinsmen. McMullen, "Historical and Literary Theory," 323.
29. Zhao, *Nianer shi zhaji*, 3:40.
30. Hinsch, "The Origins of Han-Dynasty Consort Kin Power," 1–24; Hou and Goodman, "Rethinking Chinese Kinship," 30; Gu, *Handai funü shenghuo qingkuang*, 228–50. In Engesi, "Jiazu, sichan yu guojia de qiyuan," 231–34, fn. 214, the translator gives a long footnote discussing the concept of the avunculate in Chinese history. Liu Xiang criticized empresses whose primary loyalty rested with their natal families. He thought that after a woman married she was primarily a member of her husband's family and her blood kin were secondary. It seems that this was a minority view at the time. Ban, *Hanshu*, 36:1961.
31. Li, "Nüren de Zhongguo zhonggushi," 477–81; Sun, "Tangdai benjia dui nüxing hunyin," 104–7.
32. Holmgren, "Imperial Marriage in the Native Chinese and Non-Han State," 62, 65.
33. Although Emperor Hui married, almost nothing is known about Empress Zhang. The standard histories do not even provide her given name. Like her husband, she was dismissed as a nonentity. Ban, *Hanshu*, 2:90, n. 2.
34. Takigawa, *Shiki kaichū kōshō*, ch. 10; Ban, *Hanshu*, ch. 4.
35. Ban, *Hanshu*, 4:126.
36. Dou Yifang. Loewe, *A Biographical Dictionary*, 78–79.
37. For example, Emperor Wen ignored Empress Dou's advice regarding a controversial expedition against the Xiongnu. Ban, *Hanshu*, 4:126.
38. Ban, *Hanshu*, 4:125.
39. Hinsch, "Textiles and Female Virtue," 170–202.
40. Ban, *Hanshu*, 4:134; Loewe, *A Biographical Dictionary*, 469.
41. Rosemont and Ames, *The Chinese Classic of Family Reverence*, 110.

42. Ban, *Hanshu*, 30:1718–19.
43. Wu, *Handai nüxing lijiao yanjiu*, 143–46; Gu, *Handai funü shenghuo qingkuang*, 76–92, 261–72.
44. Brown, "Sons and Mothers," 66, 70, 72–75, 139.
45. Le Blanc, *Huai-Nan Tzu*.
46. Hinsch, "The Criticism of Powerful Women," 96–121.
47. Ban, *Hanshu*, 4:123; Di, "Handai gongnü de chulu," 139–40. Minor consorts and serving women often left the palace and returned home when an emperor died.
48. Ban, *Hanshu*, ch. 6.
49. Ban, *Hanshu*, 22:1031.
50. Later historians assumed that Emperor Wu managed to prevent his mother from participating in politics and they praised him for this decision. Liu, "Wei Jin yihuan shijia dui houfei zhuzheng," 29.
51. Kamiya, "Keimon no watashi," 80–95.
52. Li, "Furen meidao kao," 1–32.
53. Loewe, "The Case of Witchcraft," 159–96. Yan, *Quan Han wen*, 4:40, lists the justifications used to depose empresses during the Han dynasty.
54. She was known as Lady Gouyi and Zhao Jieyu. Ban, *Hanshu*, 67A: 3956–57; Wong, "Zhao Gouyi," 247–49; Loewe, *A Biographical Dictionary*, 708.
55. Liu, "Wei Jin yihuan shijia," 29–30.
56. Ban, *Hanshu*, ch. 63.
57. Ban, *Hanshu*, ch. 8.
58. Ban, *Hanshu*, ch. 10.
59. Raphals, *Sharing the Light*, 78–86; Loewe, *A Biographical Dictionary*, 704, 717.
60. For an example from the Tang dynasty see Yan, *Quan Han wen*, 11:108–9. The Qing dynasty historian Zhao Yi marveled at the low birth of so many Western Han imperial consorts. Zhao, *Nianer shi zhaji*, 3:36.
61. Habberstad, "Recasting the Imperial Court in Late Western Han," 239–62.
62. Even before the Eastern Han had ended, some thinkers were already blaming China's problems on the defective system of government established by Emperor Guangwu. Du, "Lun Zhongchang Tong de zhiguo sixiang," 57–60, 65.
63. Fan, *Hou Hanshu*, ch. 2.
64. Fan, *Hou Hanshu*, 10A:407–14; de Crespigny, *A Biographical Dictionary*, 634–38; McMahon, *Women Shall Not Rule*, 102.
65. Fan, *Hou Hanshu*, 10A:415; de Crespigny, *A Biographical Dictionary*, 160–61; McMahon, *Women Shall Not Rule*, 102–4.
66. Fan, *Hou Hanshu*, 4:165–95.
67. Fan, *Hou Hanshu*, 23:812–21; de Crespigny, *A Biographical Dictionary*, 170–72.
68. Deng Sui. De Crespigny, *A Biographical Dictionary*, 121–28.
69. Fan, *Hou Hanshu*, ch. 5.
70. Fan, *Hou Hanshu*, 10A:417–20.
71. Yan Ji. Fan, *Hou Hanshu*, 10A:420–30; de Crespigny, *A Biographical Dictionary*, 935–36.
72. Fan, *Hou Hanshu*, 6:249–74.

73. Liang Na. Fan, *Hou Hanshu*, 10B:438–40; de Crespigny, *A Biographical Dictionary*, 454–56; McMahon, *Women Shall Not Rule*, 105–6.
74. Fan, *Hou Hanshu*, 34:1178–87; de Crespigny, *A Biographical Dictionary*, 450–53.
75. Fan, *Hou Hanshu*, ch. 7.
76. Fan, *Hou Hanshu*, 10B:445–46; de Crespigny, *A Biographical Dictionary*, 160–61.
77. Fan, *Hou Hanshu*, ch. 8.
78. Fan, *Hou Hanshu*, 69:2239–53; de Crespigny, *A Biographical Dictionary*, 169–70.
79. Fan, *Hou Hanshu*, 10B:449–52; de Crespigny, *A Biographical Dictionary*, 309.
80. Yi, "Hou Hanshu de shuxie nüxing," 17–41.
81. Liu, "Wei Jin yihuan shijia," 32.
82. Wei, *Weishu*, 48:1073.
83. Hinsch, "The Origins of Han-Dynasty Consort Kin Power," 1–24.
84. Nishijima, *Baihua Qin Han shi*, 64.

CHAPTER 4

Medieval Empresses

AFTER THE COLLAPSE OF THE HAN DYNASTY, CHINA FELL INTO DISAR-
ray for 350 years. Chinese historians usually refer to this era by the unwieldy name "Wei, Jin, Northern and Southern Dynasties." More concisely, it is also called the "Six Dynasties" after the major political units of the time. In the West, historians often label this period the "early medieval era." Whatever name is used, this long age of disunion saw important changes. Chaos demanded innovation. North and south were divided so each era developed differently. Politics, culture, social structure, and gender relations all varied substantially by region.

The fall of the Han allowed rulers to cast aside precedent and behave in ways that would previously have been unacceptable. When the warlord Cao Cao died in 220, his son Cao Pi should have dismissed the women in his father's palace to avoid accusations of incest. For a man to have sexual relations with his father's concubines would previously have been seen as deeply depraved. However, Cao Pi had little concern for old-fashioned propriety so he took his father's minor consorts as his own.[1] However, some people still adhered to the old ethics. When the empress dowager found out about the situation, she expressed disgust and she did not mourn Cao Pi after his death.

Cao Pi understood that many of the problems of the Eastern Han were attributable to the excessive powers of empresses dowager. Accordingly he issued an edict declaring female participation in government to be the root of chaos, and he prohibited women from interfering in politics.[2] Henceforth, memorials would not be sent to the empress dowager,

CHAPTER 4

and her relatives could not hold office or receive titles. Cao Pi hoped that these measures would prevent empresses dowager and consort kin from usurping the government once again as they had so many times in the past.

Despite the Han dynasty's shortcomings, it had endured for more than four centuries and provided the only available template for the institution of empress. The wives and mothers of emperors could sometimes still employ that dynasty's procedures to exercise power. In 254, the ambitious strongmen Sima Shi and Sima Zhao tried to depose the Cao Wei regime, intending to enthrone a pliable puppet.[3] However, Empress Dowager Guo foiled their plans. She wanted to preserve the Cao line and demanded that they select Cao Mao as ruler. Although still a boy, he was intelligent and capable, making him the best possible candidate. This event demonstrated that the empress dowager retained the authority to appoint the emperor and could play a positive political role.

Early medieval elites relied heavily on marriage ties to bind society together.[4] Northern emigres to the south stressed Confucian propriety and the rites, leading to the increasing standardization of southern marriage customs.[5] Stringent class endogamy maintained elite privilege generation after generation, allowing great families to perpetuate their status by carefully arranging marriage relations. Yet, within the elite, families tended to marry with a wide range of partners to gain useful allies.[6] In both north and south, different types of elite families mixed. As marriage ties gained importance, people often married off their children while still young to gain the benefits of new kinship as soon as possible.[7] Emperors and empresses often married in childhood.

The Southern Dynasties had native rulers who sought to preserve Chinese civilization from the threat of barbarization so their institutions maintained a degree of continuity with the Eastern Han. Yet, circumstances had changed considerably so even Southern Dynasties rulers had to cast off many Han precedents and adopt new measures that suited the situations they faced.

As during the Han, many members of the southern elite still adhered to a system of descent that was close to bilateral. People had close connections with both paternal and maternal kin.[8] The standing of both parents affected the status of their children, making it imperative for members of the elite to marry well. As before, wives remained loyal to their natal kin and men had close relationships with their maternal uncles.[9] During the Han, bilateral descent had given rise to powerful consort kin factions so officials of the Southern Dynasties tried to diminish the links between men and their maternal kin. Over time literati educated in the Confucian canon and court officials interested in orthodox kinship rules managed to impose an increasingly patrilineal system of descent on society. People mourned maternal kin less intensely, and the bond between men and their maternal kin weakened.

Filial piety had previously been an important virtue but in this era it became a paramount political and social principle.[10] The ruling elite promoted filial piety to reorganize their broken society into an orderly hierarchy. The patriarchal image of the ruler also made filial piety a way to attract loyalty to the weakened state. Daoists, Buddhists, and Confucians all emphasized filial piety in their belief systems.[11] Writers recorded stories of filial paragons, many of which described a man's devotion to his mother. Some of these moral exemplars went to outrageous lengths to fulfill their filial obligations. One poor man reportedly abandoned his wife and children so that he could spend all of his money on his mother's funeral.[12] Today he would be seen as eccentric or irresponsible but at that time people regarded him as a moral hero. The ideal mother had a similarly strong devotion to her offspring. According to one account, an elderly woman began to lactate and considered this an inauspicious sign.[13] Later she received word that her son had been defeated in battle. This story presents the relationship between mother and son as so intense that a supernatural bond connected them. The birth of rulers was also often described in miraculous terms, making the mother seem like a mythic figure.[14] Due to the importance of the mother-son bond, a man could be sentenced to death simply for cursing his mother.[15]

Rising devotion to mothers altered kinship ties. For example, filial piety brought stepmothers and stepsons closer, making their relations more harmonious.[16] This recalibration of family bonds affected relations between emperors and empresses dowager. Princes studied the *Classic of Filial Piety* (*Xiaojing*) as a cornerstone of their early education, inculcating obedience to maternal figures.[17] The emperor was expected to pay regular courtesy visits to the empress dowager and treat her with deference.[18] Despite increasing wariness toward female power, some ambitious women nevertheless managed to use filial values to empower themselves.

In the era immediately following the end of Han, none of the empresses from the kingdoms of Cao Wei, Shu, and Wu came from a high background.[19] The rulers of Cao Wei deliberately avoided taking wives from powerful lineages.[20] To the contrary, they pursued a policy of mésalliance, choosing spouses whom they happened to find attractive from ordinary families. One empress was an orphan and another a former courtesan. In an age obsessed with genealogy, an empress with humble origins lacked prestige, and the low birth of her relations precluded them from high office and noble title. Due to their modest backgrounds, empresses and consort kin did not cause problems during the Cao Wei era. By altering the marriage system, the rulers of this regime avoided the rise of powerful empresses dowager and consort kin factions.

After the demise of the Three Kingdoms, the rulers of the Eastern Jin, Liu Song, Southern Qi, and Chen dynasties all followed Eastern Han norms and took their empresses from important families.[21] Because emperors wed for political reasons, they looked on these unions as marriages of convenience. An emperor treated his wife politely but no one expected the couple to be intimate.[22] It seems that most empresses in this era did not have sexual relations with their husbands. The emperors of the Southern Dynasties preferred to have sex with harem women, who bore their children.[23] Because of this arrangement, empresses dowager were usually not the mothers of emperors. Nevertheless, an emperor was expected to treat the empress dowager as a surrogate mother. The distance between imperial spouses had advantages for empresses. Five Eastern Han emperors had more than one empress, but the marriages of rulers during the Southern Dynasties were more stable. It became customary for a ruler to have a single empress for his entire reign.

Given the proven dangers that high-born consorts posed to dynastic stability, it might seem odd that southern emperors would select their spouses from prominent backgrounds particularly since some of the

Southern Dynasties were founded by military adventurers with obscure origins. Yet, the modest family background of these rulers made them eager to marry women from the great clans. At the time, people considered marriage a way to confirm status. If the great families accepted imperial parvenus and married their daughters to them, they put emperors on the same social footing as the old families. Such a prestigious union elevated the ruler's standing in the eyes of his subjects and guaranteed that the heir had an impressive genealogy on his mother's side.[24]

This practice also benefited the great families as marrying with the imperial line allowed them to maintain their high status in an age of flux. They could also use this connection to gain office and privilege.[25] Empress Zhao of the Liu Song dynasty was the daughter of a local official in charge of a prefecture.[26] After she became empress, her father obtained a high post in the central government and her mother was ennobled.[27] It seems that southern rulers empowered their in-laws because they saw them as useful allies and wanted to strengthen them. However, the elevation of consort kin had limits. Emperors refused to give their in-laws the immense land grants that had been a common perquisite under the Han. Moreover, compared to the Eastern Han elite, most of the early medieval great families had relatively shallow roots and had not been prominent for very long.[28] In this age of flux, families rose and fell and it became more difficult to remain eminent over the long term.

The imperial marriage system of the Southern Dynasties may have outwardly resembled that of the Eastern Han but it had a very different outcome. Whereas consorts and their kinsmen dominated the government for most of the Eastern Han, the empresses of the Southern Dynasties were far less powerful. In fact, none came close to the importance of the greatest consorts of the Eastern Han. Empresses dowager had previously gained power by appointing a child emperor, declaring a regency, and seizing control of the state. People still believed that the empress dowager had the right to appoint the emperor. However, women usually did not serve as regents under the Southern Dynasties. If the emperor was a minor, there were usually several regents, only one of whom was a consort kinsman, so it was difficult for the empress dowager's clique to dominate the government. Because empresses dowager did not benefit from naming a child emperor, they usually appointed an adult. Empress Dowager Chu Suanzi appointed three emperors and each was an adult.[29] Sometimes powerful men even used an empress dowager as a tool for legitimizing their own ambitions. The rebel Xiao Yan used Empress Dowager Wang Baoming to overthrow the Southern Qi dynasty, then declared himself the founding emperor of the new Liang dynasty.[30]

Other measures limited empress power even further. Imperial consorts lacked the immense income that had been standard during the Han.[31] And whereas Han empresses dowager had exposed themselves openly at court, it had become customary for them to conceal themselves demurely behind a curtain erected behind the emperor. The empress dowager used this awkward arrangement to communicate with high officials while remaining hidden from view.[32] The inability to interact directly with powerful men put palace women at a disadvantage.

During the Southern Dynasties, most empresses dowager served as figureheads, and they used their authority to maintain dynastic continuity. Barred from taking control of the government, they turned their attention to symbolic and cultural matters. Empresses had to abide by ceremonial formality, and officials dealing with them employed formulaic language and ritualized etiquette.[33] They took part in symbolic rituals such as the sericulture ceremony that emphasized the importance of female domestic labor.[34] Empresses sometimes made prophetic statements based on visions they had encountered in dreams, but these statements had limited political impact.[35] Instead of trying to run the government, they sought to earn praise by practicing calligraphy, reading the classics and historical texts, devoting themselves to textile work, and patronizing religion.[36] Some consorts comported themselves humbly and wore simple clothes to win a reputation for integrity. The biography of Shen Wuhua, wife of the last emperor of the brief Chen dynasty, set down the qualities of an ideal empress, praising her as wise, talented, and widely read.[37] She was devout and did not feel jealous when her husband ignored her. The reduced significance of empresses had advantages for consort kin. Whereas the relatives of empresses were repeatedly massacred during the Han, this sort of carnage never occurred under Southern Dynasties. Weakened consort kin had fewer enemies.[38]

The Toba (Tabgach), a clan of Xianbei nomads, took advantage of China's internecine chaos to conquer the north and establish the Northern Wei dynasty, sending vast numbers of refugees fleeing southward. The Toba and other northern peoples ruled north China until reunification under the Sui dynasty in the sixth century. This was the first time that a large swath of China had been under foreign domination so it served as a prototype for subsequent conquest dynasties. Portions of China were under foreign rule for about half of the remainder of imperial history.

During this tumultuous era, north China underwent momentous changes. Faced with a fractured society and economic collapse, the Wei regime had to construct a stable system appropriate to new conditions. In doing so, they created very different modes of administration, taxation, and land tenure. Buddhism also became popular at this time, challenging established values and institutions.

Confusion and hardship made marriage practices more diverse than before.[39] Monogamy broke down and some men took two or more wives. Divorce and remarriage both increased, making families more complex. More children were raised by stepmothers and had siblings born to their father's multiple wives. The steppe customs of nomadic conquerors differed substantially from the classical Chinese rites, forcing ethnic Han to confront unfamiliar ideas about marriage and family.[40] As Confucianism declined, people exhibited less concern about premarital chastity and separation of the sexes.

Although the southern elite continued to keep concubines, there were far fewer concubines in the north. Nomadic peoples did not traditionally practice concubinage so these women had a low status in northern society and their sons shared their degraded status.[41] A man did not want his son to inherit his mother's low standing so if his wife could not bear a son, he would likely remarry rather than take a concubine.

Paradoxically, even though the impact of Confucianism declined, its influence spread. After nomads settled in China, their scions absorbed aspects of the local culture including Confucianism. As nomads acculturated they did not indiscriminately reject one culture for another. Instead families and individuals selected values from each culture and modified them to suit their specific circumstances.[42] As part of this reassessment, many people of nomadic extraction enthusiastically embraced Chinese filial piety, gladly showing devotion to both father and mother. The Wei emperors endorsed the *Classic of Filial Piety* and had it recited at court.[43] *Records of Wei* (*Weishu*) even includes a chapter celebrating devoted sons, many of whom gained distinction by being particularly solicitous or deferential toward their mother.[44]

Under foreign occupation, elite social structure underwent fundamental changes in the north.[45] Most visibly, society fragmented among different ethnicities. People of the same background tended to intermarry, maintaining separate ethnic identities and divisions over generations. Southern families sought marriage partners of comparable financial standing but northerners generally considered power more important than wealth. The Toba and other steppe peoples often chose marriage partners strategically to achieve political, social, and economic goals.

Steppe peoples viewed marriage very differently from ethnic Han, and their values affected the composition of the northern elite. Most importantly, the nomads who settled in China traditionally practiced polygyny, with each wife having equal status.[46] A wife was seen as a full member of her husband's household so a widow rarely remarried outside her husband's family.[47] When a man died, a brother or another family member would usually marry his widow to keep her in the family with a levirate union. Since nomadic peoples did not have concubinage, when they entered China they did not feel the need to strictly distinguish wife from concubine, and this ambiguity affected the status of empresses.[48]

Although it is difficult to compare female roles and prestige across cultures, nomadic men generally allowed their women more autonomy than their Chinese counterparts.[49] Each wife had her own yurt and she worked in the open, casually interacting with men. Women rode horses, practiced archery, and managed herds. Men were accustomed to strong and resourceful women, and a capable, high-born wife could exercise a degree of authority. The lyrics of folk songs show that women expressed love freely. Premarital sex was common, and women sometimes eloped. Some Xianbei wives even had extramarital affairs. After the conquest of North China, these alien customs affected the mindset of the new elite.

Before entering China, nomadic peoples were already using marriage as a political tool so they continued to arrange marriages to pursue practical goals.[50] The Tuoba elite usually took their wives from neighboring lineages, tribes, and countries, arranging each marriage on an ad hoc basis according to their circumstances at the time. They saw in-laws as useful allies. Some clans repeatedly intermarried with the same group of affines to strengthen a useful bond while others took their wives from various clans to expand their political connections. The early rise of the Tuoba was largely due to support from powerful affines, whom they united into a strong military force by forging strategic kinship connections.

Steppe peoples frequently confronted war and hardship so they chose competent adults as leaders. This practice continued after they conquered north China.[51] Because the emperors of the conquest dynasties were adults, the Northern Dynasties had no need for regents, so consort kinsmen had less importance than before. The Wei emperors were acutely aware of the corrosive effect of empress regencies and consort factions during the Eastern Han so they pursued a strategy of deliberate mésalliance.[52] They took wives and lesser consorts from unimportant families that lacked an official or military background.[53] In fact, Wei harem women generally came from very humble families. Some were even born into slavery.[54] Whereas Eastern Han empresses had grand pedigrees, the Wei emperors chose their wives for their looks and demeanor. The officialdom did not take these lowly women seriously, making it difficult for them to accrue power.

The Tuoba originally practiced fraternal succession.[55] After establishing the Wei dynasty, they adopted the Chinese concept of primogeniture to ensure smooth succession. However, they modified this practice to maintain dynastic stability. To prevent an empress dowager from declaring a regency and seizing the government, they did not allow the son of an empress to inherit the throne. Moreover, the mothers of eldest sons were never given the title of empress except posthumously.

Northern emperors appointed empresses only intermittently. These women were usually childless and not allowed to serve as titular mothers of the heir. Given the proven threat to institutional continuity that empresses posed, many rulers hesitated to name an empress at all. During the fifth century, two out of six northern emperors never declared his spouse an empress.[56] Others degraded the position by naming more than one empress.[57] Emperor Xuan of the brief Northern Zhou dynasty gave five women this title, ranking them according to seniority. However, if his intention was to make these women irrelevant, his plan backfired as he produced five consort factions that competed for dominance, destabilizing the court.[58]

A ruler could degrade the prestige of his empress by choosing her randomly. On several occasions a Wei emperor had artisans craft gold-colored statues of several candidates for the position of empress. Courtiers then examined these images and conducted a divination ceremony.[59] The woman represented by the most auspicious statue became empress. This strange beauty contest was intended to humiliate the winner. Members of the court did not bother to examine the women in person nor did they take into account their personality, talent, virtue, education, or family background. The arbitrariness of this process emphasized the unimportance of the empress, letting everyone know that she was not to be taken seriously.

The most extreme way to prevent the emergence of a powerful empress dowager was to murder the mother of the crown prince.[60] During the Han dynasty, Emperor Wu set a cruel precedent by killing his heir's mother to ensure that she would not declare a regency and take over the government.[61] Emperor Daowu, founder of the Northern Wei, revived this practice, justifying it by referring to Emperor Wu's precedent. Emperor Wu had an unusually long reign and many martial successes so his actions were considered a worthy template for the new regime. Daowu seems to have feared that consort kinsmen would interfere in the new Wei system as the maternal kinsmen of chiefs had previously played important roles in Tuoba tribal politics. After Daowu selected his heir, he ordered the boy's mother to commit suicide.[62] Thereafter, all empresses were childless, and the heir's mother was expected to die by ingesting poison. A woman from the harem who had never had sexual relations with the emperor, and sometimes also a wet nurse, would raise the heir.[63] The boy did not necessarily even know the identity of his biological mother. Sometimes the heir's stepmother would be declared empress. By distinguishing between the empress and the mother of the heir apparent, the Wei decreased the influence of the empress and her kinsmen.

As the Tuoba ruling elite became more assimilated to Chinese culture, they began to feel embarrassed by the lowly background of their wives and they compensated by marrying their children into important families.[64] Over time the Wei emperors began to take higher status wives, allowing some consort kinsmen to gain power and prestige.[65] Some prominent families intermarried repeatedly with the imperial line and became extremely powerful. As before, during the late Wei dynasty, consort kin were corrupt, arrogant, and despotic, sending the dynasty into decline.[66]

After the fall of the Northern Wei, most harem women came from modest backgrounds but emperors often selected their wives from high-status families. The genealogy of some empresses stretched back to the Han.[67] Women from such exalted backgrounds could not be expected to commit suicide so the court began to have empresses dowager. Emperors also had sexual relations with their spouses so empresses began to bear sons.[68] As the backgrounds of the empresses rose, they could participate in politics. Some northern empresses acted as regents, issued memorials, and assembled factions.[69]

Han Chinese far outnumbered conquerors from the steppe so rulers of nomadic extraction feared that their people would lose their ethnic identity or be overthrown by hostile subjects. To keep their Han subjects from overwhelming the ruling minority, northern governments discouraged or forbade steppe peoples from marrying Chinese.[70] Nevertheless, the rulers of conquest dynasties realized the utility of allying with the native elite so they often married their daughters into important Chinese families. When Tuoba Wei was contemplating an invasion of the south, they even systematically married their kinsmen into important Chinese social networks to forge a coalition.[71]

Chapter 4

The Northern and Southern Dynasties had very different rules governing the behavior of consorts, and the roles played by wives and harem women changed over time. Whereas southern empresses were ethnic Han, most politically active northern consorts came from steppe families.[72] Yet, even though nomad culture generally placed fewer restraints on women, northern consorts found it difficult to participate in politics. Even though the Wei took on the trappings of a Chinese dynasty, the government functioned as a military dictatorship. Because the administration was constructed around the military, women were locked out of core institutions.[73] Moreover, the Tuoba lacked any tradition of having an empress or empress dowager nor did they have any experience with a female regency so they resisted female power. Most women of nomadic extraction were also poorly educated or illiterate, making it difficult for them to understand complex documents and intervene in the bureaucratic process.

The Northern Wei had twenty-two empresses, and the official dynastic history *Records of Wei* (*Weishu*) records their biographies. Nothing is known about the empresses and minor consorts of the dynasty's first eight emperors.[74] Most of the subsequent biographies are scanty, and sometimes the historian does not even bother to record the date of an empress's death. These women had biographies in the standard dynastic history not because they were significant but simply because they had received the title of empress. According to Chinese historiographic convention, an empress ought to have a biography in the official history however unimportant she may have been.[75] Likewise, depictions of historical emperors sometimes included their wives even if they had lacked a political role.[76] Most Northern Wei empresses had nothing to do with affairs of state. Their public role was limited to ceremonial activities such as religious rituals and symbolic displays of filial piety.[77] The official biographies of these women laud them for their alleged virtues rather than competence.[78] Only four Northern Wei empresses managed to participate in politics to any degree.[79]

Many northern empresses identified themselves closely with Buddhism. When this religion first reached China, many people regarded it with skepticism. But during the Northern Wei, Buddhism became wildly popular among both the Han and steppe peoples. Barred from participating in government affairs, many empresses turned their attention to religion. Some became munificent patrons and spent immense sums constructing lavish temples and monasteries.[80] Others refurbished existing religious sites, filling them with fine religious art and luxurious furnishings.[81] Some of the most impressive sculptures in the famed Longshan shrines were commissioned by empresses and harem women.[82] Empresses visited temples, convened conclaves of monks, and financed the hunt for hitherto unknown sutras.[83] Some temples in the capital had close links to the inner palace. Harem women sometimes took the tonsure and became nuns at these elite monasteries. Nuns from favored temples also visited the palace to lecture the palace ladies on Buddhist teachings.[84] This outpouring of female piety had an impact on high-placed men. Sometimes an emperor would engage in Buddhist patronage to display filial piety. Emperor Xiaowen built a temple to his deceased grandmother Empress Feng and commemorated it to her.[85]

Ambitious Wei consorts may have faced many obstacles but they also enjoyed some advantages. The Xianbei initially lacked much understanding of Confucianism so ideological restraints on consorts weakened at this time. The Xianbei were accustomed to dealing with confident and resourceful women, and this mindset sometimes made them amenable to obeying an assertive empress. Also some empresses had personal qualities that they used to their advantage. A woman who was decisive, charming, or capable could gain the support of those around her. If she attracted the support of important men, she could use them as intermediaries to influence policy.

Two empresses managed to dominate northern China in this era. Empress Dowager Wenming (née Feng) used novel strategies to obtain power within the Northern Wei system. Unlike the dynasty's earlier empresses, who had humble roots, Wenming came from a minor aristocratic background. After one of her husband's consorts bore a son, the woman was executed in line with dynastic custom. The empress dowager then chose Wenming, a young woman at the time, as empress. She mistakenly assumed that the youthful empress would remain apolitical.

However, Wenming was educated, capable, and ambitious, and she used these qualities to accrue power.

When Emperor Xianwen ascended the throne at age eleven, Wenming became empress dowager.[86] Since the beginning of the Wei, empresses dowager had been banned from declaring a regency. However, Wenming organized a coup that brought down the appointed regent. She took over his position but abdicated after just one year. The circumstances of her abdication remain unclear. Some historians believe that Wenming gave up power voluntarily but most likely she faced strident opposition and renounced her authority under duress. It seems that after the emperor gave birth to an heir, courtiers determined that the empress dowager was no longer necessary to ensure an orderly succession so they forced her into retirement.

After Emperor Xianwen retired, his young son replaced him as Emperor Xiaowen. Empress Dowager Wenming had Xianwen assassinated and declared a second regency. She sidelined the titular boy ruler, took control of the state, and ran the government herself. Amid the resulting chaos, Wenming put down an attempted coup, saving the dynasty from being overthrown. She avoided one of the mistakes of Eastern Han empresses dowager. Previous empresses dowager had often been pushed aside by male kinsmen so she kept her natal family from becoming too powerful, thereby safeguarding her own authority.

Wenming was ethnic Han, and she aggressively promoted the Sinicization of the Northern Wei state. In doing so, she undertook wide-reaching political, economic, and social reforms.[87] She initiated this ambitious restructuring to bring the dynasty's institutions and practices in line with Chinese norms.[88] The revised system of government was more centralized, making it easier for the center to manage a diffuse and fractious multi-ethnic state. She also encouraged the Xianbei to speak Chinese, wear Chinese clothes, marry Chinese spouses, and take Chinese surnames.

One might think that imperial historians would have approved of Empress Dowager Wenming as she sought to restore orthodox culture to the heartland of Chinese civilization. Yet, they were highly critical of her. Although powerful men had previously tolerated Eastern Han empresses dowager who declared regencies and seized the government, over time overt displays of female power had become unacceptable. The standard histories portray Wenming as cruel and capricious, implicitly condemning all powerful women by association.[89] Historians also stressed that she showered some of the men around her with favors and paid them undue attention, implying that she was louche.[90]

The other important female figure from this era was Empress Dowager Ling (née Hu), originally a concubine of Emperor Xuanwu.[91] After Xuanwu's death, her son became Emperor Xiaoming. Even though Ling had never been empress, she assumed the title empress dowager and declared a regency. Ling often behaved like an emperor rather than an empress dowager, performing imperial rituals, practicing archery daily, and meeting with courtiers in the hall used by emperors.[92] Unlike Wenming, Empress Dowager Ling failed. During her reign, rebellions broke out and the realm became increasingly anarchic.[93] Moreover, Ling infuriated her son by taking a lover.[94] When the emperor came of age, he tried to have his mother's lover killed but she discovered the plot and poisoned her son. However, in doing so she cut her tie to the imperial line and her regency became illegitimate. A rogue general attacked the capital, massacred the officials and their families, seized the empress dowager, and drowned her in the Yellow River.

The chaos of Empress Dowager Ling's reign cast the Northern Wei state into disarray. The dynasty's remaining emperors were powerless figureheads. Rival warlords fought for supremacy, and northern China splintered into unstable kingdoms. Because Empress Dowager Ling was the last major ruler of the Tuoba Wei regime, historians have blamed her for bringing down the dynasty.[95] The conventions of Confucian historiography required that a failed dynasty end with an evil ruler whose wickedness lost it the mandate of heaven. Rather than casting one of the weak final emperors in this role, imperial historians made Ling the villain. Unlike the final puppet emperors, Ling had control of the government. Not only did she handle matters badly, but the fact that she was a woman made her ineptitude and malfeasance seem even worse from the standpoint of traditional historiography.

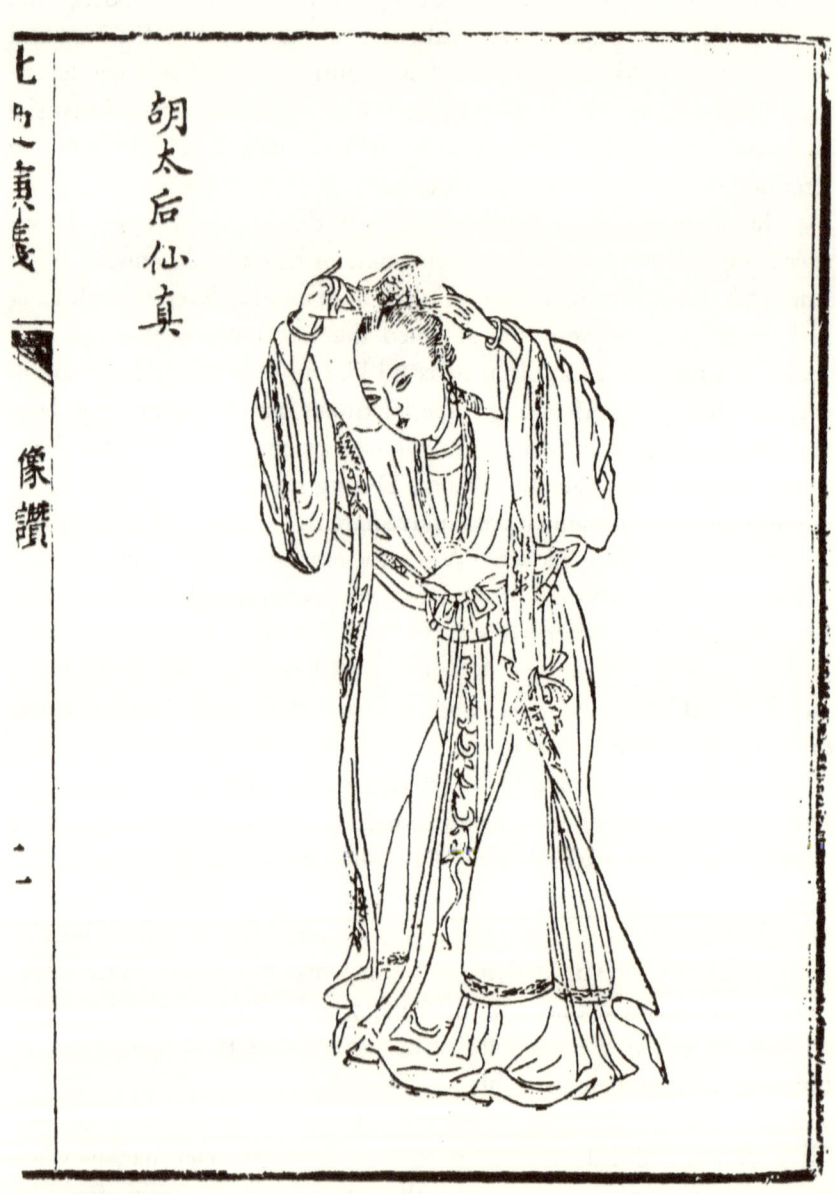

Qing dynasty woodblock illustration of Empress Dowager Ling.
SOURCE: PUBLIC DOMAIN.

To be fair, Empress Dowager Ling does not deserve all of the blame for the fall of the Northern Wei. Although she made several major errors, the dynasty faced growing challenges that she could not possibly overcome, such as an unsound land system and increasingly arrogant gentry. Even so, not all historians are interested in nuance. Some prefer to turn the past into a fable with a clear moral. By blaming Empress Dowager Ling for the fall of the Northern Wei, they reinforced the ancient belief that female power inevitably brings calamity.

Yang Jiang, father of an empress of the ephemeral Northern Zhou, overthrew that regime and reunited China under the Sui dynasty, styling himself Emperor Wen. Although the Sui lasted less than four decades, it nevertheless left an important legacy, re-establishing national unity under ethnic Han rulers and putting in place a workable administrative system. The Sui and subsequent Tang both modeled many of their institutions on the Han dynasty as that had been the only successful government of a unified China up to that time. Because the Han system empowered empresses dowager, some Sui and Tang women had opportunities to gain authority.[96]

The forthright Empress Wenxian, Emperor Wen's wife, intimidated her spouse. Many historians regard her as the most fearsome empress in Chinese history.[97] Even so, her husband loved her deeply. The couple came from similar backgrounds, married young, and shared danger and hardship during their ascent. Although Empress Wenxian is usually portrayed as a virago, she should not be reduced to a one-dimensional stereotype.[98] Wenxian was a devout Buddhist who often treated others with great kindness.[99] She also valued diligence and frugality.[100] However, historians criticized her for intervening in state affairs. Although she was not allowed to enter the audience chamber due to her sex, she waited outside and used eunuch messengers to monitor the proceedings. If she disagreed with something that the emperor did, she would let him know. Unlike most monarchs, Emperor Wen paid close attention to his wife's counsel.

Chapter 4

As Wenxian aged she became increasingly jealous. She detested the fact that the emperor kept a harem as was customary. When her husband became too close to one of his concubines, Wenxian had the woman killed. Her obsession with infidelity made her hate concubinage in general. Even though it was common for wealthy men to take one or more concubines, she urged her husband to punish any official who impregnated a woman other than his wife. This fixation even led Wenxian to interfere with the imperial succession. She loathed the crown prince because he had numerous concubines, so she assembled a clique to depose him. This scheme succeeded. The crown prince was toppled and replaced by Empress Wenxian's son Yang Guang, who would later become Emperor Yang.

Empress Wenxian's intrigues had fateful consequences. Yang turned out to be a terrible emperor. To make matters worse, competing factions centered around the kinsmen of five of his consorts and plunged the court into confusion. Emperor Yang bankrupted the government with massive construction projects and distant military campaigns. He exhibited unusual cruelty. And he infuriated his subjects by relishing ostentatious luxury even as China descended into chaos. After peasant revolts broke out, one of his generals staged a coup and assassinated the hated tyrant. A member of the military aristocracy, Li Yuan, declared himself Emperor Gaozu of a new dynasty that he called Tang. The Sui immediately collapsed, and Li reunited China under the new dynasty.

In fighting for supremacy, Gaozu was aided not just by his son but also by his martial daughter the Pingyang princess.[101] Unusually Pingyang organized and led her own army, which contributed significantly to her father's success. Her participation in warfare broke with ancient traditions barring female leadership on the battlefield. Pingyang's family background seems to have emboldened her to take up the sword. The Li family came from the northwest region, which was heavily influenced by steppe culture. Moreover, when Li Yuan rebelled he had few trustworthy allies so he depended heavily on his family. Once the realm had been pacified, however, he handed over responsibility for warfare to professional generals. Gaozu gave his daughter the title of princess, and Pingyang seems to have led a conventional life thereafter.

The early Tang was a highpoint of female power. Unfortunately, the period's unusual historiography complicates the task of understanding the lives of empresses at that time. Unlike most dynasties, the Tang has two official histories. *Old Tang Records* (*Jiu Tangshu*) and *New Tang Records* (*Xin Tangshu*) were both compiled by Song dynasty historians about a century apart. Song dynasty values and ideas differed considerably from those of the Tang in many respects, particularly due to the rise of Neo-Confucianism, leading readers to wonder at the accuracy of these two works. Historians continue to debate the relative merits and deficiencies of the two Tang histories.[102] Compared with earlier standard histories, both Tang compilations put far greater stress on ethical propriety. The editors expected more sacrifices from women and took a dim view of female sexuality. These values influenced their portrayals of powerful women.[103]

The culture and values of the ruling line influenced the behavior of Tang empresses. The dynastic founder Gaozu came from an obscure background, and historians can only speculate on his roots.[104] Some believe that the Tang ruling line were barbarized Han who had assimilated the steppe culture that prevailed in the northwest borderlands. Others think that they were descended from Tuoba who had adapted a Chinese identity. Whatever Li Yuan's origins, he and his descendants had little interest in cultural orthodoxy. The Li family readily accepted a complex interplay of Chinese and foreign cultures. This attitude made the Tang highly cosmopolitan and helps account for its dazzling cultural achievements. Confucian scholarship was also revitalized at this time, and these conservative values increasingly influenced government and society. Most obviously, the law began to adapt overtly Confucian values as officials believed that Confucian morality and rites should constitute the basis of government.[105]

The relations between husband and wife changed somewhat under the Tang. In antiquity, the wife had a tenuous position in her husband's household as she was still considered a member of her natal family. This kinship arrangement helps explain the behavior of Han dynasty empresses who favored the interests of fathers and brothers above that of their sons. Whereas a son belonged to his father's family, his mother still owed allegiance to the family of her own father, so their interests did not necessarily coincide. During the Tang, wives and husbands drew closer and this mindset began to change.[106] At the beginning of the dynasty, the height of female power, women from elite families still had very close ties to their natal families after marrying. But from the mid-Tang onward, these ties weakened noticeably.

Changing burial customs attest to this shift. Prior to this era, Confucians had criticized the burial of spouses in the same grave as it was contrary to ancient tradition, but during the Tang joint spousal burial became common.[107] Accordingly, the empress and favored minor consorts were buried in subsidiary tombs near that of the emperor.[108] And when judges adjudicated matters relating to a woman, unlike previous eras, they often ignored her natal family. By the Song dynasty, women had clearly been firmly integrated into the families of their husbands.[109]

The Tang emperors were embarrassed by their modest origins and craved acceptance. However, the great families of the Shandong aristocracy considered the Li barbarous parvenus. They shunned marriage with the imperial line, which they considered far beneath them.[110] Nevertheless, lesser members of the elite saw marriage with a member of the imperial family as both prestigious and expedient. A few families even married repeatedly with the imperial line. As a result of repeated intermarriage between imperial kin and a few favored families, some princesses ended up marrying their cousins, and emperors had particularly close connections with their mothers' kinsmen.[111] As before, men had close bonds with their maternal uncles, and the fathers and brothers of consorts used this kinship convention to demand power and privileges.[112] Many Tang consort kin joined factions and served in civil and military offices.[113]

The Wei family of Jingzhao exemplifies the marriage partners of the Tang imperial line. The Wei married with the Li at least twenty-eight times.[114] Their men took princesses as wives, and their women married emperors and princes. This ancient family had been prominent since the Western Han dynasty and had earned distinction in both classical scholarship and military pursuits. During the Tang, many Wei served as officials. They used repeated marriage with the imperial clan to bolster their political position, and they led an influential faction. Eventually, however, these tactics ruined them. Antipathy toward the Wei empresses caused widespread resentment and forced them to retire from politics.

Because early Tang empresses came from important families, they were well positioned to intervene in administrative matters, and many participated in court intrigues.[115] In contrast, many high officials were talented men from humble families so they felt abashed when confronted by an empress with a lengthy pedigree.[116] Tang empresses came from elite families so they received an education while young and often continued to study after they entered the palace.[117] Due to the era's atmosphere of cultural openness, the dynasty's early empresses were not restrained by onerous rites and rules so they could meet with powerful men.

The Tang dynasty lacked clear guidelines as to who would inherit the throne, setting the scene for inevitable succession struggles. Empresses took part in these conflicts. Emperor Zhongzong was the seventh son of the previous ruler, Ruizong was his predecessor's younger brother, and Taizong became emperor by killing his older brother in a coup. Uncertainty regarding the succession made the empress dowager an important figure at court. Moreover, unlike the Northern Wei, Tang empresses were expected to share the emperor's bed on occasion so they bore children. Emperor Gaozu had twenty-two sons by eighteen women. His empress bore four of them. When an empress's son become emperor, she took on the Han dynasty role of empress dowager to whom the reigning emperor owed filial obedience. The empress dowager presented herself as not just the mother of the sitting emperor but as the "mother of the realm," giving her maternal authority over all of China and justifying her claim to political authority.[118]

Official annals portray Empress Dou, wife of Emperor Gaozu, in one-dimensional terms. According to historiographic convention, both the dynastic founder and his wife had to be paragons of virtue to justify the new dynasty's acquisition of heaven's mandate. Accordingly, *Old Tang Records* emphasizes Dou's moral character.[119] She was supposedly educated, skilled at argumentation, and solicitous toward her mother-in-law. In other words, her official biography dutifully portrays her as talented and filial. Her husband spent much of his career fighting the wars that would unify China, so at this time military affairs overshadowed politics.

CHAPTER 4

Accordingly, Empress Dou did not have a significant role in the new government.

Empress Zhangsun, the wife of the dynasty's second ruler Taizong, was far more important. Although she had Xianbei blood and came from a military family, she had received a good education based on Confucian values.[120] Zhangsun earned lasting fame as the author of *Rules for Women* (*Nüze*), a compendium of good deeds performed by female exemplars. Zhangsun was also one of her husband's trusted advisers. She helped keep the emperor calm during difficult situations and proffered sensible advice on military and civil matters, earning her husband's respect and the gratitude of his followers. Emperor Taizong also received wise counsel from his concubine Xu Hui.[121] Late in his reign, Taizong faced serious problems, including a large-scale invasion of Korea that ended in failure. Lady Xu urged him to end the useless war and live frugally, and Taizong appreciated her prudent remonstrations.

During the subsequent reign of Gaozong, Empress Wu Zetian (Wu Zhao) rose to unprecedented heights.[122] Her usurpation of imperial prerogatives, arrogation of the male title of emperor (*huangdi*), and temporary overthrow of the Tang in favor of a new dynasty, had a huge impact on the institution of empress. Due to her enduring influence, this era stands out as a major rupture in views toward powerful women. Before Wu Zetian, empresses had often been involved in politics and sometimes took control of the state. Wu's era marked a turning point. Her violation of patriarchal traditions traumatized powerful men, and they set out to ensure that nothing like this would ever happen again. Attitudes and administrative practices before and after her reign differed markedly.

Wu Zetian was originally a concubine of Emperor Taizong. According to traditional incest taboos, a son ought to have avoided intimacy with his father's concubines. Nevertheless, when Gaozong succeeded his father to the throne, he kept Wu in the palace and she became his favorite. However, Gaozong already had an empress, surnamed Wang. Wu Zetian convinced Gaozong to depose Empress Wang and elevate her to the position. Traditionally, historians portray Gaozong as a weak-willed ruler who was easily manipulated by a wily concubine. However, there might have been more to the story. Wang and Wu belonged to rival factions so

Eighteenth-century portrait of Wu Zetian.
SOURCE: *PUBLIC DOMAIN.*

perhaps Gaozong felt threatened by the Wang faction and unseated her to weaken her powerful supporters. He then replaced Empress Wang with Wu Zetian, whom he mistakenly believed to be more supportive.[123]

In 660, Gaozong suffered a stroke that debilitated him. A few years later he handed over power to Empress Wu, and she took control of the government. Unlike her husband, Wu was intelligent, educated, and competent, and she used these strengths to accrue power and attract support. She sat in on meetings, discussed matters of state with high officials, and issued commands. Even while her enervated husband was still alive, she eliminated opponents and consolidated power. Wu even poisoned the heir apparent and exiled other princes. When Gaozong died in 683, Wu Zetian had already become firmly entrenched as the real ruler of China.

Gaozong's will named an heir who became Emperor Zhongzong. However, Gaozong had ordered his successor to defer to Empress

Chapter 4

Dowager Wu's judgment in major matters so she retained supreme authority. Zhongzong was as mediocre as his father so his wife, Empress Wei, tried to follow Wu's example and wrest authority from her incompetent spouse. The titular emperor acquiesced and helped her place supporters in key positions. In response to this challenge, Wu deposed Zhongzong and placed one of her sons on the throne as Emperor Ruizong. This time Wu made no attempt to hide the fact that she was the true ruler of China. She confined the puppet emperor to the inner palace and he never appeared in public or met with government ministers. Wu Zetian reigned as emperor in all but name.

In 690, Wu felt confident enough to do away with the Tang dynasty. She could not legitimately reign within the framework of the Tang as tradition required that the ruler be both male and a descendant of the dynasty's founder. Wu met neither of these conditions so she deposed Emperor Ruizong, abolished the Tang, and declared herself the emperor of a new dynasty called Zhou. She immediately began constructing a different type of government. Whereas the Tang rulers had used Daoism as a political ideology, Wu emphasized Buddhism, granting titles of nobility to nine senior monks. She also enshrined her ancestors in the imperial ancestral temple, giving the illusion that she came from an imperial lineage. However, the system she instituted was so unusual that basic matters such as succession remained unclear throughout her reign, sowing doubt and confusion.

Wu knew that the great families detested her illegitimate regime so she used civil service examinations to locate and elevate talented men from lesser backgrounds. Until this time, men from the lower gentry had few opportunities for government service as emperors had reserved important posts for aristocrats. Wu understood that if she gave talented men unexpected career openings, they would be grateful and serve her loyally. Her use of examinations to identify talent had wide-reaching consequences.[124] Song dynasty rulers built on Wu Zetian's arrangements and made civil service examinations the core of their administrative system, fostering meritocracy, promoting social mobility, and making the elite more open and diverse.

Wu Zetian had two lovers and gave them both important political roles. Even though her behavior violated the norms of widowhood and female chastity, courtiers nevertheless flattered her paramours. Wu would brook no opposition to her favorites. When she found out that three of her family members had secretly criticized this unusual state of affairs, she ordered them to commit suicide.

As Wu Zetian aged, she could no longer handle matters as before. Under a normal dynasty, robust institutions would keep the government running smoothly under a declining monarch, but Wu's illegitimate regime had little support among those who mattered. As soon as she showed signs of physical decline, disenchanted officials and generals began to plot against her. Eventually, they deposed her and restored the Tang dynasty. Zhongzong became emperor once again and Wu was demoted from emperor to empress dowager. After her death, she was not buried in a tomb of her own in the fashion of an emperor. Instead, she was buried with Emperor Gaozong, her husband.[125] These funeral arrangements signified that she had never reigned as a legitimate emperor but was merely a consort who had overstepped her proper place.

Wu Zetian stands alone in the annals of Chinese history. This incomparable monarch remains highly controversial and historians continue to debate her reign and legacy. Some scholars have tried to depict her as a proto-feminist.[126] Indeed, in a few ways Wu tried to give ordinary women a higher social position such as by requiring children to mourn mothers and fathers for the same length of time.[127] But, in general, Wu Zetian showed no interest in improving the lives of women. She kept most of the patriarchal structure of government and society intact, expediently manipulating it to further her own interests. In this respect, she followed the examples of earlier empresses, none of whom were feminist revolutionaries.

Because Wu Zetian's reign was so exceptional, she had to employ a unique set of techniques to keep herself on the throne and handle government affairs. These measures reveal how an empress could successfully empower herself and control proud men who resented her. Her most useful method of rulership was also the most straightforward. Wu Zetian kept herself in power largely by doing a good job. She was intelligent, educated, and a competent writer on religion and politics.[128] Although some texts were probably ghostwritten in her name, others are undoubtedly genuine.[129] Wu's writings show her to have been knowledgeable and gifted, and she used these traits to her advantage when handling affairs of state.

Even imperial historians who hated Wu Zetian admitted that she was judicious in selecting and promoting talented officials.[130] Wu had no patience for ineptitude and quickly removed incompetent ministers. By expanding the pool of potential bureaucrats beyond the high aristocracy and giving men from the lower gentry an opportunity to advance, she accessed a huge, untapped pool of enthusiastic and loyal talent, and her officials managed the government and economy efficiently. Wu's government emphasized agriculture and took concrete measures to make farming more productive.[131] She was also a successful conqueror. During her reign, China annexed new regions of Central Asia and waged successful wars on the Korean peninsula. By projecting Chinese power far beyond its traditional limits, she portrayed herself as a victorious martial emperor.

Wu Zetian also deployed terror to her advantage. As a woman taking on the role of a male ruler, she faced the ire of Tang loyalists and the conservative male elite. Particularly at the beginning of her reign, when she still faced stiff opposition, Wu used violence to cow her critics. A squad of secret police monitored the court, and they dealt with criticism ruthlessly. Anyone who disparaged one of her favorites might face execution.[132] Boxes were installed outside government offices for people who wanted to anonymously denounce anyone they deemed disloyal. Wu even dealt harshly with supporters who disappointed her. When an elderly nun under her patronage failed to predict a fire in the palace, Wu had the hapless woman and her students enslaved. The court was repeatedly roiled by torture, bloodbaths, and mass exiles. Wu even killed members of her own family. She executed two sons, a baby daughter, and several grandchildren.[133] However, when Wu felt more secure in her position, she instituted a more benign style of rule.

Wu Zetian's cruelty was not unique. At the beginning of the Han dynasty, Empress Dowager Lü had also used violence as a political tool. But the early Tang court was riddled with cliques, exacerbating the violence. Uncertainty over succession to the throne also intensified factional struggles. Once this sort of political violence began, it tended to increase in scope and consume a wider range of victims.

The most vexing problem that Wu faced was the blatant illegitimacy of her reign. For a woman to call herself emperor, she had to contrive ways to prove that she had the right to sit on the throne. Wu repurposed the symbols and rites of male rulers and used them to bolster her claim to power.[134] She conducted the ancient *fengshan* sacrifice, until then a prerogative of male rulers.[135] She also highlighted sacrifices to her own ancestors and those to her husband's deposed clan to display filial piety.[136] Wu even resurrected ancient symbols of political legitimacy. She cast a set of nine archaic bronze tripods such as ancient rulers had used to symbolize royal authority.

Wu Zetian also used auspicious reign titles and changed them frequently. The early Tang emperors rarely changed their reign titles, but over the course of Wu's reign she employed nineteen reign titles. These designations commemorated the appearance of good omens and miracles, announced major policies or triumphs, bragged about her good health, and declared that the realm was at peace.[137] Reign titles served as a public-relations tool to communicate Wu's aspirations and achievements to the public at large.[138]

Aside from appropriating the traditional legitimation techniques of emperors, Wu Zetian also manipulated female stereotypes to portray herself as mother of the realm. A supporter claimed to have discovered a rock in the sacred Luo River inscribed with a mysterious message referring to her as the "sacred mother" (*shengmu*).[139] She used this supernatural omen to take on the identity of a holy matriarch. Moreover, as powerful women were often accused of licentiousness, Wu tried to cultivate an image of moral probity. She revived the earlier system of official commendation for rewarding paragons of filial piety and righteousness, giving it renewed emphasis.[140]

In many times and places, powerful women have turned to religion to justify actions that those around them considered unorthodox. Political ideologies, symbols, and rituals tended to be closely linked to masculine privilege, but religion provided an alternative trove of ideas and imagery that women could deploy to their advantage. Wu Zetian relied heavily on creative religious ideology to justify her authority.[141] Her religious views changed over the years.[142] When her husband was still alive, she followed Tang custom in stressing Daoism and Confucianism. After his death, she made Buddhism the primary tool of legitimation. Although Buddhism was useful to her, her fervent piety was not cynical. She seems to have been genuinely devout. However, sincerity did not preclude manipulating Buddhism for her own benefit.

Early in her reign Wu announced that she was an incarnation of Maitreya, a buddha who would eventually appear to restore the dharma. To prove this claim, her supporters forged the *Great Cloud Sutra* (*Da yun jing*). This text conveniently predicted that a woman would one day reign as emperor, bringing peace, health, and stability to the world.[143] To promote the Maitreya cult, she added a giant statue of the buddha to the Longmen Grottoes, a major center for Buddhist worship. She circulated additional forged texts that also prophesied the eventual arrival of a great female monarch who would reign as a *chakravartin* (*zhuanlun wang*), the ideal universal Buddhist ruler.

Wu Zetian's Buddhism was not entirely self-serving. She became extremely close to Fazang, an erudite monk of Central Asian extraction and one of the most important thinkers of that time.[144] Fazang was twenty years younger than the empress and outlived her by seven years so he was a prominent presence at court throughout her reign. Wu took note of Fazang's talent when he was just a novice, and with her backing he rose quickly to become a leading cleric. Fazang was a gifted theorist. He earned an important place in the history of Buddhist thought as the founder of the *Avataṃsaka* school, a branch of Buddhist philosophy based on the *Avataṃsaka sutra*, a profound meditation on metaphysics. This is still considered one of the most difficult branches of Buddhist thought. Under Fazang's tutelage, Empress Wu patronized the newly popular *Avataṃsaka* school and made it a keystone of her religious ideology. She commissioned a new translation of the sutra, an extremely long text, and this massive project employed twenty-five Chinese and foreign scholars. Fazang felt indebted to the monarch for supporting his pet project so enthusiastically that he worked hard to help legitimate her rule as repayment. Fazang and other prominent religious figures tried to portray Wu's reign as the birth of a Buddhist empire that would spread the faith throughout the world.

Empress Wu also solicited support by encouraging the veneration of Buddhist relics.[145] In particular, she urged worshippers to venerate a holy artifact stored in the Famen Temple near Chang'an, a religious center with close links to the palace. She distributed relics to various temples to publicly demonstrate her piety and gain the support of the faithful. The veneration of relics helped justify Wu's claim to be a *chakravartin* as it seemed that China had become the center of the Buddhist world. She also undertook an ambitious building campaign to erect religious monuments and structures, most famously reconstructing the Giant Wild Goose Pagoda, which had collapsed not long after its completion. She built a large complex in Luoyang intended as a Buddhist version of the Bright Hall (*mingtang*) where Zhou dynasty kings conducted important rites.[146] Wu also commissioned numerous eleven-faced images of the bodhisattva Guanyin, many of them unusually large and lavish.[147] Promoting this female religious figure helped further the ideology of female rulership. Wu paid for numerous other Buddhist images, making her one of the most important patrons in the religion's history.[148] She also oversaw the replication and distribution of an unprecedented number of sutras using innovative printing techniques.[149]

Wu Zetian had eclectic beliefs and did not limit herself to orthodox Buddhism. Although she demoted Daoism from its previous place as de facto state religion, this rich body of religious thought nevertheless intrigued her. One reason she noticed Fazang was his mastery of Daoist thought in addition to Buddhism.[150] As Wu grew older, she turned increasingly to Daoism as it included practices that promised longevity and even immortality. Fazang used his familiarity with these techniques to hold his patron's attention. He also performed esoteric rites and magic, such as imploring for rain and cursing China's enemies.

Wu Zetian promoted the cult of the deity Xiwangmu (Queen Mother of the West) and identified herself with this popular goddess.[151] Xiwangmu was a popular divinity whose worship extended back to antiquity. During the medieval era, the Xiwangmu cult was absorbed into religious

Daoism, and believers made her the most important female deity of their faith.¹⁵² Religious writings were usually composed by men so many Chinese goddesses seem like male fantasies. However, Xiwangmu was different. An independent, dynamic, and powerful female persona made Xiwangmu the ideal religious alter ego for an ambitious empress. Poems about outstanding women often alluded to Xiwangmu so people were already accustomed to the idea that exceptional mortal women could take on aspects of her identity. Wu used this literary convention to her own advantage, associating herself with Xiwangmu to justify her authority.¹⁵³

The extraordinary reign of China's only female emperor fascinated writers of both history and fiction. Attitudes toward Wu Zetian shifted over the centuries.¹⁵⁴ During the late Tang era, literary portrayals largely adhered to standard historical accounts. However, Song and Yuan writers took a more critical attitude toward both the audacious female monarch and the Tang dynasty in general. They not only criticized Wu for overstepping her proper place but also portrayed her strange reign a symptom of the malicious foreign influences that disfigured Tang culture. The Ming dynasty saw the rise of the erotic novel, and writers described her imaginary sexual exploits. Qing writers continued to demonize the female emperor, depicting her rule as a catastrophe that brought misery to the common people.

The popular image of Wu Zetian became increasingly distorted and negative with the passage of time. People ended up regarding her as foolish, incompetent, and sexually depraved, and they saw her usurpation of the Tang as a cautionary tale. In reaction, men began to take a much more negative view of female power. The reign of Wu Zetian stands out as a major turning point in the history of Chinese empresses. Henceforth, rulers and officials became much more critical of female power, and they instituted stringent safeguards to curb women's ambitions. Barred from gaining political authority, empresses behaved more passively than before and sought to gain respect for displays of virtue and prudence rather than seeking to gain power.

After the restoration of the Tang, Emperor Zhongzong reigned a second time. Emboldened by Wu Zetian, the women around him continued to dominate the weak-willed monarch.¹⁵⁵ Because Zhongzong's wife, Empress Wei, had consoled her husband during his incarceration under Empress Wu, he gave her considerable authority out of gratitude. She and her kinsmen tried to dominate the state apparatus.[156] However, they faced competing factions that were also headed by women. Wu Zetian's daughter, the Taiping Princess, wanted to follow her mother's example and seize control of the state.[157] Various other palace women also assembled cliques that struggled for supremacy. The officialdom regarded Empress Wei, the Taiping Princess, and other ambitious harem women as exceedingly corrupt and resented them for undermining the norms of government.

After Zhongzong's death, his younger brother became Emperor Ruizong. Confrontation between opposing cliques eventually led to violence, and the Empress Dowager Wei was beheaded during an armed struggle inside the palace. The new emperor understood the threat posed by competing factions and was determined to restore order. Ruizong's sister, the Taiping Princess, realized that the emperor was determined to bring her down so she plotted to have him poisoned. When this scheme failed, she committed suicide. The death of the Taiping Princess marked the end of the exceptional era of female power that marked the early Tang dynasty.

Imperial historians largely judged the significance of historical figures by their political influence. Yet, influence is not necessarily positive. The preface to the section containing empresses' biographies in *Old Tang Records* emphasizes the destructive impact that powerful women had on the dynasty's government.[158] While the official biographies of some early Tang palace women are lengthy and detailed, those who came after Empress Wei and the Taiping Princess receive only cursory treatment. From the reign of Ruizong onward, Tang officials restored patriarchal administration and blocked women from accruing power. The dynasty's later empresses rarely became involved in politics.[159] Even the educational level of palace women declined.[160] While some early Tang consorts had considerable learning, later emperors did not encourage consorts to study as they realized that palace women might use knowledge to empower themselves.

After Wu Zetian, most emperors of the revived Tang dynasty did not dare appoint an empress as they feared that a woman might use this title to accrue power and destabilize the government. Out of thirteen later Tang emperors, only three designated an empress.[161] Moreover, for the remainder of the dynasty, emperors did not take their spouses from the most outstanding families.[162] Instead they repeatedly intermarried with a circle of elite provincial families to bind the periphery to the center. The emperors chose spouses from backgrounds that were respectable but not too grand, deliberately limiting their prestige. This strategy succeeded, and late Tang palace women and consort kin had little influence.

After the early Tang, the most important incident involving a woman involved the controversial Yang Yuhuan, known to posterity as Yang Guifei.[163] Of all the famous women in Chinese history, her popular image perhaps differs the most from reality. Beautiful and charismatic, Yang was either betrothed to the eighteenth son of Emperor Xuanzong or else married him.[164] However, after Xuanzong saw her, he wanted her for himself. Yang divorced her husband and entered a Daoist convent to symbolically annul her previous marriage. Then she became a concubine of the emperor.

As Xuanzong's favorite, Yang helped entertain important officials, including the powerful General An Lushan, sometimes engaging him in boisterous fun. Once she wrapped the obese general in swaddling clothes and joked that she had given birth to a giant baby, much to the amusement of the palace ladies and eunuchs. However, Yang Guifei's cousin, Yang Guozhong, an important official, clashed with An and executed some of the general's staff. These provocations pushed An Lushan into rebellion. His army marched on the capital, sending the emperor and court fleeing for safety.[165] During the ensuing pandemonium, discipline broke down among the troops accompanying the disgraced emperor. The soldiers killed Yang Guozhong then demanded the death of Yang Guifei, whom they accused of complicity in inciting this disaster.[166] Faced with mutiny, the beleaguered Emperor Xuanzong ordered his beloved concubine to be strangled.

Yang Guifei has been unfairly portrayed as one of the most colorful villains in Chinese history. Since antiquity, women had been blamed for dynastic decline and calamitous events. Writers harnessed this long-standing prejudice and cast Yang Guifei as a major cause of the An

Lushan Rebellion. Most influentially, the Bai Juyi wrote a poem that maligned her with lies and exaggerations, depicting Yang as a key figure at court who misled the emperor and fomented crisis. This famous poem popularized the image of Yang Guifei as a depraved beauty who played a major role in momentous events. Subsequent poems and stories expanded on this theme, depicting her attractive visage as a false mask hiding dangerous wickedness.[167]

Despite her inflated posthumous reputation, Yang Guifei was a trivial presence at court who certainly did not deserve blame for the catastrophic events that led to her execution. Although she accommodated the general who eventually rebelled, she was carrying out her proper role. At the time An Lushan enjoyed the emperor's favor so she did her duty by entertaining an honored guest. And although she was a cousin of the chancellor Yang Guozhong who clashed with An, she did not have anything to do with his policies. Yang Guozhong may have goaded An Lushan into rebellion, but Yang Guifei was innocent.

The An Lushan Rebellion debilitated the Tang. The dynasty managed to survive the crisis but was terminally weakened. Many local officials and warlords became autonomous, and emperors struggled to

Thirteenth-century painting of Yang Guifei mounting a horse.
SOURCE: PUBLIC DOMAIN.

CHAPTER 4

the state together. To encourage national unity, the government enthusiastically patronized Confucianism, stimulating a revival of classical ethics and scholarship in the latter part of the dynasty.[168] As a result, people began to expect women's behavior to conform to Confucian ideals, which altered their views of womanhood. In the early part of the dynasty, women gained praise for their talent or beauty, but the Confucian revival made virtue the primary standard of judgment. In subsequent eras, the influence of Confucianism continued to grow, affecting perceptions of female power. Exaggerated stories about Wu Zetian and Yang Guifei were used as cautionary tales to show the dangers of female influence. The authorities of later eras heeded these warnings, and women's participation in government declined.

NOTES

1. Liu, *Shih-shuo Hsin-yü*, 342 (19.4); Liu, *Shishuo xinyu huijiao jizhu*, 19:567–68.
2. Chen, *Sanguozhi*, 2:80; Liu, "Wei Jin yihuan shijia," 30.
3. Cutter, "Sex, Politics, and Morality," 79–113.
4. Deng, "Cong *Shishuo xinyu*," 40–44.
5. Miyakawa, "The Confucianization of South China," 31–33, 38.
6. Ochi, *Gi Shin Nanchō no kizoku sei*, 183–93; Zhu, *Wei Jin nanbeichao shehui shenghuo shi*, 246–49; Lee, "Women and Marriage," 62–63; Zhang, *Jiating shihua*, 39.
7. Zhu, *Wei Jin nanbeichao shehui shenghuo shi*, 242–54.
8. Pan, "Jiazu," 13:231–34, n. 214. For example, see Liu, *Shih-shuo Hsin-yü*, 218 (8.22), 242 (8.139), 398 (24.15); Liu, *Shishuo xinyu huijiao jizhu*, 8:372, 8:519, 24:646. People also mourned extensively for maternal kin. Yan, *Quan Jin wen*, 32:317.
9. Fang, *Jinshu*, 60:1633; Li, *Nanshi*, 19:534, describes incidents that demonstrate married women's loyalty to their natal kin.
10. Ochi, *Gi Shin nanchō no hito to shakai*, 41–61.
11. Yoshikawa, *Liuchao jingshen shi yanjiu*, 419–35.
12. Shen, *Songshu*, 92:2263. Also Shen, *Songshu*, 91:2243, 91:2257; Fang, *Jinshu*, 38:1126; Xiao, *Nan Qi shu*, 55:956–58.
13. Shen, *Songshu*, 76:1969.
14. Shen, *Songshu*, 27:780. Also 27:760–75.
15. Shen, *Songshu*, 54:1534.
16. Li, "Lun Wei Jin shiqi de jimu zi guanxi," 45–47.
17. Yao, *Liangshu*, 7:165.
18. Li, *Nanshi*, 11:318.
19. Bielenstein, "The Six Dynasties, Volume 2," 16–17; Misevic, "Oligarchy or Social Mobility," 217–21.
20. Cutter, "To the Manner Born?" 70.

21. Bielenstein, "The Six Dynasties, Volume 2," 16–28, gives basic information regarding all of the empresses of the Six Dynasties.

22. For example, the proper mourning of empresses and their kinsmen was considered an important matter and received considerable attention from the court. Yan, *Quan Jin wen*, 29:282, 30:291, 32:317, 32:319, 78:829, 82:868–69, 120:1329, 129:1387, 130:1398, 130:1400, 132:1422, 132:1428, 133:1432, 135:1456, 135:1463, 136:1469, 145:1573, 145:1579, 146:1587; Shen, *Songshu*, 15:397–403.

23. Not everyone liked this arrangement. Li, *Nanshi*, 14:386.

24. Chennault, "Lofty Gates or Solitary Impoverishment?" 258, 267–68, 308–9, 323; Misevic, "Oligarchy or Social Mobility," 213–15; Mather, "Intermarriage as a Gauge of Family Status," 212–14.

25. It was expected that an empress would be close to her father. Yan, *Quan Jin wen*, 131:1416, 132:1423, 134:1445.

26. It was not uncommon for an empress to come from the family of an important local official. Some local magnates were very wealthy and powerful. Fang, *Jinshu*, 32:983, 32:985.

27. Li, *Nanshi*, 11:317. Also see Shen, *Songshu*, 41:1280–83. For a discussion of taking an empress see Yan, *Quan Jin wen*, 145:1578.

28. Misevic, "Oligarchy or Social Mobility," 224, 226, 228–29, 230, 232.

29. Bielenstein, "The Six Dynasties, Volume 1," 69, 76–78, 81–82.

30. Bielenstein, "The Six Dynasties, Volume 1," 188–89.

31. Fang, *Jinshu*, 31:953.

32. Fang, *Jinshu*, 8:191; McMahon, "Women Rulers in Imperial China," 195–96; McMahon, *Women Shall Not Rule*, 147.

33. Shen, *Songshu*, 15:407–8.

34. This ceremony was based on the ceremony described in the *Rites of Zhou* (*Zhou li*). Yan, *Quan Jin wen*, 66:685; Shen, *Songshu*, 14:355–56, 17:482.

35. Xiao, *Nan Qi shu*, 20:390; Yao, *Liangshu*, 7:157; Lu, *Power of the Words*, 42–43. The cruel and jealous Empress Chi, wife of Emperor Wende of the Liang dynasty, allegedly was transformed into a dragon when she died and lived in a well in the palace. Thereafter, she communicated with the emperor through dreams. Li, *Nanshi*, 12:339. Some consorts engaged in unorthodox shamanistic and magical practices. Fang, *Jinshu*, 31:956.

36. Fang, *Jinshu*, 31:948, 31:950, 31:952, 31:955, 32:975; Yan, *Quan Jin wen*, 153:1675; Li, *Nanshi*, 12:338; McMahon, *Women Shall Not Rule*, 120–21.

37. Li, *Nanshi*, 11:344; McMahon, *Women Shall Not Rule*, 174.

38. Bielenstein, "The Six Dynasties, Volume 2," 28. Consort kin still had many privileges, and were often above the law. Li, *Nanshi*, 47:1177.

39. Zhang, *Jiating shihua*, 41–42, 46.

40. Wang, "Beichao funü hunyin shulun," 9–16.

41. Lee, "Women and Marriage," 170, 172; Li, *Wei Jin Sui Tang hunyin xingtai*, 182–85.

42. Holmgren, "Family, Marriage and Political Power," 11.

43. Li, *Beishi*, 4:137, 4:148, 22:829.

44. Wei, *Weishu*, ch. 86. The author emphasized that the filial son cares for both father and mother. Wei, *Weishu*, 60:1347.

CHAPTER 4

45. Li, *Wei Jin Sui Tang hunyin xingtai yanjiu*, 167–70, 177–81.
46. Holmgren, "Imperial Marriage in the Native Chinese and Non-Han State, 77.
47. In spite of levirate, it seems that women maintained membership in their natal families as well. A married woman had membership in both the family of her husband and also that of her father. Zhang, *Cong Tuoba dao Bei Wei*, 20, 220–21.
48. Holmgren, "Social Mobility in the Northern Dynasties," 27.
49. Barfield, *The Perilous Frontier*, 25; Zhuang, "Beichao shidai Xianbei funü," 62–68; Song, *Bei Wei nüzhu lun*, 46.
50. Holmgren, "Political Organization of Non-Han States in China," 11; Barfield, *The Perilous Frontier*, 26; Xie, *Beichao hunsang lisu yanjiu*, 15–17; Eisenberg, *Kingship in Early Medieval China*, 29; Zhang, *Cong Tuoba dao Bei Wei*, 29–30, 227–28.
51. Holmgren, "Imperial Marriage in the Native Chinese and Non-Han State, 77; Holmgren, "The Harem in Northern Wei Politics," 76.
52. For example, a memorial discussing the fall of the Han dynasty emphasized the excessive power of consort kin. Wei, *Weishu*, 48:1073.
53. Holmgren, "Imperial Marriage in the Native Chinese and Non-Han State, 79–80; Holmgren, "The Harem in Northern Wei Politics," 78.
54. Li, *Beishi*, 14:524–25.
55. Holmgren, "Women and Political Power in the Traditional T'o-pa Elite," 43.
56. Holmgren, "The Harem in Northern Wei Politics," 76–77.
57. Bigamy became common among the elite in the Six Dynasty era. Xue, "Wei Jin beichao hunyinzhong de erqi xianxiang," 77, 79–80. The Qing dynasty historian Zhao Yi criticized imperial bigamy in this era as a flagrant violation of ritual norms. Zhao, *Nianer shi zhaji*, 15:207.
58. Eisenberg, *Kingship in Early Medieval China*, 161–63; McMahon, *Women Shall Not Rule*, 172.
59. Wei, *Weishu*, 13:321, 325; Holmgren, "Women and Political Power," 56–57; McMahon, *Women Shall Not Rule*, 137–38.
60. Li, *Beishi*, 51:1844.
61. Li, *Beishi*, 1:26. This Han dynasty precedent was used to justify the Wei practice.
62. Holmgren, "The Harem in Northern Wei Politics," 76; Holmgren, "Political Organization of Non-Han States in China," 13; Holmgren, "Women and Political Power," 57–58; Eisenberg, *Kingship in Early Medieval China*, 29, 50–51; Golavachev, "Matricide among the Tuoba-Xianbei," 1–42.
63. Doran, "Royal Wet Nurses," 198–224. Zhao, *Nianer shi zhaji*, 14:186, comments on the Wei custom of the emperor treating a wet nurse as a surrogate mother and even sometimes making these women a type of empress dowager.
64. Holmgren, "Race and Class in Fifth Century China," 86–117. For example, Wei, *Weishu*, 30:709.
65. Sometimes the father of an empress was ennobled. Wei, *Weishu*, 83B:1832, 1833; Li, *Beishi*, 62:2213.
66. Holmgren, "Northern Wei as a Conquest Dynasty," 23. For examples of repeated marriage of a consort family with the imperial line, see Wei, *Weishu*, 83A:1815, 1819, 1820, 1829. For an example of malfeasance by a consort kinsman, see Li, *Beishi*, 55:2011.

67. Misevic, "Oligarchy or Social Mobility," 237, 240, 245–47. For some examples, see Wei, *Weishu*, 75:1664; Linghu, *Zhoushu*, 9:143,147.
68. Li, *Bei Qi shu*, 9:124.
69. Li, *Beishi*, 4:144–45, 5:175.
70. Holmgren, "Imperial Marriage in the Native Chinese and Non-Han State," 80, 87.
71. Holmgren, "Race and Class in Fifth Century China," 97–102.
72. Duan, "Beichao zhi Sui Tang shiqi nüxing," 111.
73. Holmgren, "Women and Political Power," 63.
74. Wei, *Weishu*, 13:321.
75. Holmgren, "Women and Political Power," 57.
76. Shanxi sheng Datong shi bowuguan, "Shanxi Datong Shijiazhai," 26.
77. Wei, *Weishu*, 56:1238; Li, *Beishi*, 8:283.
78. Linghu, *Zhoushu*, 9:141.
79. These were Empresses Xianming, Chang, Feng, and Hu. Song, *Bei Wei nüzhu lun*, 46–48.
80. Li, *Beishi*, 27:992; Wang and Cao, *A Record of Buddhist Monasteries in Luo-yang*, 15; Lewis, *China Between Empires*, 110. Zhou, "Bei Wei Luoyang nüxing zhi fojiao xinyang," 177–84; Lee, *Empresses, Art, and Agency*, 10–11, recounts the Buddhist activities of Empress Ling.
81. Wang and Cao, *A Record of Buddhist Monasteries in Luo-yang*, 17.
82. McNair, "Early Tang Imperial Patronage at Longmen," 65, 68–70.
83. Wei, *Weishu*, 9:225; 77:1703; Wang and Cao, *A Record of Buddhist Monasteries in Luo-yang*, 261.
84. Wang and Cao, *A Record of Buddhist Monasteries in Luo-yang*, 73.
85. Lewis, *China Between Empires*, 192; Wang and Cao, *A Record of Buddhist Monasteries in Luo-yang*, 171.
86. Wei, *Weishu*, 13:328–30; 14:358, 108A:2751; Kang, "Bei Wei Wenming taihou ji qi shidai (shangbian)," 461–75; Holmgren, "The Harem in Northern Wei Politics," 85–89; Li, *Bei Wei Pingcheng shidai*, 198–225; Zhou, *Taihe shiwunian*; Holmgren, "The Lu Clan of Tai Commandary," 295; McMahon, *Women Shall Not Rule*, 139–40; Eisenberg, *Kingship in Early Medieval China*, 61–62, 71, 79, 85–90.
87. Kang, "Bei Wei Wenming taihou ji qi shidai (xiabian)," 56–66, discusses her reforms.
88. Barfield, *The Perilous Frontier*, 125.
89. Wei, *Weishu*, 31:741, 44:994; Li, *Beishi*, 34:1255.
90. Wei, *Weishu*, 93:1988–90; Li, *Beishi*, 33:1215.
91. Wei, *Weishu*, 13:337–40; Holmgren, "Empress Dowager Ling"; Wang and Cao, *A Record of Buddhist Monasteries in Luo-yang*, 27, 29, 33; McMahon, *Women Shall Not Rule*, 143–45.
92. Li, *Beishi*, 44:1620. Empress Dowager Ling's archery was controversial. An official sent in a memorial advising her that according to Confucian tradition, archery was an inappropriate pursuit for women. He advised her to cultivate passive feminine virtues instead, citing Empresses Ma and Deng of the Han dynasty as worthy role models. Wei, *Weishu*, 67:1492.

CHAPTER 4

93. Wei, *Weishu*, 19B:482, 519.
94. Wei, *Weishu*, 66:1475, 93:1007.
95. Holmgren, "Empress Dowager Ling," 127, 140.
96. Wright and Twitchett, "Introduction," 14.
97. Wei, *Suishu*, 36:1108–9. Zhao Yi singled out Empress Wenxian as the most jealous empress in Chinese history, and Arthur Wright considered Emperor Wen the most "henpecked" Chinese emperor. Zhao, *Nianer shi zhaji*, 15:208–9; Wright, "T'ang T'ai-tsung and Buddhism," 240.
98. Wright, *The Sui Dynasty*, 71–73; McMahon, *Women Shall Not Rule*, 182–83.
99. Wright, *The Sui Dynasty*, 89.
100. Wei, *Suishu*, 7:145.
101. Liu, *Jiu Tang shu*, 58:2315–16.
102. Mou, *Gentlemen's Prescriptions for Women's Lives*, 136–40.
103. Holmgren, "Widow Chastity in the Northern Dynasties," 185–86.
104. Chen, *Multicultural China in the Early Middle Ages*, 6–14.
105. Duan, *Tangdai funü diwei yanjiu*, 27.
106. Sun, "Tangdai benjia," 104–7; Li, "Nüren de Zhongguo zhonggushi," 477–81.
107. Yao, *Tangdai funü de shengming licheng*, 118.
108. Chen, *Gaogui de zangyi*, 111–58; Kitamura, *Tōdai kōtei misasagi no kenkyū*, 134–52.
109. Ōsawa, *Nansō chihōkan no shuchō*.
110. Li, *Wei Jin Sui Tang hunyin xingtai yanjiu*, 237–54.
111. Guo, "Lun Tangdai gongzhu de hunyin xingtai," 92.
112. Wu, *Tangli zheyi*, 512–20.
113. Wechsler, "Factionalism in Early T'ang Government," 108, 111; Niu, "Tangren de 'lihun' chuyi," 25–26. Ouyang, *Xin Tangshu* chapter 206 is devoted to important consort kin.
114. Wang, "Tangdai Jingzhao Weishi," 109–12.
115. Ren, "Lun Tangdai qianqi shangceng nüzi," 109.
116. Ren, "Lun Tangdai qianqi shangceng nüzi," 108.
117. Ouyang, *Xin Tangshu*, 76:3470–71; Ren, "Lun Tangdai qianqi shangceng nüzi," 108–9.
118. Liu, *Jiu Tang shu*, 87:2844.
119. Liu, *Jiu Tang shu*, 51:2161–62.
120. Liu, *Jiu Tang shu*, 51:2164–67; Zeng and Liu, "Zhangsun huanghou," 13–15; Huang, "Tangdai nüxing yu wenxue," 4, 9–26.
121. Liu, *Jiu Tang shu*, 51:2167–69.
122. Liu, *Jiu Tangshu*, chapter 6. Wu Zetian remains a highly controversial figure. She has been the subject of a large body of research, and historians have written numerous biographies that depict her in various ways. See Rothschild, *Wu Zhao: China's Only Woman Emperor*. Fong, "Re-Gendering Chinese History," 361–79, gives a revisionist interpretation of her reign.
123. Wechsler, "Factionalism in Early T'ang Government," 89–90; Eisenberg, "Emperor Gaozong, the Rise of Wu Zetian," 46–47.
124. Twitchett, "The Composition of the T'ang Ruling Class," 64.

125. Kitamura, *Tōdai kōtei misasagi no kenkyū*, 52–58, describes Wu Zetian's mausoleum. On pages 134–52 the author describes how Tang consorts were usually buried.
126. Chen, "Empress Wu and Proto-Feminist Sentiments," 77–116; Bokenkamp, "A Medieval Feminist Critique of the Chinese World Order," 383–92.
127. Kutcher, *Mourning in Late Imperial China*, 36–37.
128. Huang, "Tangdai nüxing yu wenxue," 54–78.
129. Twitchett, "Chen gui and Other Works," 33–109.
130. Fitzgerald, *The Empress Wu*, 114–15.
131. Yang, "Wu Zetian yu Tangdai nongye," 450–58.
132. Fong, "Four Chinese Tombs of the Early Eighth Century," 307–21, describes the tombs of two victims who were executed for criticizing one of Wu's favorites.
133. Chen, "Succession Struggles and the Ethnic Identity," 390; Chen, *Multicultural China*, 19–20.
134. Guisso, *Wu Tse-t'ien and the Politics of Legitimation*, 53, emphasizes the importance of charismatic legitimacy to her reign.
135. Doran, *Transgressive Typologies*, 123–25.
136. McMahon, "Women Rulers in Imperial China," 198–201.
137. Bao, "Tangdai zhengzhi yu furui," 87–92, analyzes Dunhuang's document S.6502 to explore how Wu used omens to legitimize her reign.
138. Rothschild, "An Inquiry into Reign Era Changes," 123–24, 133, 141–42.
139. Liu, *Jiu Tang shu*, 24:924; Kory, "A Remarkably Resonant and Resilient Tang-Dynasty Augural Stone," 99–124; Rothschild, "Beyond Filial Piety," 149–68.
140. Lou, "Zhengsheng yuannian chi," 11–17, discusses Dunhuang document S.1344, an edict by Wu Zetian concerning the commendation system.
141. Bokenkamp, "A Medieval Feminist Critique of the Chinese World Order," 383–92; Rothschild, *Emperor Wu Zhao and her Pantheon*.
142. Guisso, *Wu Tse-t'ien and the Politics of Legitimation*, 49.
143. Guisso, *Wu Tse-t'ien and the Politics of Legitimation*, 44; Bao, "Tangdai zhengzhi yu furui," 87–92.
144. Chen, "Fazang (643–712) the Holy Man," 11–23; Chen, "More than a Philosopher," 322–38.
145. Chen, "Śarīra and Scepter," 36–37, 129–32.
146. Forte, *Mingtang and Buddhist Utopias*.
147. Lee and Ho, "A Colossal Eleven-Faced Kuan-yin," 3–6.
148. Qiang, "Gender Politics in Medieval Chinese Buddhist Art," 28–39; Kucera, "Recontextualizing Kanjingsi," 61–80; Karetzky, "Wu Zetian and Buddhist Art," 113–50.
149. Barrett, *The Woman Who Discovered Printing*.
150. Chen, "Fazang (643–712) and Wuzhensi," 179, 196; Chen, "Fazang (643–712) the Holy Man," 22–23.
151. Rothschild, "Wu Zhao and the Queen Mother of the West," 29–56; Barrett, "Breaking the Reputation of Female Rule in China," 183–93.
152. Cahill, *Transcendence and Divine Passion*.

CHAPTER 4

153. Cahill, "Performers and Female Taoist Adepts," 155–68. Subsequently, other empresses invited comparisons between themselves and Xiwangmu although they were more restrained than Wu Zetian. McMahon, "Women Rulers in Imperial China," 203.

154. Han, "Wu Zetian gushi de wenben yanbian yu wenhua neihan"; Han, "Ming Qing xushi wenxue zhong Wu Zetian," 32–35.

155. Lewis, *China's Cosmopolitan Empire*, 34, 38–40, 180; Wang, "Lun Tangdai gongfu shezheng," 67–70.

156. Liu, *Jiu Tang shu*, 150: 2171–75.

157. Liu, *Jiu Tang shu*, 183:4738–39.

158. Liu, *Jiu Tang shu*, 51:2161; Chen, "Problems of Chinese Historiography," 91.

159. Duan, *Tangdai funü diwei yanjiu*, 156–67.

160. Duan, *Tangdai funü diwei yanjiu*, 163.

161. McMahon, *Women Shall Not Rule*, 223.

162. Mao, "Tangdai houbanqi houfei zhi fenxi," 175, 183, 186, 189; Mao, "Guanzhong jun xing hunyin guanxi," 130–32; Tackett, *The Destruction of the Medieval Chinese Aristocracy*, 144, 169. Over time the emperors took spouses of decreasing status. Before the An Lushan rebellion, 91.7 percent of empresses came from families whose members had served as high officials. None came from nonofficial families. After the rebellion, 33.4 percent came from nonofficial families. Zhang, *Songdai hunyin jiazu shilun*, 44.

163. Liu, *Jiu Tang shu*, 51:2178–81.

164. Levy, "The Selection of Yang Kuei-fei," 411–24.

165. Kroll, "The Flight from the Capital and the Death of Precious Consort Yang," 25–53, translates the account of the emperor's flight and the death of Yang Guifei.

166. Xie, "Zailun Tang Xuanzong Yang Guifei yu Anshi zhi luan," 147–53, explores accusations that Yang Guifei deserves some blame for the rebellion.

167. Ma, "Fact and Fantasy in T'ang Tales," 167–69, 180; Shi, *Yang Taizhen waizhuan*; Xiang, "Rensheng jiaguo liang changhen," 38–45.

168. Chiu-Duke, "The Role of Confucian Revivalists," 52–53, 76.

CHAPTER 5

Empresses Contained

DURING THE VIOLENT FALL OF THE TANG DYNASTY, REBELS MASSACRED the aristocracy and officialdom, extinguishing families that had been prominent for centuries. When the founder of the Song dynasty reunited the nation in 960, the old order had been destroyed so he had to reimagine Chinese society, culture, and government. The obliteration of the old aristocracy may have been traumatic but it opened the way for innovation and allowed China to became more dynamic, prosperous, and meritocratic than before.

Under the Song dynasty system, the central government's bureaucratic apparatus became far more effective, altering relations between the palace and officialdom. People close to the emperor, such as empresses and consort kinsmen, lost power while government ministers became increasingly important.[1] When officials read histories of past dynasties, they noted the numerous catastrophes that had occurred when empresses and their families undermined well-ordered institutions. Wu Zetian cast a particularly long shadow, and responsible men were determined to prevent a woman from ever accruing so much power again. They decreased the stature of the empress, relegating her to a marginal place in state institutions.[2] In addition, they limited the status, wealth, and privileges of princesses to curb female power in general.[3] This restructuring made it almost impossible for a woman to follow the example of Wu Zetian and threaten the dynasty.

Song authorities may have been wary of female power but they also put great stress on tradition and orthodoxy so they revived the practice of naming an empress.⁴ Although Song consorts lacked the powers of their early Tang predecessors, many nevertheless had a hand in government matters. Most visibly, palace women repeatedly interfered with the imperial succession. The Song allowed female regencies, and nine empresses dowager served as regents. The high number of regencies resulted from the dynasty's ambiguous rules of succession. Because the Song lacked strict primogeniture, many rulers were not eldest sons. Some came to the throne seemingly by chance so their legitimacy seemed questionable. Empresses dowager could potentially exploit these shortcomings to gain authority. In response, many Song emperors appointed a successor while they were still alive, reducing the empress dowager to a symbolic role.

Song rulers increasingly emphasized Confucian ethics, and they required harem women to conform to stringent regulations.⁵ These rules made it difficult for a woman to take over the government. Moreover, unlike as in the early Tang, a Song empress could no longer appear ambitious.⁶ Whenever a consort seemed to overstep her symbolic role, she faced strong pushback from high ministers. When Empress Li, wife of Emperor Taizong, plotted to depose the heir apparent and replace him with her preferred candidate, the chancellor opposed her. Later when Empress Liu tried to interfere in succession after the death of Emperor Zhenzong, she was also thwarted by officials.

Empresses knew that to avoid trouble they had to put on a self-effacing front and behave cautiously. They usually acted with restraint and exercised power indirectly if at all. Some consorts engaged in politics obliquely by promoting religious personages and practices that had political ramifications.⁷ They also went to great lengths to construct a benign public image, presenting themselves as sagacious, maternal, and enlightened patrons of the arts. Because female regents avoided controversy, imperial historians largely approved of their actions.⁸ The men who wrote the dynasty's history may have been critical of female power in general, but they believed that these benign empresses had conducted themselves appropriately and upheld the dynasty's institutions.

A poem by Empress Yang, wife of Emperor Ningzong, projects a beneficent but unthreatening persona. In this short work of just four lines, she manages to portray herself as cultured, ascetic, and virtuous.⁹

Provisions for my Kunning Palace: just a single goat.
Since assuming the proper seat, I manage literary affairs.
Cherishing life and frugality, I pursue models of the
 ancient past;
As exemplar for the palace ladies, I apply only light rouge.

Empress Yang wrote this poem not to describe her actual personality but to craft a useful public image so she was deliberately disingenuous. In fact, Yang was one of the dynasty's most energetic consorts. Yet she knew that pretending to be passive and unambitious would help stave off criticism.

Many Song empresses came from relatively low backgrounds.[10] Their modest origins reflected the dynasty's culture and values. The Song elite was more fluid than the Tang aristocracy, and they put far less emphasis on genealogy. Emperors took their spouses from families that were respectable but modest. Only 26.8 percent were born into the families of high officials. During the Southern Song, only 11.8 percent came from families that had produced high ministers. Some consorts came from military families. Many were from respectable families that had gone into decline.[11] Emperors often promoted a woman already in the harem to the position of empress rather than seeking someone from an important family as had been customary during the Tang.[12]

Empresses from unimpressive families came into the palace with no powerful allies. Their modest backgrounds also restricted the rise of their kinsmen. Moreover the examination system had become fundamental to bureaucratic recruitment, preventing consort kin from automatically ascending to the highest levels of government. Empresses presented the insignificance of their natal families as a sign of their commitment to upholding the dynasty.[13] Instead of relying on their blood kin, they emphasized ties with their husbands.[14]

Tang aristocrats considered moral character heritable and often attributed a woman's virtues to good ancestry. Ethical views underwent a major shift during the Song, and people began to see virtue as an individual characteristic.[15] Due to the reassessment of morals, even though Song empresses had unimpressive genealogies, they could nevertheless

CHAPTER 5

be considered paragons of virtue. Other empresses undertook uncontroversial artistic pursuits such as perfecting their calligraphy or patronizing talented artists.[16] Because Song empresses were so cautious and self-effacing, historians have tended to underestimate their political activities.[17]

Empress Liu was the most powerful consort of the Song, and she serves as a case study of the opportunities and limitations that palace women faced.[18] There had been no empress dowager regent since Wu Zetian, so the Song lacked set procedures for handling a female regency. Empress Liu exploited this ambiguity to gain authority. However, the officialdom was still traumatized by the reign of Empress Wu and guarded against overt displays of female power, so Liu knew that she could not imitate the formidable dowagers of earlier times. She had to reinvent the role of female regent, gaining power while appearing unthreatening.

Because Empress Liu had such a colorful life, many authors wrote fictional stories about her. They shrouded her ascent in mysticism, asserting that before she entered the palace, she visited a temple where a monk foretold her rise to wealth and power.[19] Her real story is even more intriguing. Empress Liu came from a lowly background. She was orphaned in infancy, married a silversmith, then entered the palace as a concubine of the heir apparent, who eventually became Emperor Zhenzong. Liu had a talent for holding the emperor's attention. In her youth, she entertained him with her musical talents, and in middle age she used her intelligence to retain his respect. She received a good education in the palace and used her learning to make herself useful and stay in the ruler's good graces. After Zhenzong's first empress died, he promoted Liu to fill the position despite opposition from suspicious critics. Although Liu did not bear children, she adopted Zhenzong's heir, who eventually succeeded him as Emperor Renzong.

Zhenzong suffered from poor health so he relied heavily on his intelligent and capable spouse. As his health declined, she accrued power. On his deathbed, Zhenzong declared that Empress Liu would act as regent for his successor Renzong as he was still a child. Liu adopted Renzong and became his titular mother. Even though Renzong resented the dowager regent, filial piety obligated him to obey her. Liu never relinquished her regency and retained control of the government for eleven years until her death in 1033.

Empress Dowager Liu managed to exercise power for such a long time through a combination of skill, diligence, and prudence. When she was in control, the government ran smoothly and China enjoyed a welcome interval of peace so imperial historians considered her a successful ruler. Yet, in spite of these accomplishments, her long regency provoked criticism. Liu knew that if she appeared too high-handed, opposition would only intensify so she tolerated censure to avoid being branded a tyrant.

Empress Liu patronized the arts strategically and used this to promote a sense of legitimacy.[20] She revived the term "two saints" (*er sheng*), which had been used occasionally during the Northern Wei and Sui dynasties, to describe herself and her son.[21] By presenting mother and son as a closely bound pair, united by common virtues, she justified her extended regency. Liu took this image even further by comparing herself to the Sage Mother, a goddess who had attracted a large following during the Tang dynasty. By associating herself with this deity, Liu created a public façade grounded in both religious and maternal ideals.[22] She also copied Wu Zetian in inviting comparisons with Xiwangmu and Maitreya.[23] However, Liu's ideological program was far more subtle than that of Empress Wu as she did not want to awaken bad memories.

Liu did not involve her family in politics. As an orphan, she had little connection with people outside the palace. The lack of a consort kin faction assuaged critics and made her authority less conspicuous. Liu cleverly combined power with reserve so that she could quietly achieve her goals while evoking minimal opposition. However, after her death, pent up criticism burst forth and many people condemned her for maintaining a regency after her adoptive son had entered adulthood.

Empress Dowager Liu faced a problem that had not caused so much trouble for earlier female regents. During the Song, the standards of female reclusion tightened significantly due to the Confucian revival, making it impossible for the empress dowager to meet directly with high officials. For her regency to function, she had to find ways to

Empress Liu.
SOURCE: PUBLIC DOMAIN.

communicate with government ministers.[24] To solve this quandary, Liu relied heavily on palace eunuchs, giving them greater responsibility so that they could be more useful to her. Liu also met frequently with the wives of high officials. As titled ladies, the wives of important men were allowed access to the inner palace so they acted as intermediaries for their husbands. Liu also used slave women as messengers. Ironically their low position gave them far more freedom of movement than their female superiors so they could easy gain access to important people.

Empress Cao.
SOURCE: *PUBLIC DOMAIN.*

Chapter 5

Empress Dowager Cao, wife of Emperor Renzong, was the only other powerful Song consort.[25] Her husband's successor, an adoptive son who became Emperor Yingzong, suffered from chronic poor health and psychological problems, rendering him unable to carry out his imperial role. The empress dowager stepped forward to declare a regency and keep the government running. Cao wanted to depose Yingzong and appoint a capable ruler but the top officials resolutely opposed such a move. They did not want to set a precedent that might allow a future empress dowager to dethrone the emperor and seize control of the government. Also, the ministers may have liked having such a weak ruler on the throne as it gave them more authority. Isolated in the palace and cut off from the outside world, Empress Dowager Cao needed the cooperation of the bureaucracy to implement her orders so she acquiesced to their wishes. When Yingzong's health improved to the point at which he could handle some basic duties, officials forced Cao to end her regency and she faded into the background.

During the chaotic era known to history as Five Dynasties and Ten Kingdoms, nomadic warlords fought for control of North China. Conditions quickly shifted so these rulers had to reimagine gender relations. Some petty rulers allowed their wives and mothers to participate in politics in traditional steppe fashion.[26] Most conspicuously, in many tribes it was traditional for the ruler's widow to serve as regent after his death, ruling temporarily until the next male ruler was chosen.[27]

The Khitan people established a kingdom to the northeast of Tang and Song that flourished from the early tenth into the twelfth century. Khitan rulers styled their regime, the Liao dynasty, in the Chinese fashion. Yet, even though they established a Chinese administrative framework, they also maintained many native customs and values, allowing women to play roles within this fusion state.

Elite Khitan marriage and family practices had a particularly large impact on women's status.[28] The Khitan rulers of Liao took Chinese surnames, allowing them to imitate certain aspects of Chinese kinship. The ruling line traditionally practiced polygyny, with each wife theoretically enjoying equal status. Traditionally, Khitan men had often married two or more sisters, and sons engaged in levirate marriages after a father's death.[29] Once the Khitan established Liao, however, rulers named one of their spouses an empress in the Chinese fashion.

The Khitan originally belonged to eight kinship groups, and rules governed how their members intermarried.[30] The ruling line, surnamed Yelü, married almost exclusively with a designated consort clan, the Xiao. A man surnamed Yelü reigned as emperor and consort kinsmen surnamed Xiao served in the highest offices. The Yelü adopted this arrangement to reduce the power of the emperor's male kinsmen and keep them from challenging him. Because the regime's founder gained supremacy over his uncles and brothers only with the help of his wife's relatives, the emperors regarded their in-laws as useful allies.

The Liao emperors treated their agnates with respect but forbade them from holding meaningful office. A ruler married a woman from the family of the dynasty's first empress, and her kinsmen were expected to support the emperor in return for tangible privileges.[31] Due to repeated intermarriage between these two lineages, it was not unusual for a person to marry an uncle or cousin. The unusual Liao system bound together status, office, and marriage more closely than any other Chinese dynasty. Although this arrangement was intended to safeguard the authority of the emperors, it did not always work as intended. Consort kinsmen sometimes used their hereditary power to take control of the government.[32]

Khitan women had a somewhat contradictory social position. In some ways, a wife was far below her spouse. Liao emperors and princes even had the right to kill refractory wives and concubines. This prerogative was a remnant of the ancient custom of human sacrifice. When a prominent man died, his wives were often murdered to accompany him to the afterlife. This custom continued up to the Liao dynasty, and several empresses ended up being sacrificed upon the deaths of their husbands.[33] The powerful Empress Chunqin avoided this fate by cutting off her hand and placing it in the coffin of the deceased emperor, thereby symbolically fulfilling her duty of ritual suicide.

Given the tradition of sacrificing widows of the ruler, it seems incongruous that some Liao consorts ended up extremely powerful.

CHAPTER 5

Palace ladies continued many nomadic practices, hunting and riding as before.[34] They were not confined and restricted as were Song empresses, allowing them considerable freedom of action. The Khitan royal marriage system, with members of two clans intermarrying each generation, gave the empress dowager an impeccable pedigree and guaranteed her the support of the officialdom. Two Liao empresses dowager declared regencies, temporarily shifting power from the imperial clan to consort kin.[35] Unexpectedly, Liao empresses usually remained independent of their powerful kinsmen.[36] When they sought power, they rarely relied too heavily on their natal families as they did not want male relatives to dominate them.

In general, Liao consorts were more powerful than those of other dynasties.[37] The dynasty's officials even compared the emperor and empress to heaven and earth, using Chinese metaphysics to justify a significant role for women in government. Several factors contributed to female empowerment. Khitans had great respect for their mothers and showed them deference so women had a relatively high position in the overall kinship structure. The mothers of emperors used this feature of Khitan culture to their advantage. The basic structure of the Liao government also gave women opportunities to exercise power. Although the Liao adopted the appearance of a Chinese dynasty, many institutions developed out of tribal government. The relative informality of decision making allowed women to participate in important matters. Moreover, the mothers and wives of Khitan khans traditionally had a say in succession, and they maintained this right after the establishment of Liao. Also, many consorts were extremely aggressive and charismatic, and they used these traits to accrue power. In sum, even though Liao consorts took on the identity of a Chinese-style empress, they often behaved very differently.

Liao empresses most often affected policy by assisting and advising their husbands. Women from the elite consort clan came into the palace with high status, knowledge, and a network of connections that they could use to influence the ruler. A few became primary advisors of the ruler. Such was the case with Empress Chunqin, who aided her husband, the dynastic founder Emperor Taizu.[38] Chunqin was intelligent and proffered good advice, urging her spouse to select talented officials and construct an efficient bureaucratic system to underpin the new dynasty.

Unusually, Liao empresses sometimes ordered military campaigns and even led them personally.[39] Nomadic culture accepted female participation in warfare. Liao was surrounded by enemies and frequently went to war. Empress Chunqin exemplifies the martial Liao empress. She led a campaign against enemy troops at the beginning of the dynasty and returned victorious, giving her a major role in establishing Liao. Because her husband was often away from the capital on military campaigns, she kept the machinery of government running in his absence. Subsequent empresses were sometimes involved in military matters as well. Empress Dowager Chengtian, regent for the young Emperor Shengzong, commanded a force of ten thousand cavalry and led Khitan forces to defeat the Chinese army when they invaded Liao.[40]

Several Liao empresses served as regents. They also tried to influence the imperial succession although not always successfully. When Emperor Taizu died, his wife became Empress Dowager Chunqin. She used this role to become even more important, establishing a precedent that a Liao empress dowager could exercise power. However, when Chunqin demanded that one of her sons replace her deceased husband as emperor, powerful rivals opposed her choice and civil war ensued. Chunqin lost this conflict and ended up banished to a remote outpost. Historians blamed her for plunging the state into discord.[41]

Although Chunqin made some faulty decisions, her bold actions at the beginning of the dynasty made it acceptable for Liao empresses to exercise power. Nevertheless, the importance of Liao empresses should not be overstated. Their participation in politics was always conditional and depended on their personal character and circumstances of the time. Empresses did not have specified powers within the Liao system. They usually acted in a supporting or advisory capacity, and men made the final decisions. Only when the emperor and his senior officials were particularly weak or mediocre did women act directly.

After settling in China, the Khitan and other foreign conquerors had to address the question of Sinicization. Would they adopt the culture of their numerous Han subjects or try to maintain their traditions, customs, and lifestyles? Each conquest dynasty handled this problem differently. Although the question of acculturation affected everyone from the steppes who settled in China, it had a particularly large impact on their women as the cultures of China and the steppe had extremely different gender norms.

In some respects, women had a high standing in Khitan society. Parents traditionally had absolute authority over their children, who had the duty to obey their mother and father.[42] The Liao state was grounded in the patriarchal authority of Khitan culture, making this dynasty's emperors particularly powerful. At first, Liao institutions were firmly grounded in Khitan culture. Unlike some conquering peoples who resided in China, the Khitan embraced Chinese-style education.[43] Emperors wanted to elevate the Khitan elite so that they could rule a large and complex state. As Liao emperors became familiar with Chinese ideas and values, they integrated these principles into their system. Khitans even accepted the Chinese view that women should also be educated so that they could oversee their children's education, and it became customary for elite Khitans to use a Chinese curriculum to educate their daughters. Some women used their learning to write about political matters, presenting their writings to the ruler to persuade him to institute a particular policy.[44]

As Khitans gained familiarity with Confucian values, they put some of these ideas into practice. The imperial clan began to employ Chinese ritual in their wedding ceremonies.[45] They also saw women's sexual integrity as symbolic of a community's honor and abused the women of their enemies to humiliate them.[46] Some Liao epitaphs for women praised their commitment to widow chastity. Khitan women used Confucian rhetoric to denounce remarriage, and the government eventually prohibited titled ladies from remarrying.[47] When Empress Xuanyi, wife of Emperor Daozong, was falsely accused of having a sexual liaison, her husband ordered her to commit suicide.[48]

Even though Confucian ethics put women under increasingly stringent moral obligations, they also gained new powers. Liao empresses dowager could use filial piety in the Chinese manner to position themselves above the sitting emperor. As Khitan invaders assimilated to

Chinese culture, their empresses became increasingly similar to those of native Chinese dynasties.

In the early twelfth century, Jurchen nomads became the rising power in the region. First they defeated the Khitans and absorbed Liao, then they invaded China, overwhelmed Song forces, captured the northern half of the country, and established the Jin dynasty. Although Jurchen and Khitan cultures were similar in some ways, the dynasties that they founded had different institutions. Notably, Jin empresses had a less significant political role than their Liao counterparts.

Before conquering China the Jurchens were organized into clans, each with a different surname, which were subdivided into smaller lineages. Clans were exogamous so each member married a spouse from a different clan.[49] Like the Khitans, the Jurchens used marriage as a political tool to gain allies and stabilize the state. The Jurchen ruling line traditionally married with a small group of counterparts, and Jin emperors continued to select their spouses from important families.[50] However, they were less concerned about the origins of their concubines and took women into the harem from a wide range of backgrounds. As a result, the culture of the Jin palace reflected the ethnic diversity of the realm.

The marriage strategy of Jin emperors shifted over the course of the dynasty. They abandoned polygyny and each emperor declared one woman his official spouse. The official history of the dynasty lists twenty empresses and three other significant consorts.[51] Forty percent of these women were not ethnic Jurchens. They came from prominent families among peoples living to the northeast of China. Due to their homeland's geography, Jurchens had a different world view from the Chinese. They put great stress on the stability of their northern flank and used marriage to bind themselves to important khans in that sensitive region.[52] Over time, however, Jurchen rulers became increasingly more oriented toward China. Toward the end of the dynasty they took large numbers of Han women into the palace and the harem became much more overtly Chinese.

Because Jurchen khans traditionally took spouses from important families, their wives had status and prestige, allowing some to intervene in important matters.[53] Most importantly, the spouse of the Jurchen tribal ruler tried to negotiate a compromise when there was discord among her husband's clansmen. During the first half of the Jin dynasty, consorts remained politically active to a degree. Although Jin empresses never served as regents and they lacked explicit political roles, they advised their spouses and participated in power struggles within the palace. But, over time, Jin empresses became increasingly passive. The emperors denied power to Chinese women, so as the number of Han in the harem increased, fewer consorts were in a position to exert influence. In addition, the Jin instituted a new legal code that gave women fewer rights, reflecting the Jurchen view that women should be subservient to men. This attitude further degraded female power.[54]

As with the Khitans, Chinese culture influenced the Jurchens after they settled in China. Jurchen women were traditionally uneducated so most women in the harem were initially illiterate and lacked dignified deportment. The Jin palace initially had an embarrassingly low level of culture.[55] To elevate the atmosphere of the harem, the emperors established a palace school to give consorts an extensive, Chinese-style education. The Jin also integrated Confucian principles into their political structure, putting particular emphasis on filial piety toward mothers.[56] As Jurchen women assimilated these teachings, they began to embrace Confucian values such as wifely fidelity.[57] Yet, despite the move toward Confucianization, Jin empresses dowager were never able to use filial piety to declare regencies or dominate a sitting emperor.

In the thirteenth century, Mongol horsemen swept down from the north, overcame both Jin and Southern Song, and founded the Yuan dynasty, becoming the first foreign conquerors to govern all of China. The Mongols had an immense Eurasian empire and their political institutions had evolved considerably before they entered China, so the position of Yuan empresses had been largely determined before the dynasty was established.

As with other nomadic peoples, Mongol women had considerable freedom in some respects.[58] They rode well, worked alongside men, and provided invaluable logistical support during military campaigns. Customarily a khan's wife temporarily gained power upon his death.[59] It was expected that the deceased man's senior wife would declare a regency and hold the tribe together until an assembly of tribal elders could meet to choose their new leader. Due to long distances and poor transportation, selecting a successor could sometimes take years so a woman might act as regent for a long time. Mongol succession had vague guidelines, and many senior men were eligible to succeed a previous ruler. Because the regent presided over the succession, she was well placed to influence the selection of a new khan.[60] After the ruler began his reign, however, the regent lost her authority and the patriarchal system resumed.

The competence of Hoelun, Genghis Khan's mother, shaped his attitude toward women. Hoelun supervised a large camp with ten thousand soldiers under her command.[61] Her skill at managing this important base convinced Genghis to give his wives similar responsibilities. Mongol society was traditionally polygynous, and Genghis used marriage as a political tool. Previous Mongol leaders had stressed family background but Genghis emphasized talent above all.[62] He realized that many women had great potential and used his wives and daughters to help manage his empire.

Genghis married and divorced strategically to ally himself with powerful khans. Each of his wives received a portion of conquered territory to manage, and his daughters gained authority over their husbands' peoples.[63] Wives of the ruling line also received spoils of war, gifts from their subjects and envoys, and a share of tax revenue, making them extremely wealthy.[64] These outspoken women participated in important deliberations, and men valued their advice. Empowering women freed up important men to go on long campaigns, allowing the Mongol army to continuously expand their state.

Ögedei Khan, Genghis's son and successor, had a more traditional view of women.[65] He regarded them as inferior to men and stripped his female relatives of much of their previous authority. Ögedei and subsequent khans placed strict limits on the behavior of their wives and daughters. As Mongol noblewomen lost status, they argued and persecuted one another, struggling for a share of the shrinking amount of power and prestige.

In earlier times, Mongol khans had integrated their wives into their own families. However, they came to realize the usefulness of close affinal ties and encouraged their wives to maintain close links with their natal families. Even so, khans traditionally chose spouses from politically unimportant backgrounds to prevent the emergence of powerful consort kin.[66] Some wives came from defeated peoples or declining kingdoms on the periphery of the Mongol realm.[67] Yuan emperors learned from the mistakes of the Liao dynasty and avoided strengthening a single clan through repeated intermarriage. Instead, they took wives from various lineages. The Yuan emperors had multiple wives, in line with Mongol polygyny, but named only one of them empress, in conformity with Chinese custom.

By the time the Mongols established a dynasty in China, the wives of khans had lost their previous stature and power. The most important Yuan consort was Chabi, wife of Kublai Khan (Emperor Shizu).[68] Chabi

Chabi.
SOURCE: *PUBLIC DOMAIN.*

had unusual authority for a Yuan consort, probably due to her elevated background. She was a niece of the senior wife of Chingghis Khan so she and her husband were cousins. Even though the Mongols had settled in China, Chabi presided over a wifely camp in the traditional fashion, giving her a high degree of autonomy. She acted as a trusted advisor to her husband and counseled him to treat his Chinese subjects compassionately. She also promoted Tibetan Buddhism, giving her a lasting impact on Chinese culture.

Subsequent Yuan dynasty empresses had a lower profile.[69] Because the court had relatively little interest in Confucian propriety, empresses and princesses were not cloistered. They enjoyed riding and archery and appeared openly before the court. However, freedom of movement did not translate into authority. The involvement of Yuan empresses in politics was usually limited to influencing the imperial succession in favor of their sons. Yuan empresses may have lacked power but they were extremely wealthy. As before, each Mongol empress controlled a domain that provided her with a sizeable income. They distributed much of this wealth to favorites and petitioners.

Conquering a vast Eurasian empire made the Mongols confident in their own culture and abilities so they were less attracted to Chinese culture than other nomads. Many Mongols had little interest in assimilating into Chinese society and maintained many native customs and values. Even so, they were strongly attracted to the Confucian principle of filial piety.[70] During the Yuan, several scholars wrote new annotations for the *Classic of Filial Piety*. Children were required by law to show respect for parents, and Yuan popular culture embraced this virtue. During this era, filial piety also became increasingly directed toward mothers partly due to the high status of mothers in Mongol culture. Yet, despite the prominence of filial piety, Yuan empresses did not use this concept to dominate their sons. The Mongols limited filial piety to family life. Their institutions guaranteed that men would control the government apparatus.

In the fourteenth century, the Yuan regime collapsed after less than a century of rule. After a period of turmoil, China was reunited under the Ming, a native dynasty. The dynastic founder Zhu Yuanzhang, who styled himself the Hongwu emperor, set down institutions intended to prevent empresses from gaining control of the state. Most importantly, he decreed his successors should marry women from modest backgrounds. As a result of this pronouncement, Ming emperors pursued a novel marriage strategy. Whereas some rulers of conquest dynasties had married women from lowly backgrounds, previous emperors of Han extraction had tended to choose spouses from prestigious families. The Ming was the first native dynasty whose emperors married women from obscure families.[71] Most empresses were born into low-ranking military families near the capital. Rulers tended to choose a spouse with good looks and mild character as they wanted someone who could play the role of empress without causing trouble. This strategy succeeded. Most Ming empresses were passive and did not become involved in politics.

Calculated mésalliance also helped prevent consort kin from gaining power.[72] Some empresses came from families that were so poor that they had previously sold daughters into concubinage. With neither education nor connections, such lowly consort kinsmen found it difficult to participate in affairs of state. Prominent eunuchs also helped keep consort kin in check as eunuchs and consort families were usually rivals. When the Chenghua emperor disregarded the injunction of the dynastic founder and married a woman from an important family, consort kinsmen ended up dominating the court, proving the wisdom of the standard arrangement.[73]

Even though Ming emperors chose women from ordinary families, they still wanted their in-laws to appear respectable, so an empress's closest kinsmen received a noble title and land grant. Initially, this was a modest domain but over time these land grants increased in size. When a woman became empress, her family members experienced a sudden and dramatic rise in status. However, they knew that their good fortune was temporary. When an empress died her family lost their privileges and could experience an equally abrupt decline. Because their privileges were so fleeting, Ming consort kin leveraged their position to quickly make as much money as possible in the hope that they could permanently join the elite. Ming consort kinsmen frequently abused their privileges to solicit bribes and steal land, and the sitting empress would shield them from accountability.

The Ming system degraded the position of empress in another way as well. Even though sitting empresses usually bore sons, Hongwu had declared that only the son of a principal wife was qualified to ascend the throne. For this reason, many emperors deposed their empress and named the mother of the heir as empress in her place. They did so to make the heir eligible to inherit the imperial mantle. This unusual practice made Ming empresses extremely insecure. Everyone knew that there was a good chance that an empress would eventually be deposed, lessening her prestige and influence.

The Ming ideology of government reflected the declining political importance of women.[74] Ancient thinkers portrayed consorts as central figures in the dynastic cycle who could either contribute to the government's success or help bring down the state. Ming ideology portrayed women differently. Having been insulated from administration, women were no longer considered significant political actors.

When the Ming began, it seemed that empresses might regain some of their former privileges. The dynasty's founder Hongwu was an illiterate rebel. He relied heavily on his spouse, Empress Ma, as she was educated and competent. He sometimes took her advice, so she influenced some important decisions. *Ming History* (*Mingshi*), the dynasty's official chronicle, gives Ma the longest biography of all the dynasty's empresses.[75] Nevertheless, Hongwu resented Ma's interference, and his antipathy toward female power led him to forbid empresses dowager from declaring a regency. Thereafter, most Ming empresses were very passive.[76] No dowager ever acted as official regent although one exercised power equivalent to regency.

Previous emperors had usually paid the most attention to their empress or a favored minor consort, who was often the mother of the heir. The Ming instituted novel practices intended to decrease female power. Emperors were expected to divide their time among numerous harem women so that none would stand above the rest. Moreover, emperors deliberately ignored the woman who gave birth to the heir apparent. As a result of this novel arrangement, the empress, mother of the heir,

Caption: *Empress Ma.*
SOURCE: *PUBLIC DOMAIN.*

and favorite companions of the emperor were different women.[77] Palace women vied intensely for power and often challenged the supremacy of the empress. Because the empress came from such a low background, other palace ladies did not feel obligated to show her respect, and their rude treatment degraded the standing of the empress even further.

Few Ming empresses did anything worthy of note nor did they usually attract much attention. Empress Ji, popularly known as Li Tangmei, gained some recognition due to her unusual background.[78] Ji came from the Yao people of Guangxi in the distant south and was the only ethnic Yao ever to become empress. People in the capital were fascinated by her exotic origins, and she became a character in popular fiction about the era.

In spite of the barriers blocking female ambition in the Ming system, Empress Zhang, wife of the Hongxi emperor, nevertheless managed to exercise significant power.[79] Although Zhang came from an obscure family in accordance with dynastic convention, she had more education than most Ming empresses and was also familiar with the mechanics of government. After less than a year her husband died and Zhang's son replaced him as the Xuande emperor. Although Xuande was an adult, his mother counseled him on major policies and Xuande willingly deferred to her. When Xuande suddenly died, a child ascended the throne as the Yingzong emperor and Xuande's wife, Empress Sun, became empress dowager.[80] The dowagers Zhang and Sun did not get along and they vied for supremacy. Officials invited Empress Zhang to declare a regency but she wisely refused as the dynasty's founder had clearly forbidden this. Nevertheless, she acted as regent in all but name. Zhang cooperated with officials and eunuchs to keep the government running smoothly. She approved major policies and stamped documents with a large jade seal in the fashion of an emperor. Zhang behaved prudently, made good decisions, and kept her family from accruing much power.

While Empress Dowager Zhang was alive, her rival Empress Dowager Sun had little authority. After Zhang's death, however, Sun participated in one of the most important events of the Ming dynasty.[81] Following the death of Empress Dowager Zhang, Yingzong began deciding matters himself. He wanted to prove himself a great conqueror so he undertook an ill-advised campaign against nomads to the north. During a battle gone awry, Mongol troops captured him. The high ministers considered Yingzong a reckless fool and declined to ransom him. Instead, they deposed the captive ruler and put his younger brother on the throne as the Jingtai emperor. A year later the Mongols released

Empress Zhang.
SOURCE: *PUBLIC DOMAIN.*

Yingzong to sow dissention in China. Jingtai refused to step down and he confined Yingzong to house arrest in a side palace. Six years after Yingzong's return, Empress Dowager Sun and her brothers led a coup that deposed Jingtai and restored Yingzong. Because Sun had helped overthrow a sitting emperor, historians condemned her.[82]

With the exception of Empresses Ma, Zhang, and Sun, Ming consorts had almost no power. Their role was usually symbolic. At most, they could only influence minor matters. Blocked from participating in government, some sought recognition as paragons of domestic feminine virtue. Empress Xu, wife of the Yongle emperor, gained lasting fame by writing *Teachings for the Inner Quarters* (*Neixun*), a book on Confucian female conduct that stands out as probably the most influential Ming dynasty text on women's matters.[83]

Other empresses turned to religion for fulfillment. The religiosity of certain consorts went against official policy. Ming officials wanted to keep women secluded and prevent licentiousness so they discouraged women from visiting temples, practicing folk religion, meeting with clerics, or becoming Buddhist nuns.[84] Yet, Empress Dowager Zhang became a Daoist priestess and commissioned a large scroll painting of her ordination to publicize her piety. She used religion as a political ideology, justifying her power by depicting herself embodying the sacred.[85] Empress Dowager Xiaoding, mother of the Wanli emperor, was the dynasty's most enthusiastic patron of religion.[86] Xiaoding built so many new temples that she sparked a revival of Buddhism. However, government funds paid for this building spree, draining the treasury just as China was trying to cope with challenges that would eventually bring down the Ming dynasty. For this reason, historians criticize her as an irresponsible wastrel.

The Ming system had multiple safeguards that generally succeeded in keeping empresses from participating in government.[87] However, weakening empresses and consort kin so much had an unanticipated outcome. Empresses were traditionally opponents of palace eunuchs. Ideally, each side kept the other in check. But degrading the powers of empresses allowed eunuchs to gain an unprecedented importance.[88] The Ming stands out as the highpoint of eunuch power. Castrated men hollowed out the dynasty's institutions, shocked onlookers with their shameless corruption, and fomented chaos that helped bring down the dynasty.

When the Ming finally collapsed, Jurchen horsemen once again invaded China. This time they succeeded in conquering the entire realm.

In 1644, they established the Qing dynasty, which encompassed not just China but the larger Manchu empire as well. Although the Qing gave one imperial spouse the title of empress in conformity with Chinese custom, Manchu rulers took measures to prevent these women from becoming involved in administration.

The Manchus were a tiny minority living among their far more numerous Chinese subjects so their leaders feared that they would assimilate and lose their unique identity. To maintain ethnic distinctions, Manchus were forbidden from marrying Han women. The emperors followed this rule as well and took their wives from Manchu families or from members of the Mongol and Chinese banners.[89] This arrangement helped the rulers keep in touch with their roots, renew links with the steppe elite, and prevent powerful Han families from dominating the palace and court. The emperors chose spouses from modest backgrounds to avoid having to deal with powerful consort kin. Moreover, Qing palace women were isolated from the outside world to an unusual degree to keep them from fomenting intrigues or plotting with their natal families. Emperors also downplayed distinctions between the empress and minor consorts and often promoted a minor palace lady to the rank of empress. Muddying the distinction between empress and minor harem women reduced the prestige of the emperor's official spouse.

According to Chinese custom, a boy born to a concubine was considered the son of his father's official wife. This fiction gave a concubine's son the same rights as his half-brothers born to the wife. However, the Manchu palace did not adopt this practice, reducing the position of the empress dowager. Only one Qing emperor was born to an empress. The rest were the sons of other harem women. An emperor usually elevated his own mother to the rank of empress dowager alongside the wife of his deceased predecessor so there were usually two or more empresses dowager at any given time. These women competed for preeminence, diminishing the status of each.

As any of the emperor's many sons might potentially succeed him, this practice further degraded the empress by denying her sons special inheritance rights. Whereas Ming emperors usually designated an heir apparent, their Qing counterparts preferred not to publicly name a successor during their lifetime. Some emperors named a successor in their will. This practice prevented a future emperor's mother from amassing power and constructing a faction in advance of his reign.

From the beginning of the Qing system, empresses lacked a high position. Nurhaci, the first Manchu emperor, married sixteen women. One was posthumously awarded the title of empress because her son became emperor. Gundai, Nurhaci's second-ranked wife, was accused of stealing some of her husband's valuables.[90] Although Nurhaci did not execute her, she was publicly disgraced. Her misconduct tainted her children and one of them killed his mother to remove the stigma. This incident demonstrates the low position of the ruler's wives at the beginning of the dynasty.

The Jurchen conquest of China was extremely bloody, and the Chinese looked back on the atrocities that accompanied unification with disgust. After pacifying the realm, Qing emperors had to rule an enormous population that detested them. The Qing government employed many strategies to gain the trust and respect of their Chinese subjects. Emperors put great stress on ethics, portraying their regime as a morally upright force that had rescued Chinese from the decadence of the Ming. Much of this moral program focused on women. The government banned female singers and dancers from the palace and eventually prohibited officials from associating with them.[91] They also promoted widow chastity and other extreme expressions of female rectitude. Keeping women away from the machinery of the state was another way for the Qing to appear exceptionally virtuous. Ancient historians had warned of the corrosive effects of palace women on gullible rulers so the Qing took care to avoid displays of female authority or ambition.

Qing empresses rarely had much power. Any influence they had was usually very oblique.[92] Empress Xiaozhuang, one of the wives of the dynastic founder Hong Taiji, was lauded as the archetypal Qing empress, and subsequent consorts emulated her.[93] Xiaozhuang became empress dowager during the reigns of her son Shunzhi and grandson Kangxi, whom she took pride in raising. She did not interfere directly in government matters but sometimes gave the emperor prudent advice. She was a conservative who counseled caution. She urged rulers to select good

CHAPTER 5

officials, take care when altering the administrative system, maintain a strong military, and stay true to their Manchu roots. Xiaozhuang had spent her early years on the open plains and felt uncomfortable amid the luxury of the imperial palace so she lived an unusually simple life despite her high position. Onlookers considered her austerity a sign of virtue.

Empress Xiaozhuang.
SOURCE: *PUBLIC DOMAIN.*

Empress Dowager Chongqing, wife of Yongzheng and mother of Qianlong, served as a different sort of role model.[94] Although her husband did not title her empress, she was his senior spouse and ran the harem. During his reign, she confined her activities to quotidian matters within the inner palace. Her son Qianlong loved and respected his mother. He often visited her and took her along when he traveled. When Chongqing became unable to travel in old age, her son stopped traveling and only resumed his journeys after her death. Qianlong showed his esteem for his mother by arranging an unusually opulent party to celebrate her sixtieth birthday. Yet, even though mother and son shared a close bond, it seems that Chongqing had nothing to do with policy. Instead Qianlong used his devotion to his mother as a way of publicly displaying his filial piety. Chongqing played the role of the ideal mother, and Qianlong took on the part of the dutiful son. In this way, they could both claim to be paragons of Confucian virtue.

The dynasty's only politically active empress dowager unexpectedly became one of the most famous, powerful, and important female figures in Chinese history. Empress Dowager Cixi oversaw the government at a time of unprecedented national crisis when aggressive foreign powers challenged China with modern weaponry. Cixi's response helped shape contemporary China. Cixi's historical impact makes her one of the three most significant Chinese empresses alongside Empress Lü of the Han and Wu Zetian of the Tang.

Cixi was born into one of the most important Manchu families.[95] Based on her lineage and poise, Cixi was selected as a concubine for the sickly Xianfeng emperor, who already had a senior wife, Empress Xiaozhen.[96] Cixi was initially an inconsequential figure in the palace, but when she bore the emperor his first son, her fortune instantly changed. As mother of the heir presumptive, she became the second-ranking consort.

At first, Cixi followed convention and took on the image of a model Qing palace lady. She did not make any political statements and confined herself to quotidian activities in the harem. However, she learned about the challenges facing China and started forming opinions about how China should respond. Xianfeng died when his son by Cixi was only five

Empress Dowager Cixi.
SOURCE: *PUBLIC DOMAIN.*

years old. When the emperor was on his deathbed, he formed a committee of eight senior officials to serve as regents. However, the men he chose were all reactionaries who opposed any reform of the Qing system even though its shortcomings had become obvious.

Cixi's son ascended the throne as the Tongzhi emperor. Officially he was the son of his father's wife, Xiaozhen, so she became dowager empress. However, the regents gave Cixi the title of empress dowager as a courtesy. The two empress dowagers, Cixi and Xiaozhen, got along unusually well and became allies. They also enlisted the support of the powerful Manchu nobleman Xiyin, known in English as Prince Gong, who could help them deal with the bureaucracy.

When Cixi's clique felt sufficiently strong, they moved to bring down the regents. Cixi accused them of disrespecting and frightening the young emperor and deposed them. When the empresses dowager executed this coup, Cixi was only twenty-five years old. Thereafter, Cixi usually made the most important decisions and Prince Gong implemented them. However, Cixi faced a major impediment. It was not customary for Manchus to educate their daughters so Cixi found it difficult to understand the complex language of court documents. She studied the classical language in the evenings but never became proficient at writing the elaborate official language used in government communications.

History has not been kind to Cixi. Eager for someone to blame for China's humiliations during the late nineteenth century, the popular imagination has seized on Cixi as the main villain. According to historiographic convention, an evil woman appears at the moment of a dynasty's final crisis, and her malfeasance delivers a coup de grace to the tottering state. Even in her own lifetime people were already depicting the audacious Cixi in ways that fit this ancient stereotype. Recently revisionists have tried to portray her more positively, but she remains one of the most controversial figures in Chinese history.[97] All sides agree that she faced daunting challenges and ultimately failed, whatever her intentions. She was surrounded by reactionaries in denial over China's predicament. They steadfastly opposed the radical reforms necessary to strengthen China and make it a modern power. Yet, in spite of strident opposition, Cixi supported a series of steady and gradual reforms intended to create a modern state capable of resisting foreign incursions.

With hostile men staffing government bureaus, Cixi had to rely on people outside the bureaucracy to achieve her goals. She promoted literate eunuchs to key positions, and they took over many posts that had previously been held by bondservants.[98] Cixi arranged marriages between eunuchs and Manchu maidservants as a reward for their loyalty. She even allowed the adoptive sons of eunuchs to enter the bureaucracy, and they participated in political factions. However, eunuchs had a reputation for corruption and depravity, and the elite considered them harbingers of dynastic decline. Cixi's dependance on eunuchs evoked criticism and contributed to her negative reputation.

Notwithstanding her meager education, Cixi tried to cultivate the image of an erudite ruler who represented classical orthodoxy and Confucian virtue.[99] She also let it be known that she was studying English, presenting herself as modern and outward looking. Cixi was extremely enthusiastic about certain modern inventions, particularly the new medium of photography. She circulated carefully composed images of herself in various settings and poses, using this visual propaganda to present herself to the world as vigorous and moral.

Given the military threats that China faced, Cixi prioritized military reforms. The government purchased weapons and warships and began to manufacture modern arms. She also tried to establish a college to teach Western science. However, reactionary officials tried to counter every reformist policy. They opposed railways and mechanized mining because they thought that loud equipment would disturb ancestral tombs, and they also opposed abandoning the traditional curriculum grounded in the ancient classics. Instead of reform, xenophobes wanted to close China off from the outside world and seek vengeance.

The Tongzhi emperor died of smallpox in 1875 at the age of nineteen. As he had no children, Empress Dowagers Cixi and Xiaozhen arranged for a three-year-old child to be posthumously adopted as son of their late husband Xianfeng. This child ascended the throne as the Guangxu emperor. The two dowagers retained control of the government, with Cixi making major decisions. She initiated a major military campaign that succeeded in reconquering the Xinjiang region, which had fallen away from the Manchu Empire during the previous chaos. She also continued to strengthen the army and navy. At this time, China established a telegraph service, two railway lines, and a steamship service serving cities along major rivers. A small number of students began to study math and science.

Cixi had to end her regency in 1889 when Guangxu turned seventeen and officially became an adult. Strangely, when Guangxu was young Cixi had told him to call her "Papa Dearest" (*qin baba*). Later he called her "Royal Father" (*huang baba*). The Qing was notable for the intense filial devotion that men expressed toward their mothers.[100] However, Guangxu was not Cixi's biological son so she did not want to rely on a tenuous maternal role to claim authority. Instead she took on a masculine persona as Guangxu's fictive father figure.

Guangxu had been educated by a reactionary scholar who imparted to him an outdated world view incompatible with modern circumstances. In contrast with Cixi's vigor, Guangxu preferred passivity. The tongue-tied ruler found it difficult to communicate with officials and preferred formal bureaucratic routine. Japan's astonishing defeat of China in 1894 proved Guangxu's inadequacy. The bewildered emperor called Cixi out of retirement to help manage the crisis. She tutored Guangxu on statecraft and encouraged him to undertake further changes, resulting in the Reform Movement of 1898. Although most Chinese mistakenly believe that Cixi opposed these changes, in fact she helped initiate them. The government sent students abroad to study, and the military received modern training. This round of reforms also targeted the economy. The government encouraged the modernization of agriculture and commerce, and imported industrial machinery.

Cixi had to compete with the charismatic scholar Kang Youwei for Guangxu's fickle attentions.[101] Although both Cixi and Kang were reformists to some degree, they detested one another. Each wanted to dominate the malleable emperor and steer the course of events. Finally, Kang and his circle plotted a coup intending to assassinate the head of the military and capture Cixi. Maybe they even planned to kill her. However, their plot was discovered and was never carried out. Even after this conspiracy failed, Kang Youwei continued to influence Guangxu. Kang was stridently pro-Japanese as he considered Japan's rapid modernization the best blueprint for China's development. Kang even advocated union between China and Japan as he believed that close links would facilitate China's industrialization. In contrast, Cixi considered Japan a treacherous enemy and steadfastly opposed these plans. Fearing that Kang would convince Guangxu to make China a vassal of Japan, Cixi seized power outright and imprisoned the emperor in the palace. Thereafter she deftly played off various factions against one another to maintain supreme authority.[102]

Cixi's biggest challenge came with the Boxer Rebellion, which began in 1899. Furious at foreign bullying, ordinary people formed militias to fight for Chinese autonomy. Foreign observers called the rebels Boxers because they practiced martial arts exercises. The Boxers claimed to have magical powers and wanted to use them to massacre outsiders and end foreign domination. This rebellion put Cixi in a difficult position. The Boxers were Chinese nationalists and they resented the Manchus. She did not want to be perceived as pro-Western. Nor did she want a massacre of foreigners as this would invite retaliation. Lacking good options, Cixi responded cautiously. Although she officially banned the Boxer movement, she did not seek to punish the rank and file.

The Boxers entered Beijing and threatened the foreign legations there. In response, an international army marched on the capital to protect foreign diplomats. Cixi allowed the Boxers to try to stop foreign troops from entering the capital. When a Chinese soldier shot the German ambassador, Cixi decided to throw her lot in with the militias and the Qing declared war on eight invading countries. Cixi legalized the Boxer army and praised them. However, the undisciplined Boxers degenerated into a violent mob and began looting homes and shops. Foreign troops easily overwhelmed both the Chinese army and the Boxers and occupied Beijing, sending Cixi and Guangxu fleeing westward. This terrifying experience wrecked the emperor's mental and physical health. Thereafter, he suffered from debilitating aliments and rarely spoke to officials. When he said something to them, his remarks were often inaudible.

After the Boxer debacle, Cixi returned to the capital and embarked on a final round of reforms. Women gained more rights and opportunities. The traditional education system was abolished and replaced with a Western curriculum. China's fiscal and legal systems were reformed. Cities began to have streetlights, running water, telephone lines, museums, cinemas, zoos, public parks, and sporting venues, altering the lifestyle of average people. Cixi started to prepare for China to establish a constitutional monarchy with an elected parliament.

Cixi had no faith in Guangxu's ability or judgment. She feared that after her death he would lead China down the wrong path. When Cixi felt certain that she would soon die, she ordered her minions to murder the emperor. She died the day after he was poisoned. Cixi had arranged for a child emperor to succeed Guangxu and for the next empress dowager to quickly approve his abdication and abolish the Qing dynasty. Cixi dreaded a massacre of the Manchus so she wanted them to give up power voluntarily to prevent a bloodbath. Not long after Cixi's death, the Qing indeed came to an end in accordance with her plan. As arranged, it was a woman who declared the end of China's imperial system.

Notes

1. Holmgren, "Imperial Marriage in the Native Chinese and Non-Han State," 76, 88–98; Zhang, *Hunyin yu shehui*, 132–39; Zhang, *Songdai hunyin jiazu shilun*, 439–58.
2. Qi, "Songdai zhuizun huanghou fumiao kaolun," 23–29.
3. Zhuang, "Songdai gongzhu quanli pangluo yuanyin tanxi," 14–20. Zhang, *Hunyin yu shehui (Songdai)*, 106, gives basic information about Song princesses.
4. Anonymous, *Song da zhaoling ji*, chapters 11–17, contains edicts regarding empresses dowager. Chapters 18–20 have edits about empresses. And chapters 21–24 have edicts regarding lesser consorts. Huang, "Nan Song houfei xinian," gives a detailed chronology of what is known about the Southern Song empresses.
5. Zhu, "Identity, Legitimacy, and Chaste Widows," 186.
6. Liu, "Songdai houfei yu diwei chuancheng," 429, 432; Chaffee, "The Rise and Regency of Empress Liu," 25; Lee, *Empresses, Art & Agency*, 232–33.
7. Hartman, "Cao Xun and the Legend of Emperor Taizu's Oath," 76.
8. Ching-Chung, "Power and Prestige," 99; McMahon, *Celestial Women*, 3, 32.
9. Chang and Saussy, *Women Writers of Traditional China*, 110.
10. Zhang, *Hunyin yu shehui*, 105, 109.
11. Chaffee, *Branches of Heaven*, 10–11, 32, 83.
12. Ebrey, *Emperor Huizong*, 8.

Chapter 5

13. Ebrey, "Empress Xiang (1046–1101)," 196.
14. For example, Empress Yang commissioned numerous images of her late husband Zhenzong and emphasized the ancestral cult. Lee, *Empresses, Art, and Agency*, 48–49.
15. Bossler, *Powerful Relations*, 21, 24.
16. Lee, *Empresses, Art & Agency*, 19, 80–94, 160, 162–64, 169.
17. Lee, *Empresses, Art & Agency*, 18–19.
18. Tuo, *Songshi*, 255:8612–15; Chaffee, "The Rise and Regency of Empress Liu," 1–25; McMahon, *Celestial Women*, 10–14; Lee, *Empresses, Art, and Agency*, 33, 36–40.
19. Luo, "Song Zhangxiao Mingsu Taihou," 22–25.
20. Lee, *Empresses, Art, and Agency*, 41.
21. Liu, "Bei Song nüzhu zhengzhi Hong de nüxing yizhi," 73–74. Cai, *Wei Jin mingshi yu xuanxue qingtan*, 76, 114, discusses the implications of the term saint (*sheng*).
22. Lee, *Empresses, Art, and Agency*, 52–69.
23. McMahon, "Women Rulers in Imperial China," 203; Liu, "Empress Liu's 'Icon of Maitreya,'" 129–90.
24. Liu, "Songdai teshu zhengzhi shili," 100–103.
25. Tuo, *Songshi*, 255: 8620–22; Ji, *Politics and Conservatism in Northern Song China*, 77–85.
26. Davis, *From Warhorses to Ploughshares*, 14–18.
27. Miyawaki-Okada, "The Role of Women in the Imperial Succession," 147.
28. Holmgren, "Marriage, Kinship and Succession," 44; Johnson, *Women of the Conquest Dynasties*, 33–41, 80–120.
29. Yang and Meng, "Qidan yinghunzhi kaolue," 94–98.
30. Sun, "Liaodai guizu lianhun guanxi shulun," 38–41.
31. Shimada, *Ryōdai shakaishi kenkyū*, 182–98; Holmgren, "Imperial Marriage in the Native Chinese and Non-Han State," 80–81, 84; Liu and Hu, "Liaodai hunyin zhuangkuang qianxi," 140–14; Wang, *Shijia dazu yu Liaodai shehui*, 13, 29–30, 36–38, 54–55.
32. Shi, "Qidan waiqi shufang shici kao," 68–72; Shi, *Liaochao houzu zhu wenti yanjiu*.
33. Zhang, *Liaodai shehuishi yanjiu*, 133.
34. Sun, "Qidanzu de maju yu weilie," 22–25.
35. Liu, "Liaodai jiechu de houmu (huang taihou) shezheng," 56–60.
36. Holmgren, "Marriage, Kinship and Succession," 56–57.
37. Hu, "Liaodai houfei yu Liaodai zhengzhi," 68–72; Wang, "Shixi Liaodai Shulü Hou de houquan he muquan," 59–61, 65; Du and Zhao, "Qidan nüxing canzheng," 165–69.
38. Tuo, *Liaoshi*, 71:1199–1200.
39. Zheng, "Lun Qidan nüxing de minzu yishi yu junshi fengmao," 64–67; McMahon, "Women Rulers in Imperial China," 209; Johnson, *Women of the Conquest Dynasties*, 121–32.
40. Tuo, *Liaoshi*, 10:107–210, 71:1201–2; Li and Li, *Xiao taiho pingzhuan*; Liu, "Liao wangchao Qidanzu nüjie Chengtian Taihou Xiao Chuo," 118–27; Wu, "Qidan Xiao Taihou chuanshuo yanjiu," 72–75.
41. Wright, "The Political and Military Power of Khitan Empress Dowagers," 325–26.
42. Zhang, *Liaodai shehuishi yanjiu*, 134.

43. Wang, *Shijia dazu yu Liaodai shehui*, 235; Zhang, "Liaodai shike zhong suo fanying de Liaochao muyi guifan," 81; Zhou, "Qidan Chengtian Taihou de ruhua zhanlue," 32–35; Zhang, "Liaodai Qidan nüxing de jiaoyu wenti tanxi," 15–16; Shi, "Rujia sixiang dui Liaodai qidan nüxing de yingxiang," 67–70.
44. Yin and Shen, "Liaodai Qidanzu nüxing wenren chuangzuo," 141–44.
45. Kuhn, *The Age of Confucian Rule*, 147–48.
46. Kuhn, *The Age of Confucian Rule*, 63.
47. Tuo, *Liaoshi*, 30: 109, 179; Xia and Zhao, "Liao Jin Qidan Nüzhen hunzhi hunsu zhi bijiao," 78; Zhang and Zhang, *Qidan jinguo*, 159–71; Chen and Gao, "Liaodai Qidan jiating qianlun," 90.
48. Tuo, *Liaoshi*, 45:1205.
49. Tao, *The Jurchen in Twelfth Century China*, 10; Du, *Liao Jin shi yanjiu*, 255.
50. Xia and Zhao, "Liao Jin Qidan Nüzhen hunzhi hunsu zhi bijiao," 76–78; Song, *Jindai de shehui shenghuo*, 85.
51. Tuo, *Jinshi*, chs. 63 and 64; Wang, "Jindai fei Nüzhen houfei chuyi," 300–318; Xia, *Jindai Qidanren yanjiu*, 131–45; Zhang, "Qianxi Jindai houfei de xuanna tujing," 48–49; Wang, "Jindai Zhenyi Huanghou chujia yuanyin xinyi," 145–48.
52. Barfield, *The Perilous Frontier*, 112.
53. Wang, "Jindai houtei zhengzhi canyu yanjiu," 51–53; Tao, *The Jurchen in Twelfth Century China*, 69–70; Sang, "Jinshi wan yan shi hunqhi zhi shihi," 255–88; Wang, "Ershi shiji yilai Jindai funü yanjiu zongshu," 110–21; McMahon, *Celestial Women*, 44–45.
54. You, "Cong hunyinfa bijiao Song Jin funü diwei de chayi," 99–162.
55. Lan, *Jindai jiaoyu yanjiu*, 97–98.
56. Tuo, *Jinshi*, 19:179; An and Jiang, "Jindai de zhongxiao yishi pingxi," 67.
57. Xia and Zhao, "Liao Jin Qidan Nüzhen hunzhi hunsu zhi bijiao," 78.
58. Seol, "Monggol jegug eseo hwangsil yeoseongui wisang byeonhwa," 317–50.
59. Barfield, *The Perilous Frontier*, 208.
60. Barfield, *The Perilous Frontier*, 214; Kuhn, *The Age of Confucian Rule*, 92.
61. Weatherford, *The Secret History of the Mongol Queens*, 3.
62. Weatherford, *The Secret History of the Mongol Queens*, 9–10.
63. Weatherford, *The Secret History of the Mongol Queens*, 20, 27–30, 47, 70–72; Rossabi, "Khubilai Khan and the Women in His Family," 156; Broadbridge, *Women and the Making of the Mongol Empire*, 30, 32–35, 101 2, 104, 107–8, 137.
64. Broadbridge, *Women and the Making of the Mongol Empire*, 23–24.
65. Weatherford, *The Secret History of the Mongol Queens*, 89–91, 93–96, 98, 105–7, 110, 125–26.
66. Holmgren, "Imperial Marriage in the Native Chinese and Non-Han State," 84–86.
67. Broadbridge, *Women and the Making of the Mongol Empire*, 94–95.
68. Song, *Yuanshi*, 106:2693; Broadbridge, *Women and the Making of the Mongol Empire*, 239.
69. Song, *Yuanshi*, chapter 114; McMahon, *Celestial Women*, 58–59, 62–63, 65.
70. Cleaves, "The Eighteenth Chapter of an Early Mongolian Version of the Hsiao Ching," 225–2254; Li and Liu, "Yuandai tonguo nüxing xianxiao wenhua xianxiang tanxi," 114–17.

Chapter 5

71. Holmgren, "Imperial Marriage in the Native Chinese and Non-Han State," 74–75; Soullière, "The Imperial Marriages of the Ming Dynasty," 15; McMahon, "Women Rulers in Imperial China," 212; McMahon, *Celestial Women*, 75.

72. Soullière, "The Imperial Marriages of the Ming Dynasty," 37–38; Cui, "Mingdai waiqi zhuangtian chutan," 71–75.

73. Soullière, "Palace Women in the Ming Dynasty," 309–10.

74. Raphals, *Sharing the Light*, 137.

75. Zhang, *Mingshi*, 113:3505–8.

76. For biographies of major Ming consorts see Zhang, *Mingshi*, chs. 113–14. Ju, *Zhongguo huanghou quanzhuan*, 819–902; Cai, *Mingdai de nüren*, 4–67; Na, *Ming Qing houfei de aihen wangshi*.

77. Soullière, "The Writing and Rewriting of History," 2–29.

78. Zhang, *Mingshi*, 113:3521–23; Li and Qian, "Mingdai Xiaomu huang taihou," 1–5.

79. Zhang, *Mingshi*, 113:3511–13; Soullière, "The Writing and Rewriting of History," 16–24.

80. Zhang, *Mingshi*, 113:3514.

81. Soullière, "The Writing and Rewriting of History," 23–24.

82. Zheng, "Lun Xuanzong Sun Huanghou," 13–18.

83. Chang and Saussy, *Women Writers of Traditional China*, 678–81.

84. Jian, *Mingdai funü fojiao xinyang yu shehui guifan*, 22–29, 61–73.

85. Luk, "Picturing Celestial Certificates," 17–48; Luk, *The Empress and the Heavenly Masters*; Purtle, "The Icon of the Woman Artist," 292–94.

86. Chen, *Mingdai de fojiao yu shehui*, 102–9.

87. Soullière, "Palace Women in the Ming Dynasty," 382–84.

88. Soullière, "Palace Women in the Ming Dynasty," 382–83.

89. Rawski, "Ch'ing Imperial Marriage and Problems of Rulership," 170–3; Lü, "Man Meng lianhun yu Qingdai bianjiang," 65–73.

90. Pang, "The Destiny of Qing Taizu Nurhaci's Second Wife Gundai," 183–87.

91. Mann, *Precious Records*, 26, 28, 126–27.

92. Ju, *Zhongguo huanghou quanzhuan*, 915–1003; Wang and Li, *Qingdai houfei*; Peng, "Empresses and Qing Court Politics," 128–41.

93. Zhao, *Qingshi gao*, 214: 8901–3; Pozzi, "Manchu Women of the Early Stage," 192–94.

94. Zhao, *Qingshi gao*, 214: 8914–15.

95. Chang, *Empress Dowager Cixi* is the best biography in English, but the highly positive depiction of Cixi is controversial.

96. Zhao, *Qingshi gao*, 214: 8925.

97. Chung, "The Much Maligned Empress Dowager," 177–96 argues for a revision of negative portrayals of Cixi.

98. Dale, *Inside the World of the Eunuch*, 4, 26, 59, 74–75.

99. Barish, "Empress Dowager Cixi's Imperial Pedagogy," 261, 267–68.

100. Hsiung, "Constructed Emotions," 102–10; Epstein, *Orthodox Passions*.

101. Lei, *Liwan kuanglan*, describes the conflict between Cixi and Kang Youwei.

102. Rowe, *China's Last Empire*, 248.

CHAPTER 6

Palaces and Harems

THE CHINESE PALACE USUALLY HAD THOUSANDS OF FEMALE INHABI-tants but the number fluctuated considerably depending on dynastic custom and the preferences of the reigning emperor. Many palace women had a status akin to concubines. Imperial concubinage served a practical function. If an emperor had numerous sexual partners he would be more likely to produce a male heir, thereby increasing the likelihood of dynastic continuity. The reproductive aspect of imperial polygyny can be seen in the parental backgrounds of emperors during the Six Dynasties. At that time, only nine princes are known to have been born to empresses. The remaining 247 were the sons of imperial concubines. Accordingly, only four emperors in that era were the sons of empresses while twenty-one were the sons of concubines.[1] Most emperors in that period had sexual relations with numerous women so their sons were born to different mothers. Emperor Wen of the Liu Song dynasty was typical in this respect.[2] His empress gave birth to just one son. His other eighteen sons were born to eighteen minor palace ladies. Emperor Xiaowu of the same dynasty had twenty-eight sons.[3] His empress gave birth to two of them, and the remaining twenty-six were born to twelve harem women. Because imperial concubines usually came from poor families, the mothers of many princes had a low status in the palace hierarchy.

Besides the reproductive function of concubinage, this practice also had symbolic value. In this respect, China was not unique. Polygyny has been practiced by rulers around the world, as surrounding a man with numerous women visibly attests to his potency and power.[4] During the

Six Dynasties era, it was already customary for wealthy men to keep large numbers of concubines and female entertainers in their home. They even competed to show off the largest number of women to guests.[5] Due to the implicit association between the number of concubines and social status, the government occasionally tried to link the number of women to a man's official rank.[6] Some men kidnapped women to display their power or forced female civilians into concubinage as booty of war.[7] Rulers also handed out concubines to their supporters as rewards and to elevate their social position.[8] Because concubinage was so closely associated with male status, emperors displayed their supreme position by surrounding themselves with the largest number of women.[9]

In each region and era of world history, the size, composition, and function of harems varied considerably. In every case, polygyny had to be justified lest the presence of so many women make the ruler appear decadent. The ways that each monarchy achieved these goals varied, giving rise to a wide variety of historic royal harems. Moroccan sultans had numerous wives and concubines but these women were never seen in public and had no impact on government policy.[10] A Swazi king customarily married two women at the same time, and this pair of senior wives oversaw the lesser women whom he subsequently wed.[11] The Inca ruler chose his wives from among a group of chaste, unmarried women called *acllas* who had a religious status akin to nuns.[12] When an Asante king was close to death, he selected favored women from his harem to accompany him to the afterlife.[13] They were clad in lavish garments, rendered drunk on palm wine, then strangled. In each case, the ideology of the harem reflected the institutions and values of the underlying culture.

Polygyny usually degrades the status of female partners.[14] If a man brings multiple women into his household, they tend to have a lower standing than a monogamous wife. However, polygyny does not affect every female household member equally. This arrangement might bolster a senior wife's position by elevating her above the women around her.[15] Similarly a large harem could make the empress seem important in comparison to the multitudes of lesser spouses and concubines in the rear palace.

Imperial historians had little interest in the daily activities of palace women so most aspects of palace life went unrecorded.[16] Sometimes a dynastic history does not even bother to record the name of a harem woman who bore an emperor.[17] Because documentation is so scanty, it is impossible to calculate the precise number of women in the palace at any given time.[18] Generally speaking, rulers usually brought some new concubines into the palace every year, so the longer an emperor's reign, the more women lived in the palace.[19] During the Song dynasty, emperors did not expel their predecessor's concubines, so the number of palace women grew considerably over time.[20] The most extravagant monarchs had thousands of concubines. Emperor Tang Xuanzong reputedly had forty thousand women in his palace.[21] Although this number seems far-fetched, there was clearly a very large number of women residing in the palace during his reign.

Royal concubinage had deep roots in China. Archaeological remains suggest that some elite men already had concubines in the prehistoric era. Many graves from the Neolithic Qijia culture feature an adult man buried with two women.[22] Researchers suggest that they were either two wives or a wife and concubine. Similarly, the bodies of high-ranking men in the prehistoric Liangzhu culture had nearby subsidiary burials of women.[23] These women were treated as valuable burial goods that displayed a powerful man's status.

Shang dynasty kings surrounded themselves with numerous women. Oracle inscriptions mention Shang nobility and foreign peoples sending female slaves and concubines to the king as tribute.[24] This custom continued during the Zhou dynasty, and the rulers of major domains had numerous concubines and other types of women in their palaces.[25] These women varied in rank. Most had a debased status. There was already a large market in concubines at the time so it was a simple matter for a noble to procure lesser harem women. However, if a woman had been sent into a ruler's palace by another noble to forge a political alliance, she might have a status akin to that of a minor wife.

Vast numbers of women inhabited the immense palace complex of the first emperor Qin Shihuang. Their status was very low and many were sacrificed upon his death. It is not clear where these women came from, but amid the war and disruption of the late Warring States era it would have been easy to acquire numerous concubines. Some of these women were carried off as booty when rebels burned the Qin palace during the dynasty's collapse.[26]

When the Han dynasty began, the dynastic founder Gaozu had a small number of concubines. He chose his harem women personally and had an intimate relationship with each of them.[27] Over time the lifestyle of the Han emperors became increasingly lavish, and the number of women in the palace increased. The population of the Han palace fluctuated considerably with each reign.[28] Emperor Wu had several thousand palace women as did several Eastern Han emperors.[29] However, many of the dynasty's titular emperors were children so the palace probably often lacked concubines.

The palace enclosure was sacralized and regarded as central and virtuous.[30] The significance of the palace was not merely symbolic. People believed that this ritually charged space interacted with the cosmos in unique ways. Events in the palace were believed to reverberate throughout the realm so it was essential for virtue and order to be maintained in those sacred precincts. To prevent the appearance of impropriety, the palace was strictly divided into male and female sections with women confined to the rear sections and attended by eunuchs to maintain the integrity of this sacred space.[31] The architecture of the Han dynasty palace intentionally isolated the women's quarters from the outer court.[32]

During the medieval era, harem women came from a wide range of backgrounds, ranging from important families to the common people.[33] Most were chosen for their appearance or talent.[34] At this time, Korean kingdoms sent women to the palaces of northern dynasty emperors as a form of tribute.[35] It was also customary to take women prisoner when an army overran an area, and some of these captives ended up as palace concubines or servants.[36] Warlords periodically overthrew a ruling house and established a new dynasty, and some took on the deposed emperor's harem. However, the rulers of some dynasties were very particular about what sort of women they admitted to the palace. The Tuoba rulers of the Northern Wei usually did not allow Han Chinese in their harems.[37] They feared being subsumed by their Chinese subjects so they

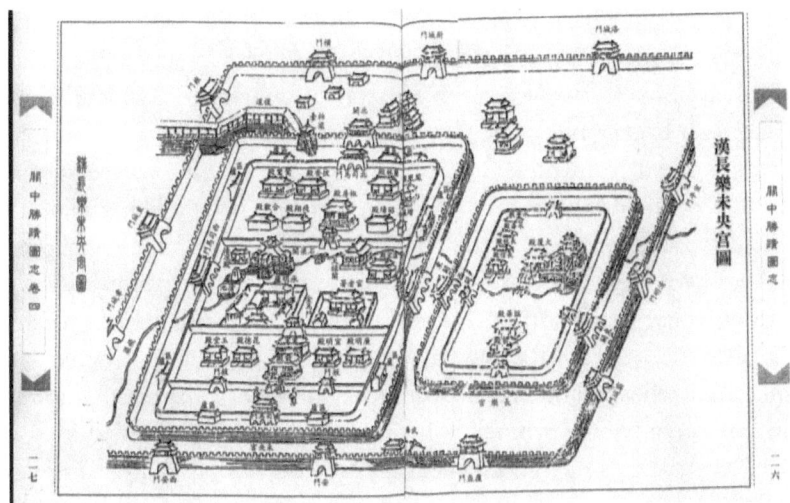

Han palace.
SOURCE: PUBLIC DOMAIN.

wanted to maintain a traditional Xianbei atmosphere in the palace to keep them in touch with their roots.

Tang and Song emperors brought women into the palace in various ways.[38] Officials selected attractive young women from ordinary families based on their appearance. Palace administrators also solicited reputable families to offer a daughter for palace service, selecting the most attractive and talented of these candidates.[39] Other women entered the palace as captives or because they were the wife or daughter of a convict.[40] Officials and the rulers of foreign regions continued to send in women as tribute.[41] Princesses and consort kin also offered up women for palace service. Emperors presented concubines and female performers to favored ministers and generals as a sign of favor.[42] And rebels targeted palace women, treating them as desirable spoils of war to be carried off along with other treasures.[43]

The rulers of the subsequent conquest regimes took different types of women into the palace. During the Jin dynasty, most empresses and minor consorts were ethnic Jurchen. The Jin palace underwent major changes over time.[44] At first, harem organization was rudimentary and women were not divided into many ranks. After the Jurchens defeated the Liao and Northern Song states, many female captives entered the palace where they assumed a debased status.[45] This practice resembled traditional Jurchen bride capture when a man kidnapped a wife and paid her family a bride price after they had been married. The Jurchens also selected women from other northern steppe peoples for palace service. Over the course of the Jin, the status of non-Jurchen women in the palace gradually rose. Eventually, many ethnic Han women became concubines and were treated with respect. Some were even selected as empresses.

Yuan rulers were notable for taking in palace women from foreign peoples as tribute.[46] Most famously the Korean kingdom of Goryeo sent numerous women to the Yuan court to symbolize political submission. Many of these tribute women were high born, educated, or trained in music, dance, tea preparation, cooking, or other useful skills. Although the kings of Goryeo considered this arrangement humiliating, it allowed them to evade Mongol occupation.

When the Ming dynasty began, Emperor Taizu wanted to safeguard China's northern borders so he took Mongol and Korean women into the palace as minor consorts.[47] He did this not to symbolize domination in the Yuan fashion but to build alliances with potentially troublesome Mongol khans and to keep Korea within China's sphere of influence. However, the Ming emperors abandoned this policy in the early fifteenth century. As the dynasty stabilized, Chinese officials took a more condescending attitude toward foreigners and did not consider them fit to live within the sacred confines of the palace.

The Zhengde emperor abused the recruitment system to extort money from wealthy families.[48] It had long been customary for palace officials to select young women from respectable families as minor consorts. However, Zhengde had officials seize women with no intention of making them part of his harem. Their families had to pay out a large ransom to get them back. Wealthy men bribed members of the emperor's circle to avoid having their daughters detained. If a woman's family did not pay for their daughter's release, she was sent to work in the imperial laundry, which also served as the palace prison. Women there had to perform hard labor and received little food. Some starved to death.

Traditionally, the Manchus practiced levirate and other forms of polygyny so the Qing emperors considered concubines akin to minor wives. Most women entered the Qing palace as servants.[49] A few were promoted to the status of concubine because they attracted an emperor's notice but most remained in a servile role. A lowly woman who gave birth to a future emperor could become empress dowager despite her background.[50] Moreover, as conquerors of China, Manchu emperors considered it their prerogative to require Han women from good families to serve as harem women.[51] They considered this a kind of tribute from the Chinese to their Manchu overlords. The Chinese gentry detested having their daughters forced into minor positions in the palace, seeing this as akin to kidnapping or blackmail. Sometimes they married off a daughter prematurely to render her ineligible for palace service.

Monogamy became the norm during the Han dynasty. Henceforth, usually only one of the emperor's partners was designated an official wife. Even most foreign peoples adopted monogamous marriage when they settled in China.[52] Aside from the empress, other harem women either had lesser titles, were untitled concubines, or performed specialized functions, working as entertainers, wet nurses, teachers, female officials, or servants.

Many palace women held a nebulous position somewhere between wife and concubine. Although concubines were not true wives, an emperor sometimes conducted an attenuated marriage ceremony when a concubine entered the palace for the sake of propriety. This custom had ancient roots. During the early Eastern Zhou dynasty, many nobles practiced *ying* marriage, which anthropologists describe as sororal polygyny or accompanying concubinage.[53] At that time, there were two kinds of group weddings. Either a bride was attended by servants, who constituted part of her dowry, or she came into marriage accompanied by younger sisters or nieces.[54] In the latter case, one woman was designated the main wife and her relations became minor spouses or respected concubines.[55] The women accompanying the main bride took part in the marriage ceremony.

CHAPTER 6

Aside from *ying* marriage, Zhou dynasty concubines who entered the palace could also undergo a simplified wedding. Although women from lesser backgrounds did not receive this honor, when a woman from an important lineage entered a nobleman's palace as a concubine, she might undergo a simplified marriage ceremony as a mark of honor.[56] This custom endured into the imperial era. Although most women entered the palace without any ceremony, some underwent a token wedding that included the presentation of a betrothal gift, an act that traditionally distinguished wife from concubine even though they were not officially designated a wife.[57]

Aside from the queen and concubines or lesser spouses, many other women lived in the palace as well. During the Zhou dynasty, the rulers of major domains had female musicians and performers to provide entertainment.[58] Performances had yet to be commercialized because the economy was insufficiently developed, so singing and dancing occurred in ritual and religious contexts as well as in palaces.[59] Rulers frequently presented performers as gifts to nobles, showing that these women had a servile status like slaves. These exchanges allowed people to encounter the performing arts of different regions, helping to create a common Chinese culture.

After China's unification, the emperors of Qin and Han continued to maintain troupes of female entertainers in the palace.[60] The numbers of palace performers fluctuated with each reign, depending on a ruler's inclinations. As before, these women had a low position. The mercurial warlord Cao Cao executed a female singer simply because he detested her bad temper.[61] During the Six Dynasties era, palace musicians and dancers featured prominently in descriptions of palace life and court poetry.[62] Poets emphasized their beauty and used them to symbolize sensuality and the extravagance of palace life. In subsequent dynasties, female performers continued to entertain at court banquets and other palace festivities.[63] Toward the end of the imperial era, however, palace entertainers lost favor. Because courtesans had become associated with the decadent excesses of late Ming dynasty culture, the Qing palace did not have resident singers or dancers.[64]

The palace complex was an immense space. In addition to harem women and entertainers, numerous female servants and artisans lived on the periphery of the palace grounds. Others came in from the outside each day to work. Besides performing necessary tasks, legions of palace servants also served as status symbols. Having a huge female staff confirmed the unique position of the emperor. Servants were traditionally considered marginal members of the employer's household. Likewise, palace serving women were minor members of the imperial establishment.[65] In the early imperial era, the palace had large workshops whose artisans produced luxury goods such as silk fabric and lacquerware for use by the emperor and harem. Most palace artisans were women.[66] As the commercial economy grew, the palace could more easily procure luxury goods through commercial channels and the tribute system, so the number of palace female artisans declined.

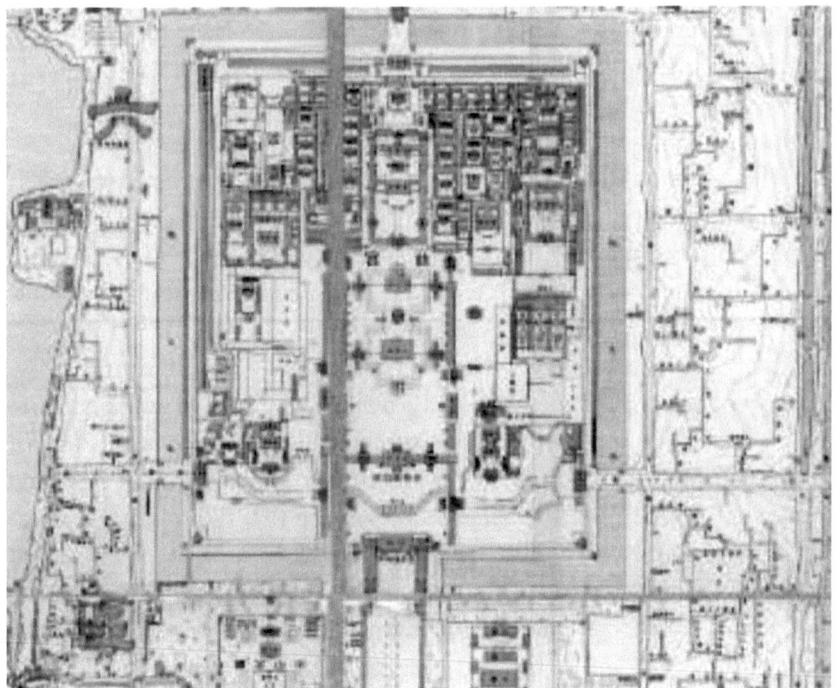

The Qing Dynasty Palace
SOURCE: *PUBLIC DOMAIN.*

Chapter 6

It was customary for the wealthy to hand over a newborn infant to a wet nurse for feeding and care. The wet nurse would often continue to serve as a nanny when the child was older. In the palace, wet nurses and the infants in their care lived in special quarters.[67] Wet nurses had an ambiguous social position. Even though they were charged with care of the emperor's children, they came from the bottom of society. Some were even slaves or the wives of convicts.[68]

When a child emperor ascended the throne, his nursemaids continued to attend him.[69] Even after an emperor grew to maturity, he might maintain a strong and affectionate bond with his wet nurse. Some monarchs treated their wet nurses as surrogate mothers, favoring them with wealth, privileges, and titles.[70] A few wet nurses were even designated empresses dowager and participated in politics.[71] The contradiction between these women's base origins and subsequent privilege provoked dismay among the officialdom. In the third century, there was even a debate over whether a wet nurse should be mourned as a surrogate mother or whether her obsequies should be curtailed due to her lowly origins.[72] Historians took a dim view of wet nurses and tended to blame them for schemes and political problems, often unfairly.[73]

Most women resided in the palace temporarily, and they usually left when they grew old or lost favor.[74] After departing the palace, a woman usually returned home to live with her family. If she was young enough she would be married off. Some became nuns. Emperors sometimes presented minor palace women to important personages and foreign leaders as gifts.[75] Wei rulers demonstrated their compassion by marrying excess palace women to poor men and widowers who were otherwise unable to wed.[76] It is not recorded what these women thought of this fate. Emperor Wen of Han, famed for his benevolence, set an example by expelling numerous women from the palace and ordering them to marry.[77] Henceforth, it was not uncommon for numerous women to be sent away at the same time. There was often a major turnover in the palace when an emperor died. Concubines and serving women of the deceased monarch were usually sent home to avoid the impression that the new monarch was having sexual relations with his predecessor's harem women, which would have constituted incest.[78] Officials periodically complained about the large number of women in the palace as they considered an expensive harem a tangible symbol of dynastic decay, and emperors occasionally expelled some palace women to appease critics.[79] Women were also sometimes sent away during austerity campaigns to reduce palace expenditures.[80]

⸻

In wealthy households, concubines and female servants frequently caused scandals.[81] The immense scale of the palace intensified these problems. Housing thousands of women together in a confined space and forcing them to compete for one man's attention guaranteed endless trouble. Jealousy, backstabbing, manipulation, and factionalism were commonplace. Harem managers tried their best to foster harmony.[82] Most importantly, they instituted a hierarchy of ranks upon the various secondary consorts and minor concubines to impose a semblance of order.

In prehistory and high antiquity, many palace women had an extremely low status not much different from that of slaves. Some were even murdered for ceremonial purposes, attesting to their degraded position. In certain stratified Neolithic cultures such as Liangzhu and Qijia, the burials of prominent men sometimes had subsidiary graves of women presumed to be human sacrifices.[83] The victims had likely served the deceased in life, and they were forced to accompany him in death. During the Shang dynasty, society became even more unequal, and human sacrifice became a standard practice. The burial of an important man was often accompanied by the sacrifices of women to mark his status.[84] And during the subsequent Western Zhou dynasty, it was common to sacrifice women upon the death of an important nobleman.[85] The tomb of the Marquis of Zeng contained the remains of thirteen women.[86] Many of the victims were young, and archaeologists assume that they were concubines, performers, or servants.

Human sacrifice declined over the course of the late Eastern Zhou. Mourners began placing symbolic figurines of people, animals, and valuables in tombs in lieu of real items, and small statues of women became acceptable substitutes for sacrificial victims.[87] However, there was one last major instance of human sacrifice during the Qin dynasty. Like other domains in the Zhou realm, the kings of Qin had originally practiced mortuary human sacrifice but this custom had decreased during the Eastern Zhou as in other states.[88] Emperor Qin Shihuang revived the archaic custom. When he died, all of the palace concubines who had not born children were sacrificed and placed in his tomb.[89] Although the main tomb has yet to be excavated, the remains of female sacrificial victims in it might number in the thousands. The Han dynasty abandoned mortuary human sacrifice, and thereafter the murder of harem women for funerals was rare.

Ancient human sacrifice shows that the female attendants of an important man were treated as luxury goods rather than as human beings worthy of empathy. Over time, the status of women around the ruler increased, and they received more respect. One reason for this shift was the practice of comparing a ruler's harem women to his officials. During the Zhou dynasty, it became common to liken these two roles. Although a concubine and a government minister had very different roles, the ancients believed that they nevertheless shared fundamental similarities as they had analogous ties to the ruler. Readers today are often surprised by early poetry that uses romantic or even sexual imagery to describe the relationship between a ruler and a high official. Ancient readers knew to interpret these passages as political allegories so authors used sexualized imagery to emphasize the importance of this tie.[90] This analogy had a major impact on the status of harem women. Because people saw them as analogous to government functionaries, they were ranked and ordered in the manner of bureaucrats. And thinkers emphasized that because a ruler's harem women and his officials were analogous, both should be loyal and obedient.[91]

Shang kings classified the harem into ranks because these women attended them in various capacities.[92] The attention given to a king's top consort shows that she had a status comparable to that of a queen. In addition to the senior wife, there were also many other women in the palace. King Wuding is believed to have had between fifty-eight and sixty-three consorts. Usually only one consort became integrated into the sacrificial system after her death. Even so, three kings had two consorts memorialized in the ritual calendar, and one monarch had three consorts join the system. It is unclear why the number of consorts in the sacrificial system differed for these kings. Perhaps they had multiple senior wives. Or maybe one consort died prematurely and was replaced by another so both women were considered eligible to join the posthumous sacrificial system. The burials of the royal consorts also differed considerably, attesting to a difference in ranks. Some had a large tomb of their own filled with an array of lavish burial items while others were buried in subsidiary positions within the king's tomb.[93]

The kinship customs of the Zhou people affected palace organization. Zhou kings distinguished between wife and concubine, each of whom had distinct rank and status.[94] The king's wife received the title *hou*, equivalent to a queen. Lesser consorts were called *fei*, a term for royal concubines.[95] Although a comprehensive hierarchy had yet to emerge, *fei* had different ranks. A concubine's status could change if she was favored by the ruler, bore a son, or if her son was promoted. Ordering the harem not only improved palace administration but also helped ensure the stability of the realm as the rankings of harem women could influence the royal succession. The Zhou practiced primogeniture, which they codified into the rites.[96] Usually the eldest son of the ruler's wife became the apparent heir. If he was incompetent, the succession devolved to his full younger brothers in order of their ages. Below them were the sons of concubines, who were ranked in order of age.

When Qin Shihuang annihilated the Zhou aristocracy, the traditional rites went into abeyance. The Qin imperial system included a new type of palace organization.[97] Qin Shihuang is not known to have named an empress. It is not clear how harem women were ranked, although they clearly had very low standing because many were sacrificed upon his death. It was left to the Han dynasty to put in place a system of harem ranks appropriate to the new imperial system. Most importantly, there was only one Han empress. Below her were numerous concubines of various ranks. The system of palace ranks fluctuated over the course of the Han, changing in response to political intrigues, factions, and the ambitions of ambitious women.[98]

The Six Dynasties also had dynamic palace organization.[99] By this time it was assumed that a ruler would have a large harem divided into ranks. Even warlords established a tiered harem to take on the appearance of a rightful monarch.[100] The Jin dynasty initially lacked harem ranks but over time they implemented a system different from that used during the Han.[101] Emperor Wu of Jin had three senior harem women, each with a distinct title. Below these were lesser concubines with graded appellations. Female titles corresponded to the ranks of male officials in the bureaucracy, drawing an explicit comparison between harem women and government ministers. In the south the Liu Song dynasty revived the Han dynasty system of titles.[102]

From the reign of Emperor Taizu of Wei, the Northern Dynasties also classified palace women into ranks, although the grades and titles differed from those used in the south.[103] The number of palace women far exceeded that in previous eras and was rarely matched in subsequent dynasties. Each of the Northern Dynasties had a somewhat different system of palace organization and harem titles.[104] Toward the end of this era, the Latter Zhou dynasty responded to intensifying crises by decreasing the number of women in the palace and distinguishing them according to only three titles.[105]

The Sui and Tang dynasties merged female titles into a comprehensive system so the wife of an official received a title commensurate with her husband's office.[106] The titles of imperial concubines fluctuated over time, but these women were usually divided into twenty-seven major ranks. Numerous lesser women had additional titles and classifications. Palace women had flexible ranks. A woman could be promoted if she attained the emperor's favor or bore a son, particularly the heir apparent, but she would be downgraded if she committed a transgression. The Song dynasty system followed that of the Tang in basic respects except that the number of total positions were reduced to twenty-four.[107] Moreover, each title in the harem was directly associated with a corresponding rank in the civil service.

Palace organization and hierarchy always posed problems for conquest regimes as steppe peoples traditionally lacked large harems. When the Jurchens founded the Jin dynasty, at first they did not use clearly defined palace ranks. This ambiguity resulted in confusion and chaos. Emperor Xizong had received a Confucian education so he instituted harem ranks in imitation of Chinese norms, and Jin rulers gradually expanded and refined this system.[108] In contrast, emperors of the subsequent Yuan dynasty had little interest in Chinese precedent and never established clear harem ranks in the manner of native dynasties.

The Ming revived the system of ranks used during the Tang and Song, and palace concubines received carefully graded titles.[109] However, due to a general decline in the status of palace women, their ranks were not considered analogous to grades in the male bureaucracy. The Ming introduced the novel practice of naming one woman "imperial honored consort" (*huang guifei*). The holder of this title stood above the other palace concubines in rank and was equal to the empress in prestige.[110] The Ming rulers seem to have established this new title to reduce the status of the empress by forcing her to share her honors with another woman.

Qing dynasty palace organization evolved considerably over time.[111] At first, the harem was relatively unstratified and consorts lacked clear titles. The early Manchu rulers were polygynous and all of their harem women had a status akin to wives. The Qing emperors introduced a few general titles for harem women. From the late seventeenth century onward the inner palace had one empress and seven ranks of lesser consorts. A woman generally received a particular rank according to her family background. Women in the highest ranks belonged to prominent Manchu families while minor consorts came from humble backgrounds. As rank was based on birth, harem women rarely changed their status.

Palace administration had to develop to cope with the rising number of inhabitants of the inner palace. Rulers did not see smoothly functioning palace services as merely useful. People judged a man according to the situation in the inner quarters of his home. If his household fell into disorder, this was taken as a sign of general ineptitude.[112] The same standards applied to monarchs as well. This belief made efficient palace administration a high priority.

Uncastrated men were normally barred from interacting with palace women so many palace administrators were eunuchs. Women also participated in palace administration. Female palace functionaries date to the Bronze Age. Western Zhou inscriptions mention a palace official titled *bao*.[113] The orthography of the ancient character depicts a person carrying

CHAPTER 6

a baby on her back, hinting at the original meaning of this term. People of both sexes received this title. A male *bao* seems to have been a tutor or advisor to a young ruler. Women titled *bao* raised and educated royal or noble children. Female *bao* received precious gifts from important people, showing that they were significant personages. *Bao* does not seem to have been a regular bureaucratic office. It was probably an honorific title given to people who performed specific roles. In addition to *bao*, commentators to the *Classic of Poetry* (*Shijing*) allege that there were female palace scribes in antiquity although nothing is known about them except that they were held to high standards of accuracy.[114]

The ancient trope comparing harem women to government ministers justified female participation in palace management. During the Han dynasty, women were already overseeing certain palace services. However, a dramatic increase in female palace residents during the Six Dynasties required more efficient administration so talented women served in important positions.[115] The Wei emperors put female servants in charge of handling clothing, food, and other quotidian items.[116] They also sought out literate women to keep records of palace goods. Likewise, in the south the Jin dynasty palace also had female administrators.[117] These women were so numerous that they were divided into systematic ranks, giving rise to a large and comprehensive female palace bureaucracy.

The Sui and Tang governments organized female palace officials into a graded hierarchy, with each rank having clearly defined duties.[118] Palace women had two kinds of titles. A concubine had a title that marked her rank in the harem hierarchy. In addition, a separate system of titles and ranks distinguished the different types of female palace officials. Women serving in the palace were referred to as female scribes (*nüshi*). They managed the quotidian matters of palace life, including food, carriages, lamps, gardens, medicines, music, clothing, ornaments, and rituals. Numerous specialized female professionals kept detailed records of every aspect of palace management, participating in a large and sophisticated female bureaucracy.

The Song palace maintained the basic administrative framework that developed during the Tang.[119] Female officials received titles analogous to those of men in the civil and military bureaucracies, and they worked together with eunuch administrators to keep palace life running smoothly. Although the Song distinguished harem women from administrators, emperors often took female officials as concubines so the two hierarchies sometimes intersected.

During the Ming, the female bureaucracy continued to evolve.[120] Officials divided palace organization into seven major departments staffed by women. Most were unmarried commoners capable of reading, writing, and doing basic arithmetic. A minority were talented harem women who volunteered to do administrative work. When a concubine expressed her willingness to take on managerial duties, she received special training to ensure that she had sufficient skills to carry out the duties of her post. At the beginning of the dynasty, most female administrators came from the south. After the capital was shifted to Beijing, they usually came from northern regions. An ambitious woman who studied hard and proved herself capable could be promoted because female administrators were selected and evaluated according to knowledge and competence. Higher-grade administrators managed a specific palace compound or the residence of a princess. If a woman served a prince who became emperor, she received the title madam (*furen*), placing her just below an imperial consort in status. Although these women were skilled and wielded some authority, they were of low birth so imperial consorts often treated them with contempt. They were also commonly victimized during factional battles within the tumultuous Ming palace. The Qing maintained much of the Ming system. However, because Manchu women were traditionally illiterate, female administrators were usually Han commoners.

A woman's life inside the palace varied considerably depending on her status and role.[121] The palace atmosphere was infamously louche during some eras. Later generations looked back on the Northern Qi palace as a sewer of chaos and depravity.[122] And some women violated established norms and misbehaved, sometimes in extraordinary ways. Lady Xu, a minor consort of Emperor Yuan of the Liang dynasty, ripped fetuses out of the wombs of other palace concubines, yet she herself had an affair with a Daoist cleric. Xu infuriated the emperor by having only part of her makeup completed when he arrived, then became so drunk that she vomited on her clothes.[123]

Many other palace ladies distinguished themselves as prudent and moderate. Some dressed in deliberately simple attire to display their temperance.[124] During the Song and Ming eras, Neo-Confucian influence led to an abandonment of flamboyant Tang dynasty styles. Harem women adopted sober styles of dress including garments based on prototypes mentioned in ancient ritual works.[125] Even during the infamous Northern Qi era, some women in the royal household continued to spin and weave as a tangible sign of their integrity.[126]

Perhaps the most important factor affecting the lives of palace women was their physical seclusion. Some empresses and empresses dowager lived in mansions outside the central palace grounds.[127] Yet, most harem women were strictly confined to the inner palace where they lived in compounds that shielded them from the eyes of men.[128] Women even held their own banquets and entertainments separate from those of the outer court.[129]

Popular literature depicted palace life as fiercely competitive and frustrating. Individual interests were pitted against those of the state, rank thwarted love, and factions clashed.[130] For most women, there was no escape from these struggles. The atmosphere in the palace was claustrophobic, and female inhabitants felt cut off from the outside world. A Tang poem describes women crowding around a man who had come in from the outside to sweep a courtyard. They eagerly question him, desperate to find out what is happening beyond the high palace walls.[131]

Many women were secluded in the palace against their will, making their confinement even worse. An incident that occurred during the Tang dynasty reveals that many women hated life in the palace. When an emperor allowed thousands of palace ladies to go outside and visit the residence of a high official, which had been decorated for a festival, many of them absconded.[132] Poets often described the misery of life in the harem.[133] Some were written by literati imagining the oppression of palace life. Other poems were written by the victims themselves. A poem by Empress Yang of the Southern Song dynasty expresses the jealousy she feels at having to share her husband's attentions with numerous concubines.¹³⁴

> Spring breeze is light, water flowing,
> Hand in hand we seek fragrant blossoms across the small bridge.
> But how annoying the scene of the wild pond where my eye chances upon
> Innumerable mandarin ducks resting pair by pair!

The surroundings and material goods of harem women were strictly regulated according to rank. They could not leave the palace and buy whatever they wanted. Instead they had to depend on palace officials to designate their living quarters and allocate essential items. Each woman's clothing and ornaments reflected her grade. Official histories describe these garments in detail, attesting to their significance.¹³⁵ Women traveled around the immense palace grounds in different sorts of vehicles, again distinguished by rank.¹³⁶ Officials used distinctive rites when paying their respects to women of different levels.¹³⁷ Most importantly from the standpoint of the bureaucracy, each rank of palace concubine had a different type of official seal that she used to stamp documents.¹³⁸

The palace had an array of entertainments to keep the residents amused. These differed in each period. In debauched eras, entertainments could be vulgar. During the Latter Zhou dynasty, palace ladies, officials, female entertainers, and foreign envoys playfully splashed one another with water for fun.¹³⁹ In most eras, however, such unrestrained amusements would have been unthinkable. The poetry of the Northern Song Emperor Huizong describes palace women playing musical instruments, embroidering, reading, and engaging in polite diversions.¹⁴⁰ Some pastimes seem surprising in retrospect. During the Tang dynasty, women took riding lessons.¹⁴¹ And because wrestling had become popular in the Song era, at that time the palace had a stable of wrestlers.¹⁴²

The palace also had an infrastructure for educating the female residents. Emperors usually encouraged the women around them to pursue an education to inculcate virtue, elevate the cultural and intellectual tone of the palace, enable concubines to carry out elaborate rituals, and prepare the willing for administrative roles. Consorts from privileged families sometimes entered the palace with considerable learning. Some had even studied the classics and ancient poetry.[143]

The Tang system of palace education served as the basis for subsequent arrangements.[144] The palace had an organization staffed by professional teachers who taught palace residents. A senior teacher oversaw the palace school. Beneath him were five experts in the classics; three teachers for history, philosophy, and literature; two calligraphy teachers; and one teacher each for various minor fields including various Daoist classics, law, poetry chanting, arithmetic, and the board game *weiqi* (Go).[145] Another organization had three teachers who gave music lessons. Female palace administrators also sometimes took on teaching duties in addition to their regular workload, and accomplished concubines helped teach their peers. Princes studied the most advanced subjects while princesses and harem women usually limited their education to simpler texts.

The Ming system of palace education resembled that of the Tang in most respects.[146] However, women had become more strictly secluded from men in the intervening centuries so the earliest palace teachers were women. Later, educated eunuchs took over teaching duties. The curriculum focused heavily on Neo-Confucian content. Because men could no longer come in from the outside to teach, educational standards declined. In fact, in every era the educational standards for palace women were far below those of princes and literati as few studied complicated classical texts. Nevertheless the most motivated women occasionally excelled in their studies and became learned and accomplished. Some wrote competent poetry.[147] And scholars suspect that some of the edicts supposedly written by Song emperors were in fact drafted by talented palace women.[148]

Many palace women were extremely pious. Buddhism was most popular in most eras. However, the most intense show of religious devotion occurred during the Tang when numerous palace women became enthusiastic Daoists. The Tang dynasty employed Daoism as a political ideology, which helps account for the religious fervor.[149] At that time, many princesses and harem women had close relations with Daoist nuns, and some left the palace to join the clergy. Palace women seem to have preferred Daoism to Buddhism at the time because Daoism had far fewer strictures.

Harem women turned to religion for various reasons. Some were sincerely devout. Others sought blessings or longevity. It was also believed that religious practice could benefit parents whether alive or deceased. Some women disliked palace life and saw religion as a convenient avenue for escape. And when an emperor died, many harem women entered nunneries, which ended up housing many elderly women from the palace. Because several princesses joined the Daoist clergy, the religiosity of palace ladies captured the attention of Tang writers, who composed poems about nuns from the palace.

Detailed rules specified in detail the obsequies for deceased palace women including the funeral ceremony, burial, and mourning rites.[150] Relatively few harem women spent their entire lives in the palace. Those who did were mostly skilled entertainers. When a woman died outside the palace, her family was responsible for her burial. During the Tang, if a woman died from disease or an accident while still serving in the palace, she was buried in a special cemetery for palace women.[151] The location of these burial spots shifted likely in response to urban development in the capital. Sometimes only a humble plaque marked a grave. These markers often did not even record the name of the deceased, only the date of death. However, a major consort might have a lengthy epitaph as did important female palace administrators. The language and format of these commemorations altered over time but they were always formal and idealized.[152] Empresses and the most senior consorts usually had a biography in the dynasty's official history. Ladies of the highest ranks received posthumous sacrifices.[153]

NOTES

1. Bielenstein, "The Six Dynasties, Volume 2," 36–37.
2. Shen, *Songshu*, 72:1855–56.
3. Shen, *Songshu*, 80:2057–58.
4. Divale and Harris, "Population, Warfare, and the Male Supremacist Complex," 523, notes that polygyny is 141 times more frequent than polyandry. McMahon, *Women*

Chapter 6

Shall Not Rule, 11; McMahon, "The Institution of Polygamy in the Chinese Imperial Palace," 917–19, 921.

5. Xiao, *Zhongguo changji shi,* 43–48; Yan, *Zhongguo mingji yishu shi,* 30–32.
6. For example, Li, *Beishi,* 16:609–10.
7. Liu, *Shih-shuo Hsin-yü,* 441 (27.1); Liu, *Shishuo xinyu huijiao jizhu,* 27:705. When troops of the Latter Zhou dynasty looted the Qi dynasty palace, they captured two thousand palace women. Linghu, *Zhoushu,* 6:99.
8. Wei, *Weishu,* 30: 712, 723.
9. Ebrey, "Rethinking the Imperial Harem," 189.
10. Rhorchi, "Consorts of the Moroccan Sultans," 229.
11. Flannery and Marcus, *The Creation of Inequality,* 428, 434.
12. Silverblatt, *Moon, Sun, and Witches,* 82–85.
13. Flannery and Marcus, *The Creation of Inequality,* 445.
14. Schlegel, *Male Dominance and Female Authority,* 87, 98; Quinn, "Anthropological Studies on Women's Status," 211; White and Burton, "Causes of Polygyny," 871. Yang, "Chunqiu shidai zhi nannü fengji," 24–26, asserts that polygyny among the Chunqiu aristocracy depressed the status of elite women.
15. White and Burton, "Causes of Polygyny," 884.
16. Wang, "Zhashi tuijin Mingdai gongtingshi," 406–11, discusses the materials used to write the history of Ming palace women. These include both official sources and informal writings.
17. Emperor Wen of the Latter Zhou dynasty had thirteen sons. The standard history of the dynasty gives the names of five of the mothers. The historian records that the other eight boys were born to minor harem women in the rear palace, whom he does not bother to name. Linghu, *Zhoushu,* 13:201.
18. Ebrey, "Rethinking the Imperial Harem," 178.
19. Jiang and Jiang, "Tangdai gongnü shenghuo shulue," 57; Wan, "Tangdai gongren zhi mingyun tanxi," 145.
20. Ebrey, "Rethinking the Imperial Harem," 187.
21. Ouyang, *Xin Tangshu,* 207:5856. Early medieval emperors also had large harems. Bielenstein, "The Six Dynasties, Volume 2," 30. The Northern Song palace housed between two thousand and three thousand women at any given time. Ching-Chung, "Palace Women in the Northern Sung," 81.
22. Qian, Zhou, Mao, and Xie, "Gansu Lintan Mogo Qijia wenhua mudi," 9.
23. Zhang, "Suzhou de Liangzhu yicun ji gudai wenming," 112, 115.
24. Luo, "Shilun Shangdai Yindu renkou," 347.
25. Thatcher, "Marriages of the Ruling Elite in the Spring and Autumn Period," 32–33.
26. Ban, *Hanshu,* 31:1808.
27. Ban, *Hanshu,* 46:4193.
28. Ban, Hanshu, 24A:1127, notes that spending on luxurious food and clothing in the palace increased enormously after Gaozu's frugal reign. Ban, *Hanshu,* 4:105, n. 2, 10:301, n. 2. Yan Shigu explains in his commentary that imperial concubines were sometimes called *ji.* However, unlike some commenters, he does not consider this an office but rather

a title or appellation. Also see Xiao, *Zhongguo changji shi*, 21–37; Lee, "Wet Nurses in Early Imperial China," 7–8.

29. Ebrey, "Rethinking the Imperial Harem," 178.
30. Lin, *Kongjian, shenti yu lijiao guixun*, 14–32.
31. Lin, *Kongjian, shenti yu lijiao guixun*, 45–70.
32. Lin, *Kongjian, shenti yu lijiao guixun*, 45–70.
33. Bielenstein, "The Six Dynasties, Volume 2," 36–37; Liu, "Wei Jin Nanbeichao shidai de qie," 3. For some examples see Fang, *Jinshu*, 31:953; Wei, *Weishu*, 38:878, 47:1053, 56:1243, 63:1412; Li, *Nanshi*, 12:347; Li, *Beishi*, 20:751, 21:795, 22:811.
34. For example, Fang, *Jinshu*, 39:1153, 40:1168.
35. Wei, *Weishu*, 60:1346, 100:2217.
36. Li, *Beishi*, 10:376; Shen, *Songshu*, 95:2327, 2330.
37. Holmgren, "A Question of Strength," 65.
38. Jiang and Jiang, "Tangdai gongnü shenghuo shulue," 57–59.
39. For example, Lady Xu was a favorite concubine of Emperor Tang Taizong. She was the daughter of a military officer. Xu was well educated and Taizong enjoyed her companionship. She was buried together with Taizong in a side chamber of his mausoleum. Liu, *Jiu Tang shu*, 51:2167–69.
40. When a prominent man was executed for a crime, his female family members would sometimes be enslaved in the palace. Their good upbringing made them suitable for palace service. Liu, *Jiu Tang shu*, 176:4567.
41. Liu, *Jiu Tang shu*, 15:468, 17A:523.
42. For example, Wei, *Suishu*, 52:1345, 56:1530.
43. Liu, *Jiu Tang shu*, 57:2286.
44. Wang, "Jindai fei Nüzhen houfei chuyi," 300–301, 305–12; Tao, *The Jurchen in Twelfth-Century China*, 95–98.
45. Ebrey, *Emperor Huizong*, 458, 460.
46. Xi and Temuer, "Yuandai Gaoli gongnü zhidu yu Qi zhengzhi wenhua beijing," 5–9.
47. Cui, "Mingdai hougong yizu," 151–56.
48. Geiss, "The Cheng-te Reign, 1506–1521," 433.
49. Torbert, *The Ch'ing Imperial Household Department*, 74.
50. Rawski, "Qing Empresses and Their Place in History," 40.
51. Qiu, "Yongren zırao," 421–57.
52. McMahon, *Celestial Women*, 44–45.
53. Granet, *La polygynie sororale*; Kurihara, *Kodai Chūgoku koninsei*, 301–81.
54. Chen, "Chunqiu hunyin lisu yu shehui lilun," 23–34.
55. Chunqiu inscriptions seem to distinguish wife from concubine in *ying* marriages. Cao, *Jinwen yu Yin Zhou nüxing wenhua*, 233–35.
56. Thatcher, "Marriages of the Ruling Elite," 33.
57. For example, Shen, *Songshu*, 14:341.
58. Yan, *Zhongguo mingji yishu shi*, 13–14; Xiao, *Zhongguo changji shi*, 13.
59. Zhou, "Lun Zhongguo gudai biaoyan yishu," 44–47.
60. Xiao, *Zhongguo changji shi*, 21–37.
61. Liu, *Shih-shuo Hsin-yü*, 465 (31.1); Liu, *Shishuo xinyu huijiao jizhu*, 31:738.

Chapter 6

62. Li, *Beishi*, 5:174; Shen, *Songshu*, 19:547. Emperors sometimes had sexual relations with performers. Li, *Bei Qi shu*, 11:148. For examples of poetry, see Birrell, *Chinese Love Poetry*, 232; Xu, *Jianzhu yutai xinyong*, 7:17b–18a.

63. Ebrey, *Emperor Huizong*, 294–96.

64. Mann, *Precious Records*, 26, 28, 126–27.

65. Ransmeier, "Inside the Home, Outside the Family," 279–80, 285, 287; Zhang, "Mingdai nühu de jieding ji qi shehui daiyu," 8, 10.

66. Von Glahn, *The Economic History of China*, 106.

67. In the late Western Han, a building on the grounds of the heir apparent's palace was used primarily for nursing infants. The building's walls were painted with images of nine mothers and children. Ban, *Hanshu*, 10:301, n. 2.

68. Wei, *Weishu*, 13:326; Cheng, "Jinru Songdai huangshi de rumu," 127–29, 136; Cheng, "Songdai rumu yu qie de qubie ji lianxi," 136.

69. Wei, *Weishu*, 58:1291.

70. Liu, *Jiu Tang shu*, 20B:799, 183:4724; Lee, "Wet Nurses in Early Imperial China," 24–25, 28–29; Lee, "The Epitaph of a Third-Century Wet Nurse," 460.

71. Wei, *Weishu*, 5:112, 83A:1817; Pearce, "Nurses, Nurslings," 287–309; Li, *Bei Wei Pingcheng shidai*, 135–85; McMahon, *Women Shall Not Rule*, 169; Cheng, "Jinru Songdai huangshi de rumu," 125, 137–43.

72. Lee, "The Epitaph of a Third-Century Wet Nurse," 459, 462–65.

73. Doran, "Royal Wet Nurses," 198–224.

74. Bielenstein, "The Six Dynasties, Volume 2," 38. For palace women returning to their families see Liu, *Jiu Tangshu*, 7:154.

75. Di, "Handai gongnü de chulu," 140–42; Wei, *Weishu*, 30:712.

76. Wei, *Weishu*, 7A:146, 7B:165; Li, *Beishi*, 3:95.

77. Ban, *Hanshu*, 4:123.

78. Di, "Handai gongnü de chulu," 139–42; Zhao, "Liang Han funü de zhenjie wenti," 15–16. At the end of the Western Han dynasty, all of the minor consorts were expelled from the palace. Ban, *Hanshu*, 12:360.

79. Di, "Handai gongnü de chulu," 139–40.

80. Ban, *Hanshu*, 72:3072.

81. Chaffee, *Branches of Heaven*, 58–59.

82. Ebrey, "Rethinking the Imperial Harem," 180.

83. Li, "Liangzhu wenhua shehui xingtai tanxi," 70–79; Zhao, "Liangzhu wenwu renxun," 33–35; Mao, "Huanghe shangyou de zaoqi qingtong wenming," 46; Gansu and Xibei, "Gansu Lintan Mogou mudi Qijia wenhua muzang," 12–13, 16–17. Trigger, *Understanding Early Civilizations*, 484–85, notes that human sacrifice was not uncommon in early civilizations.

84. Zhongguo, "Henan Anyang Shi Yinxu Liujiazhuang beidi," 25; Zhongguo, "Henan Anyang Shi Yinxu Wangyukoucun nandi," 3–25; Mumford, "Death Do Us Unite," 3.

85. Yang, "Churen sheng, renxun shitan," 95–96; Yin, "Dong Zhou shiqi Qin Qi xunren mu," 321–23; Mi, "Dong Zhou shiqi nüxing yiren shehui diwei," 118–20; Jin, "Dong Zhou Qi guo guizu maizang zhidu," 61–62; Yu, "Ritual Practice, Status, and Gender Identity," 123–24.

86. Thote, "Shang and Zhou Funeral Practices," 133, 135; Cook, *Death in Ancient China*, 67.
87. Cao, "Zhoudai jisi yongsheng lizhi kaolue," 21.
88. Yin, "Lun Dabaozishan Qin gong lingyuan de renxun," 82. Mumford, "Death Do Us Unite," 4–5; Zheng, *Shanggu Huaxia funü yu hunyin*, 186.
89. Li, *Taiping yulan*, 560:3A. Guo, "Qin Han shiqi de renxun xianxiang shulun," 34–35; Gan, "Luelun Qin de renxun wenhua," 14–17.
90. Raphals, *Sharing the Light*, 12; Raphals, "Arguments by Women," 179–81; Goldin, *The Culture of Sex in Ancient China*, 34–35, 37, 40–42; Li, *Women's Poetry of Late Imperial China*, 48.
91. Wei, *Weishu*, 108D:2805; Tung, *Fables for the Patriarchs*, 30–40. Sometimes scholars made a clear distinction between the ranks of imperial concubines and bureaucratic office. In Ban, *Hanshu*, 4:105, n. 2, the commentator Yan Shigu emphasized this distinction.
92. Wang, "Rank and Power among Court Ladies at Anyang," 108–10.
93. Wang, "Rank and Power among Court Ladies at Anyang," 97, 100–101, 107.
94. Van Norden, *Mengzi*, 166.
95. Chen, "Cong qingtongqi mingwen," 8–10, analyzes the origins, evolution, and orthography of these two characters.
96. Thatcher, "Marriages of the Ruling Elite," 29–30, 33–35.
97. Gao, "Qin guo hunyin zhidu yanjiu," 90–91, describes the traditional palace organization of the state of Qin prior to unification, which was similar to that of the other Zhou era states.
98. Milburn, "Palace Women in the Former Han Dynasty," 195–223; Zhao, *Nianer shi zhaji*, 4:58–59.
99. Bielenstein, "The Six Dynasties, Volume 2," 28–30.
100. Fang, *Jinshu*, 106:2777.
101. Li, *Nanshi*, 11:316–17, gives an overview of harem titles in the south. Also McMahon, *Celestial Women*, 45, 145–46; Liu, "Wei Jin Nanbeichao shidai de qie," 3, 5–6.
102. Shen, *Songshu*, 41:1269–70.
103. Wei, *Weishu*, 13:321.
104. Xiao, *Nan Qi shu*, 20:389.
105. Li, *Beishi*, 10:370.
106. Liu, *Jiu Tang shu*, 51:2161–62; Ouyang, *Xin Tangshu*, 47:1225, 76:3467; Lin, "Tangdai mingfu yanjiu," 13–22, 31–45, 58.
107. Ching-Chung, "Palace Women in the Northern Sung," 91–93; Zhu, *Liao Song Xi Xia Jin shehui shenghuo shi*, 104–5.
108. Zhang, "Jindai hougong zhidu chutan," 105, 107; McMahon, *Celestial Women*, 45.
109. McMahon, *Celestial Women*, 80; Soullière, "Palace Women in the Ming Dynasty," 242–46; Peng and Pan, *Mingdai gongting nüxingshi*, 71–98.
110. Liu, "Mingdai huang guifei fenghao chutan," 115–124.
111. Rawski, "Qing Empresses and Their Place in History," 38; Zhu, "Qingdai hougong zhidu lunshu," 323–24; Qiu, "Mingdai gonzen de rong yu ru," 91–125.
112. Li, *Beishi*, 20:736.

Chapter 6

113. Cao, *Jinwen yu Yin Zhou nüxing wenhua*, 73–75; Cao, "Baojiao de xianqu," 63–64; Xie, "Jinwen zhong suojian Xi Zhou wanghou," 143; Li, *Bureaucracy and the State*, 59; Legge, *Li Ki*, 473; Sun, *Liji jijie*, 28:763.
114. Mao, *Maoshi zhengyi*, 105–1.
115. Zhang, "Beichao gongnü kaolue," 107–111. Yan, *Quan Jin wen*, 606, documents Jin dynasty admonitions for female palace officials.
116. Wei, *Weishu*, 13:321–22; 35:808.
117. Zhang, "Sanguo Liang Jin nanchao gongü," 25–26.
118. Ouyang, *Xin Tangshu*, 47:1226–32; Zhou and Wang, *Roushun zhi xiang*, 159–70; Pan, "Tangdai de nüguan," 558–61.
119. Ching-Chung, "Palace Women in the Northern Sung," 80–81, 84; Liu, "Songdai yueshu houfei guizhi shuping," 44; Ebrey, *Emperor Huizong*, 8.
120. Soullière, "Palace Women in the Ming Dynasty," 246–62; Qiu, "Mingdai gonzen de rong yu ru," 91–125; Peng and Pan, *Mingdai gongting nüxingshi*, 223–358; Li, "Mingdai nüguan laiyuan fenxi," 63–65.
121. Wang, *Qingdai houfei gongting shenghuo*.
122. The Qing historian Zhao Yi considered the Northern Qi the most depraved dynasty. Zhao, *Nianer shi zhaji*, 15:200–201.
123. Li, *Nanshi*, 341–42.
124. Ban, *Hanshu*, 4:134; Yao, *Liangshu*, 3:97.
125. Sun, "Lixue dui Songdai nüzhuang de yinxiang," 90–91.
126. Xiao, *Nan Qi shu*, 20:391.
127. Liu, *Shih-shuo Hsin-yü*, 35 (2.13); Liu, *Shishuo xinyu huijiao jizhu*, 2:60; Yuan, "Nansong Lin'an Yang huanghou zhai," 106, 110–11.
128. Lin, *Kongjian, shenti yu lijiao guixun*, 45–70.
129. Ebrey, *Emperor Huizong*, 36.
130. Guan, "Shihuan jiding," 6.
131. Larsen, *Willow, Wine, Mirror, Moon*, 52.
132. Liu, *Jiu Tangshu*, 7:149.
133. Hu-Sterk, "Les 'poèmes de lamentation du palais,'" 7–33; Hua and Luo, "Tangdai gongyuan shi fanrong yuanyin tanlun," 104–8.
134. Chang and Saussy, *Women Writers of Traditional China*, 110.
135. Shen, *Songshu*, 18:505, 18:521; Wei, *Suishu*, 11:236, 11:247–49, 12:260–62, 12:276–78; Ouyang, *Xin Tangshu*, 24:516–18.
136. Xiao, *Nan Qi shu*, 17:336, 17:338; Wei, *Suishu*, 10:193; Liu, *Jiu Tang shu*, 45:1933, 45:1935; Ouyang, *Xin Tangshu*, 24:512–13. The vehicles used by palace women of the Liu Song dynasty were allegedly based on prototypes described in *Rites of Zhou* (*Zhou li*) and classical texts. Shen, *Songshu*, 18:495–98.
137. Shen, *Songshu*, 15:407–8.
138. Xiao, *Nan Qi shu*, 17:342–43; Shen, *Songshu*, 18:506–8; Wei, *Suishu*, 11:237, 11:243, 12:250; Guo, *Ming Qing dihou xiyin*, 66–70, 180–89.
139. Linghu, *Zhoushu*, 7:122; Li, *Beishi*, 10:377–78.
140. Ebrey, *Emperor Huizong*, 307–8.
141. Larsen, *Willow, Wine, Mirror, Moon*, 50.

142. Zhang, Hua, and Zhao, "Lun Songdai nüzi de xiangpu yundong," 76–77.

143. Huang, "Tangdai nüxing yu wenxue," 26–36, discusses the education and writings of Lady Xu, a talented concubine from the reign of Emperor Taizong of Tang.

144. Wang, "Tangdai nüzi jiaoyu xintan," 138–40.

145. During the Chen dynasty, female tutors taught palace women how to compose and perform poetry. They were expected to be able to extemporize and chant poetry at banquets. Li, *Nanshi*, 12:348.

146. Xie, "Mingdai gongting nüjiao lunxi," 95–102.

147. Kroll, "The Life and Writings of Xu Hui," 35–64; Xie, "Songdai gongting nüshiren zuopin gailan," 134–35; Xie, "Songdai gongting nüshiren zuopin leibie fenxi," 8–11.

148. Ebrey, *Emperor Huizong*, 126.

149. Schafer, "The Princess Realized in Jade," 1–23; Li, *You yu you*, 169, 172, 178–200; Li, "Tangdai gongzhu rudao," 159–90; Jiao and Zhang, "Tangdai Chang'an gongzhu daoguan," 25–30; Jiang and Jiang, "Tangdai gongnü shenghuo shulue," 57–63.

150. Yan, *Quan Jin wen*, 64:668, sets down mourning rules for imperial concubines in the Jin dynasty. Shang, "Tangdai gongren gongni mu," 211–33, describes the burial of Tang harem women.

151. Jiang and Jiang, "Tangdai gongnü shenghuo shulue," 60; Hu, "Tangdai wanggu gongnü muzhi mingwen," 137.

152. For some examples of consorts' epitaphs see Yan, *Quan Jin wen*, 93:992–95. For epitaphs of female officials see Zhao, *Han Wei nanbeichao muzhi huibian*, 123–24; Zhou and Wang, *Roushun zhi xiang*, 155–57.

153. Shen, *Songshu*, 17:467–68, 17:470–77, 19:537.

CHAPTER 7

Strategies of Restraint

THROUGHOUT HISTORY MEN HAVE CONCOCTED VARIOUS WAYS TO BLOCK women from holding power. Each culture deterred female authority differently depending on prevailing circumstances and beliefs. Ancient Romans criticized powerful women as having upended the natural order, and they disparaged the men around them as effeminate.[1] Muslim scholars quoted a hadith that claimed "those who entrust power to a woman will never enjoy prosperity."[2] Ottoman sultans wed foreign slave women knowing that their consorts' lowly background would likely prevent them from gaining power.[3] And during Europe's Middle Ages, male writers lambasted reigning queens as cruel, licentious, and destructive.[4] As new forms of government emerged, the mechanisms for disempowering women altered in tandem. During the early modern era, new institutions such as legalism and constitutionalism explicitly prohibited women from wielding power.[5]

In most political systems, even if a woman gained authority it was impractical for her to rule on her own. People usually considered it unthinkable for a woman to issue orders to important men. When a woman found herself in a position of power she usually relied heavily on her husband to defend her domain and help her fulfill her duties. Because female rulers were exceptional, men in most societies did not bother to develop highly articulated ideologies that would constrain female power.[6] In places where women rarely threatened male prerogatives, men did not feel the need to justify or defend patriarchy. Male privilege was simply the prevailing assumption.

CHAPTER 7

In imperial China numerous women gained power, presenting a notable exception to global norms. Empresses dowager, empresses, princesses, and lesser consorts sometimes intervened in the political apparatus, mostly before the Song dynasty. A few women even became de facto rulers. From the standpoint of world history, the appearance of so many powerful women over such a long stretch of time seems remarkable. Yet, the price for defying patriarchy was high. Because so many women threatened male power, men developed elaborate ideas and institutions to thwart them. Ironically, the unusually high degree of female power in China gave rise to perhaps the world's most highly developed array of anti-female ideologies. Even when the imperial era had just begun, Han dynasty officials were already warning about the deleterious influence of palace women.[7] As time went on, these complaints coalesced into ideas and measures that became increasingly more effective at blocking female ambition.

Not all criticisms of female authority can be dismissed as male prejudice. Within the context of the Chinese imperial system, women's power could have negative consequences. Most importantly, women pursued their goals informally outside the standard institutions of government. Within the imperial system, legitimate power descended along the male line, preventing a woman from ruling in her own name. To gain authority, she had no choice but to act outside regular rules and conventions, undercutting orderly governance. Female power thus inadvertently resulted in administrative decline and institutional decay. Since antiquity, Chinese moralists had declared that powerful women brought down dynasties. There was a grain of truth in this claim as women had no option but to bypass systematic administration in pursuit of their objectives.

The basis of female power was propinquity to a man who held legitimate authority. Therefore, a woman usually gained power as wife, mother, daughter, or concubine of a male ruler. The closer her relationship with the ruler, the more power she might accrue. Some women employed beauty or charm to increase their influence. Historians criticized this sort of behavior, portraying beautiful women as evil and dangerous.

Not all women relied on sensual allure. Some women were highly capable and they used their skill to appropriate authority from less-competent men. In consequence, moralists were often suspicious of female talent because they realized that it could threaten patriarchal rule.[8] Certain circumstances also gave savvy women an opening to gain power.[9] New rulers were often children and unable to handle matters on their own. A mother would sometimes take advantage of this power vacuum to seize authority from her son or grandson. And when an emperor seemed insufficiently strong or legitimate, an empress dowager could exploit his weak image to seize authority.

The ancient classics constituted the foundation of political thought in the imperial era. Each of these texts was composed by different authors in different periods for different purposes so the contents differ considerably. Although these works do not discuss women's matters systematically, they contain many ideas that formed the basis for later ideologies limiting female power. The classics became the foundation of orthodox political ideology during the Han dynasty when officials and thinkers were constructing the system of imperial rule. Significantly, at that time new views toward womanhood were emerging as well. Han dynasty scholars referred to the classics to diminish women's public role and restrict them from participating in government.[10]

Han scholars referred to the ancient *Classic of Poetry* (*Shijing*) to justify ritual restraints on women.[11] Several poems in the collection describe irresponsible rulers led astray by alluring women. Instead of devoting themselves to statecraft, these besotted men wasted time feasting and drinking in the harem.[12] Although these poems do not portray women as fundamentally evil, they are shown as uninterested in professional ethics and duty so they tend to exert a negative influence on powerful men.[13] The identity of the authors and characters of most of these poems is unclear, but during the Western Han, the Mao version of the *Classic of Poetry* attributed many pieces to specific female authors.[14] Although modern scholars consider most of these attributions highly dubious, grounding poems in a specific context turned them into clear case studies of good and bad female behavior. Although the poems portray women in various ways, the influential Mao commentary tended to associate women with licentiousness, and this reading had a profound impact on subsequent views.

The *Book of Documents* (*Shangshu*) contains some of the earliest reliable texts on governance, and these pronouncements had a major influence on the development of political discourse. This work includes a famous passage about a hen who crowed like a cock.[15] Historians eventually identified the transgressive hen with the infamous Bao Si, a royal consort who allegedly brought down the Western Zhou dynasty by encouraging the king to engage in decadent behavior.[16] This image of the licentious woman leading a ruler astray became a standard trope in historical writing and gave rise to the assumption that a powerful woman was likely to be sexually depraved. Because of this negative stereotype, when an empress gained power, if she was not careful to project an image of unimpeachable probity, she would be accused of extramarital liaisons or even of putting together a male harem.[17] Although these allegations were usually false, they nevertheless served as an effective way to denigrate female power.

Classic texts warned that a licentious woman could use music to debilitate a susceptible man, a viewpoint picked up by historians. Confucians saw proper music as restrained, courtly, and preferably performed by men.[18] The *Book of Documents* notes that women in the age of the virtuous sage ruler Shun used restrained music as a didactic medium. However, the wicked King Zhou of Shang abandoned the temperate music of his ancestors and amused the women around him with lewd tunes. This display of iniquity presaged the dynasty's collapse.[19] Likewise, when historian Ban Gu wanted to portray the Han dynasty Emperor Ai as dissolute, he emphasized the ruler's obsession with female musicians.[20] Improper music served as an analogy for the harem's sensuality, which threatened to distract the ruler and lead him away from the path of righteousness.[21]

The *Zuo Tradition* (*Zuozhuan*) relates several incidents in which a woman uses her appearance to seduce a ruler and encourage him to misbehave.[22] Women act as a destabilizing force in the narrative, and the text depicts a state's decline by stressing a ruler's inappropriate interactions with women.[23] The *Zuo* also portrays women as untrustworthy because they are torn between loyalty to father and to husband, whose interests sometimes conflict. Overall, the *Zuo Tradition* contains ample material

Bao Si.
SOURCE: *PUBLIC DOMAIN.*

justifying the exclusion of women from affairs of state. Several other Eastern Zhou dynasty texts picked up this theme and amplified it.[24]

The ritual canon had a unique role in restraining women as it set down explicit rules for the proper behavior of people occupying different social roles. Ritual texts promoted the idea of the "three obediences" or "three followings" (*san cong*), with a woman obeying her father in youth, her husband in marriage, and her son in widowhood.[25] In fact, widows rarely obeyed their sons, and wives did not always submit to their husbands. Nevertheless, the inclusion of this principle in classical ritual provided a prestigious rationalization of a woman's subjugation by male family members throughout her life trajectory.

CHAPTER 7

During the Western Han era, Sima Qian's comprehensive model of the rise and fall of dynasties cautioned against allowing women to wield power. Sima took the Mandate of Heaven theory, a foundation of political discourse since the Western Zhou, and fleshed out the details. According to this influential historical model, a dynasty begins with the reign of a benevolent ruler paired with an equally upright wife. Their goodness attracts the support of heaven, winning the new dynasty the celestial mandate necessary to succeed. Over time, however, ethical standards inevitably deteriorate. Eventually, a wicked final ruler and his evil consort bring down the dynasty. Sima Qian's interpretation of the Mandate of Heaven is notable for giving women a more conspicuous role in dynastic success and failure, positioning them closer to the center of the dynastic cycle.[26] Although he believed that the wives of dynastic founders played a significant part in initiating new eras, he put greatest emphasis on the evil women who shared culpability for the collapse of dynasties.

Sima Qian's ideas about the place of women in history grew out of his training in the ancient classics. During the Han, history was not yet an independent subject of inquiry and was still subordinate to classical studies.[27] Perhaps the most significant influence on Sima Qian's view of women was the *Classic of Poetry*. One poem in this collection blamed a woman for the destruction of the Western Zhou: "Majestic was the capital of Zhou, / But Lady Bao Si destroyed it."[28] Nor do these poems limit culpability to one woman. They blame womankind in general for exerting a destructive influence on the state.[29]

> A clever man builds a city;
> A clever woman tears it down.
> Oh, that clever woman,
> She is an owl, she is a shrike.
> The wagging tongues of women
> Are the instruments of our decline.
> No, disorder does not come down from Heaven,
> Rather it is the spawn of these women.

The poet draws an unequivocal conclusion from these accusations: "Thus no woman serves the public, / They stay with their weaving and their loom."

Sima Qian used these ancient admonitions to construct a comprehensive view of women's role in history. His interpretation had several important uses. It provided a detailed explanation for dynastic collapse, emphasized the moral structure of history, and acted as an ideology to restrain powerful women. Scapegoating women for dynastic collapse also exonerated male rulers and allowed people to look up to previous dynasties as models despite their ultimate failure.[30]

Subsequent Han dynasty thinkers accepted Sima Qian's view of women's role in the historical process. Most importantly Liu Xiang, compiler of the first book of narratives about women, integrated these notions into his portrayals of historic women.[31] But Liu took this interpretation further, linking the fall of dynasties more directly to the malfeasance of evil women. Liu did not portray women as inherently evil. He believed that like men women can act for both good and ill. However, some women are depraved, and their influence on a powerful man can have catastrophic consequences. The writings of Sima Qian and Liu Xiang had a major impact on standard views of female power. In response to these ideas, Han dynasty officials repeatedly submitted memorials reminding the ruler that female power can bring about dynastic decline.[32]

The Han endured for more than four centuries so the dynasty's ultimate fall demanded explanation. Scholars discussing this problem most often singled out moral decline as the main factor for the dynasty's decline.[33] Many medieval accounts blame empresses dowager and their kinsmen for this moral rot. One medieval historian singles out Empress Lü and the mother of Qin Shihuang for having "sullied two states," while another asserted that ever since high antiquity, the destruction of states had been brought about by women.[34] Poets sometimes conveyed a woman's beauty by ironically calling her a "city destroyer" or "realm destroyer."[35]

During the Tang, the idea that dynasties are brought down by women remained vivid. One official memorialized to the emperor that ancient rulers sent female musicians to a rival's court to lead him to decadence and ruin.³⁶ Historians often blamed empresses for upsetting the Tang political order.³⁷ Qing historian Zhao Yi blamed the fall of the Tang on emperors who were sexually enamored of wayward women.³⁸ Wu Zetian's shocking usurpation was used to validate warnings about the dangers of female power, leading rulers and officials to increase restraints on palace women.³⁹

Writers and artists transferred this view of women's deleterious historical role into various media and transmitted it to a wide audience. A series of portraits of famous emperors painted in the eleventh century portrays both good and evil rulers. While the good emperors are surrounded by male attendants, the bad rulers have female companions.⁴⁰ In the realm of literature, authors combined popular stories of mischievous fox spirits with narratives of beautiful women who brought down dynasties.⁴¹ Other writers concocted accounts of strange foreign lands, real or mythical, ruled over by women. They used these exotic images as a foil to China, contrasting the female power of allegedly barbarous foreign peoples with the restraining rites and ethics of virtuous Chinese.⁴²

The elaboration of metaphysical thought provided new ways to construct ideologies that implicitly disparaged women and limited their autonomy. Although the ideas of Eastern Zhou thinkers differed considerably, many assumed that the cosmos was made up of interacting binary elements.⁴³ They believed that people perceive a single noumenon as two dynamic principles. These paired parts had various names: heaven and earth; yin and yang; *qian* and *kun*. Initially, none of these pairs had anything to do with gender. Over time, however, thinkers began to see them as analogues to another pair: man and woman.⁴⁴

During the Han dynasty, experts in the classics imaginatively reinterpreted ancient texts to justify increasingly more elaborate metaphysical theories. By situating gender within this novel framework, they imbued womanhood with new meanings. The scholar Dong Zhongshu had a central role in the Han dynasty metaphysical turn. His views of women evolved over the course of his long official career, and he applied them differently at each stage. Most fundamentally, Dong saw the structure of the cosmos as a template for ordering human relationships.⁴⁵ Accordingly he reasoned that the interaction of women and men should follow that of yin and yang or the five phases. Dong believed that cosmological analogues to gender proved the inherent superiority of men over women. This approach to cosmology justified the imposition of stringent ritual restraints on women.

The classic annal *Springs and Autumns* (*Chunqiu*) portrayed natural disasters as signs of heaven's will. Because Han dynasty thinkers put renewed emphasis on the Mandate of Heaven theory, they saw good and bad omens as clues they could use to determine heaven's attitude toward governance and the moral tenor of society. Portent specialists attributed many natural disasters recorded in old texts to female malfeasance.[46] For example, Dong Zhongshu declared that an ancient flood had been brought about by the licentiousness of a noblewoman named Ai Jiang.[47] Her malfeasance unleashed vast amounts of yin vapor, initiating a deluge.

These scholars did not limit their portent interpretations to remote historic events. After classical scholarship established the prestige of omen interpretation, officials could use this method to criticize powerful women of the present day. They blamed the misbehavior of wayward consorts on solar eclipses and earthquakes.[48] Men began to take for granted the devastating impact that female power could have on the workings of the natural world. Emperor Cheng of the Han dynasty declared that an eclipse would surely occur whenever there was a dearth of masculinity.[49] Han dynasty portent studies had a major impact on assumptions about the impact of female power. In subsequent dynasties, people continued to blame powerful women for natural disasters.[50]

The ideologies countering female power at court could be further enhanced by generalizing their provisions to encompass not just the women surrounding the emperor but all women. Patriarchy restrained empresses as well as commoners, making it an effective political ideology.[51] Ritual texts demanded that a woman obey her husband, seclude herself from men as much as possible, and forgo activities outside the home.[52] Although these admonitions were not addressed specifically to empresses, ritual nevertheless served a political purpose by imposing burdensome restrictions on palace women. The Han dynasty government initiated a system commending women for virtues in the ritual code, promoting these restrictive ideals in society at large.⁵³ These ideals continued to influence elite views of proper gender roles, and ethicists often demanded that women conform to the classic rites.⁵⁴

The idea that female nature posed a threat to the well-being of the state made palace women a target during periodic sumptuary campaigns. In times of crisis, officials called for the expulsion of women from the palace. Many memorials equated concubines with luxury goods, portraying them as wasteful and enervating.⁵⁵ Emperors often heeded this advice.⁵⁶ During the Tang, whenever disaster struck, the ruler issued a special edict ordering the expulsion of harem women as a show of austerity.⁵⁷ They accepted the belief that undue female presence in the palace, the symbolic center of the realm, generated an excess of yin in the cosmos, giving rise to cataclysm. Although Dong Zhongshu's cosmological theories rationalized the expulsion of palace women, this practice had practical reasons as well. The Tang palace housed thousands of female inhabitants, draining state resources. Expelling some palace women served as a useful way to cut expenditures during times of disaster, allowing these funds to be put to better use.

The Tang era saw a revival of Confucian doctrine, and these ideas reached deeper into society than ever before. When the dynasty began, education inculcated aristocratic values that allowed women more autonomy. However, classical ideas eventually became resurgent. As the scope of learning narrowed, views of model womanhood simplified, shifting the focus from talent toward virtue.⁵⁸ Writers portrayed women more simplistically, employing stereotypical terms and a contracted range of roles and behaviors.⁵⁹ Confucian revivalists at this time were relatively moderate and they made limited demands on women in the name of propriety.⁶⁰ Yet, even in the early part of the dynasty, women from the upper reaches of society showed increasing interest in the Confucian rites, and more of them observed these strictures. The legal system also integrated Confucian teachings, making gender inequality a basic principle of Tang law.⁶¹ The government enthusiastically promoted Confucian ethics by expanding the commendation system for women, giving these values the imprimatur of the state.⁶²

The Song dynasty Neo-Confucian movement revived interest in metaphysics, leading thinkers to reconceptualize female ethics. Many scholars had great respect for the *Classic of Changes* (*Yijing*) and used this text's cosmology to justify gender inequality.[63] Neo-Confucians did not consider women inherently evil or condemn them outright. However, they saw them as the weaker sex, unfit to hold power, and potentially a negative influence on men. Neo-Confucians used metaphysics to rationalize stringent female ethics. Most fundamentally, they demanded that women be confined to the domestic realm. Neo-Confucians also encouraged women to be gentle and submissive and to forsake cultivating their talents and pursuing achievements.

The Neo-Confucian movement turned away from the flexible views of gender that prevailed during the Tang, imposing far more demanding strictures on women. Although the level of female education increased, women's intellectual training stressed mastery of Confucian rites and ethics. This sort of education sought to encourage passivity by instilling patriarchal standards of conduct.[64] Although aimed generally at women of all backgrounds, these trends had the effect of reducing the autonomy of empresses and other palace ladies.

Beyond the abstractions of general ideologies, each dynasty also issued specific rules and principles limiting the actions of palace women. During the Han dynasty, Emperor Wu set an influential example by removing his mother from politics, a move commended by subsequent historians.[65] However, later emperors did not follow his lead, and empresses dowager and consort kin often gained control over the government. Numerous episodes of bad government during the Han eventually inspired the rulers of subsequent dynasties to revive the policy of Emperor Wu. Cao Pi's influential edict prohibiting empress dowagers from participating in the government took this position.[66] During the fourth century, court ceremonial forbade women from even being physically visible during court proceedings. If a woman wanted to attend an audience, she had to hide behind a curtain, ostensibly for the sake of propriety.[67] Henceforth, palace women were usually invisible to the men who managed the government.

Chapter 7

The rise of bureaucratic administration during the Song dynasty empowered officials, who regarded palace women and consort kinsmen as rivals.[68] Moreover the enduring trauma of Empress Wu's reign had made clear the threat that female power could pose to male ambitions. These concerns led officials to keep palace women away from politics by enforcing a regimen of stringent limits on their movements and behavior. They confined harem women to the palace, monitored their behavior, and forbade them from communicating with officials in the outer court.

Scholars and officials excoriated female authority and leveled a barrage of criticism at any ambitious woman who tried to accrue power. The fifth-century book *The Literary Mind and the Carving of Dragons* (*Wenxin diaolong*), the most influential Chinese work of literary criticism, includes a section on historical writing that condemns female interference in politics. The author cites historical examples to prove that powerful women have a negative influence on government.[69] This sort of viewpoint became standard, and many historical works issued blanket condemnations of imperial consorts who participated in affairs of state.[70] This attitude can be seen in the portrayal of Empress Sun, the wife of the Ming dynasty Xuande emperor. Although she participated in politics to some degree, imperial historians condemned her even though she did not do anything particularly bad.[71] In the eyes of history, her crime was not a particular action but simply becoming involved in government.

To prevent a woman from gaining power, some emperors either declined to name an empress or else gave the title to several women at the same time, degrading the honor.[72] Alternatively, an emperor could have an empress but choose an official spouse who would be unlikely to gain power. Mésalliance also served as an effective strategy to keep women out of politics. Mindful of the disruptive influence of empresses and their kinsmen during the Han, many rulers of the Northern Dynasties took wives from very low backgrounds.[73] Sometimes they even wed slaves. The high born despised these women, and the women would have found it difficult to attract useful allies. The rulers of the Ming were the first native emperors to adopt this strategy and deliberately marry down. By choosing consorts from politically insignificant families, they reduced the possibility that their spouses would become politically active.[74] The Qing maintained this policy, and emperors continued to choose empresses from relatively modest backgrounds.

The palace education system also served to restrain consorts. Over time, the focus shifted away from the composition and appreciation of poetry toward the study of Confucian ethical works that taught patriarchal values. Historians presented empresses who enjoyed moral works as paragons of virtue so harem women knew that if they studied these texts and followed their injunctions, they would be remembered as model consorts.[75] Women were enjoined to observe physical restraints on their movements and cultivate a passive demeanor. Although most of these texts were aimed at ordinary women, these teachings assumed a political dimension when applied to harem women, preventing them from behaving in ways that would allow them to accrue power. Obsession with the so-called virtue of palace women largely grew out of a desire to keep women insulated from government affairs.

Finally, emperors sometimes used terror as a weapon against women. During the reigns of Emperors Wu and Xuan of the Han dynasty, palace women were accused of using black magic to harm the monarch.[76] The palace and court descended into hysteria, and thousands died in the ensuing purges. The causes of this panic remain a topic of debate. Most scholars take this hysteria at face value. They assume that people of the time believed in black magic and feared it. Recently, however, some revisionists have proposed that black magic was merely an excuse for emperors to execute their enemies and rivals, including threatening palace women and their meddlesome kinsmen.[77] Whatever the motivation for these purges, palace women and their families suffered disproportionately. Terror cowed and preventing them from exercising much influence during this era of witchcraft hysteria.

Murder was the most extreme form of terror directed at harem women. Emperor Wu of the Han killed the mother of his heir apparent to prevent the emergence of a powerful empress dowager after his death, a custom that was revived again by the Wei dynasty.[78] During the Ming, this ancient custom was revived and the dynasty's first five emperors practiced human sacrifice. When an emperor died, concubines were killed and placed in his tomb to accompany him to the afterlife.[79] Given

CHAPTER 7

the influence of Neo-Confucian ethics at the time, such cruelty seems jarring. The revival of human sacrifice at such a late date seems to have been driven by a combination of religious piety and the dynasty's unusually cruel, authoritarian mindset. Killing palace women also reduced their social standing and ensured that they would behave cautiously. A woman knew that if she stood out from her peers, she might be selected for execution. Ming human sacrifice presents one of the most extreme measures used to neutralize ambitious consorts. Female power sometimes inspired a violent reaction.

NOTES

1. Freisenbruch, *Caesar's Wives*, 9–10.
2. Gavin R. G. Hambly, "Introduction." Hambly, *Women in the Medieval Islamic World*, 9–10, 12.
3. Freely, *Inside the Seraglio*, 88–98.
4. Weir, *Eleanor of Aquitaine*, 344–45.
5. Cosandey, "De lance en quenouille," 799, 815–17.
6. In this context, ideology refers to ideas that present the self-interested behavior of one group as benefiting society as a whole. Trigger, *Understanding Early Civilizations*, 410.
7. Gu, *Handai funü shenghuo qingkuang*, 37–38.
8. Mou, *Gentlemen's Prescriptions for Women's Lives*, 66.
9. Liu, "Songdai houfei yu diwei chuancheng," 429.
10. Wu, *Handai nüxing lijiao yanjiu*, 139–43.
11. Wu, *Handai nüxing lijiao yanjiu*, 59–77.
12. Goldin, *The Culture of Sex in Ancient China*, 51. For ancient views of the moral implications of music see Li, *The Readability of the Past*, 118, 133.
13. Kinney, "The Mao Commentary to the Book of Odes," 80–82.
14. Kinney, "The Mao Commentary to the Book of Odes," 65, 67.
15. Kong, *Shangshu*, 158.2; Qi, "Cong Yinxu jiaguwen kan Shangdai funü shehui diwei," 128; Li, *Landscape and Power*, 202–3.
16. Li, *Landscape and Power*, 195–96, 199–203, 214, 232; Milburn, "The Wicked Queen," 1–25; Hinsch, "Evil Women and Dynastic Collapse," 62–81.
17. McMahon, "The Polyandrous Empress," 47, 50.
18. Lam, "The Presence and Absence of Female Musicians," 104.
19. Kong, *Shangshu*, 46.2–47.1; Ban, *Hanshu*, 22:1038–39.
20. Ban, *Hanshu*, 22:1072.
21. Li, *The Readability of the Past*, 147. For other examples of the negative impact of sensual music see Ban, *Hanshu*, 22:1039, 22:1072, 27A:1329, 27B1:1373. Also see discussions of the political impact of sensual music in Lam, "The Presence and Absence of Female Musicians," 99–100; Gu, *Handai funü shenghuo qingkuang*, 71–76.

22. Li, *The Readability of the Past*, 154–57, 159–60; Goldin, *The Culture of Sex in Ancient China*, 61–62.
23. Li, *The Readability of the Past*, 148–50.
24. Goldin, *The Culture of Sex in Ancient China*, 58; Wu, *Handai nüxing lijiao yanjiu*, 27–28.
25. Liu, *Handai hunyin zhidu*, 21; Wu, *Handai nüxing lijiao yanjiu*, 21–22.
26. Raphals, *Sharing the Light*, 15–20, 61–70; Wu, *Handai nüxing lijiao yanjiu*, 33–38.
27. Lu, *Wei Jin shixue de sixiang yu shehui jichu*, 30.
28. Waley, *The Book of Songs*, 167–70; Karlgren, *The Book of Odes*, 135–38 (Mao 192).
29. Waley, *The Book of Songs*, 284 (Mao 264); Karlgren, *The Book of Odes*, 237.
30. Li, *Landscape and Power*, 202–3.
31. Ban, *Hanshu*, 36:1957; Zhang, "Liu Xiang lishi zhexue fenxi," 26–31.
32. Liu, "Calendrical Computation Numbers," 299.
33. Holcombe, "Re-Imagining China," 7.
34. Wei, *Weishu*, 93:1986; Fang, *Jinshu*, 32:984; Li, *Nanshi*, 10:311.
35. Birrell, *Chinese Love Poetry*, 209–10, 233, 257; Xu, *Jianzhu yutai xinyong*, 6:16b–18a, 7:18b, 8:11b.
36. Ouyang, *Xin Tangshu*, 111:4297.
37. Ouyang, *Xin Tangshu*, 76:3468.
38. Zhao, *Nianer shi zhaji*, 19:256.
39. Davis, "Chaste and Filial Women," 213–17.
40. Ning, "Imperial Portraiture," 96–128.
41. Huntington, "Foxes and Sex," 101–9.
42. Jay, "Imagining Matriarchy," 220–29.
43. Liu, "An Exploration of the Mode of Thinking," 387–97.
44. Raphals, *Sharing the Light*, 139–93. Hinsch, *Women in Early Imperial China*, 153–67.
45. Gu, *Handai funü shenghuo qingkuang*, 30–33; Wu, *Handai nüxing lijiao yanjiu*, 43–44, 77–83.
46. Hinsch, "The Criticism of Powerful Women," 96–121.
47. Ban, *Hanshu*, 27A:1344. For similar portent interpretations see Ban, *Hanshu*, 27A:1322–23, 27A:1339, 27A:1343, 27C:1432, 27D:1462, 27D:1465.
48. Ban, *Hanshu*, 27E:1502, 60:2671.
49. Ban, *Hanshu*, 10:309.
50. Wei, *Suishu*, 22:622.
51. Wu, *Handai nüxing lijiao yanjiu*, 44–49.
52. Wu, *Handai nüxing lijiao yanjiu*, 21–22, 40–41, 51, 83–118, 134–38; Liu, *Handai hunyin zhidu*, 13, 21.
53. Gu, *Handai funü shenghuo qingkuang*, 38–63; Wu, *Handai nüxing lijiao yanjiu*, 134–38.
54. Wei, *Weishu*, 7B:163; Shen, *Songshu*, 60:1621, 64:1704.
55. Ouyang, *Xin Tangshu*, 107:4069.
56. Ban, *Hanshu*, 72:3072; Li, *Beishi*, 10:370.
57. Li, "Zhaihai yinsu yu Tangdai chu gongren kao," 90–95, 105.

Chapter 7

58. Wong, "Confucian Ideal and Reality," 270–71; Sun, "Lun Tangdai shehui biangeqi de nüxing jiaoyu," 41–47.
59. Mou, Gentlemen's Prescriptions for Women's Lives," 189–91; Yu, "Cong liang *Tang shu Lienü zhuan*," 30.
60. Chiu-Duke, "The Role of Confucian Revivalists," 54, 65, 92–93.
61. Zhang and Yuan, "Tangren funüguan," 12.
62. Zhang, "Tangdai cishi yu jingbiao zhidu," 146–52; Zhang, "Shilun Tangdai nüde jingbiao zhidu de fazhan," 232–38.
63. Peng and Wang, "Songdai lixue xingbie yishi tanwei," 107–9; Van Ess, "Cheng Yi and His Ideas about Women," 63–77; Tie, *Songdai shiren jieceng nüxing yanjiu*, 45–85.
64. Ebrey, "Education Through Ritual," 277.
65. Liu, "Wei Jin yihuan shijia," 29.
66. Chen, *Sanguozhi*, 2:80; Liu, "Wei Jin yihuan shijia," 30.
67. McMahon, "Women Rulers in Imperial China," 195–96.
68. Liu, "Songdai yueshu houfei guizhi," 43–45.
69. Liu, *Wenxin diaolong*, 16:291; Liu, *The Literary Mind and the Carving of Dragons*, 114–15. Liu, "Wei Jin yihuan shijia," 32–33.
70. Liu, "Wei Jin yihuan shijia," 30–31, 33.
71. Zheng, "Lun Xuanzong Sun Huanghou," 13–18.
72. Eisenberg, *Kingship in Early Medieval China*, 161–63.
73. Li, *Beishi*, 14:524–25; Holmgren, "Imperial Marriage in the Native Chinese and Non-Han State," 79–80.
74. Holmgren, "Imperial Marriage in the Native Chinese and Non-Han State," 74–75; McMahon, "Women Rulers in Imperial China," 212.
75. Ouyang, *Xin Tangshu*, 76:3468, 3470–71.
76. Loewe, "The Case of Witchcraft in 91 B.C.," 159–96; Loewe, *Crisis and Conflict*, 37–90.
77. Pu, "Wugu zhi huo de zhengzhi yiyi," 511–38.
78. Liu, "Wei Jin yihuan shijia," 30.
79. Tang, "Lun Mingdai renxun zhidu de feichu," 120–24.

Conclusion

The Power of Chinese Empresses

To understand the main iterations of female power in China, it is necessary to look beyond the stories of individual women and appreciate how the institution of empress developed. Over two millennia the role of imperial consort repeatedly altered in response to shifting conditions. Many changes came in response to power struggles. Officials usually sought to exploit or limit the power of women close to the emperor while empresses themselves did their best to overcome these constraints to empower themselves and pursue what they regarded as their best interests.

The Chinese empress had significance far beyond the history of China. Because China's monarchy has such a long and richly recorded history, it serves as a uniquely rich trove of raw material that can reveal many facts about the general contours of historic female power and how it differed from male authority. Chinese empresses faced a wide range of circumstances so they gained power in various ways. They also employed power to pursue different goals. Some tried to promote themselves and their families. Others enjoyed exercising power and deciding policy. Many empresses, cowed by restraints and expectations, merely wanted to obtain a modicum of respect.

The history of Chinese empresses calls into question one of the fundamental principles of feminist theory: the conviction that gender is paramount in determining social identity. Some scholars have expanded this assertion into an interpretive paradigm called social identity theory. They suggest that individual identity is primarily based on membership in a

Conclusion

socially significant group.¹ Feminist theorists would argue that gender is the most fundamental social division and hence the basis of individual identity.² Yet, society encompasses many other groups as well. Many scholars have objected that social class takes priority over gender and that a woman's identity is closer to that of men in the same social class than to the identity of women of different strata.³ Accounts of Chinese empresses are staggeringly rich, providing copious evidence that might be used to enhance either of these arguments. A woman could only gain significant administrative authority if she were related to an emperor, so her position amid China's strata provided an entrée for her to gain power. Yet, powerful women and men were perceived very differently, and their gender determined how they would gain and use power.

Empresses achieved high position due to the organizational principles underlying the imperial system that commenced with the unification of China. Although some royal consorts exercised power during remote antiquity, their status declined in tandem with the Zhou monarchy. Queens had become nonentities by the late Eastern Zhou. That aristocratic society tied legitimate authority to hereditary status that passed down the male line of descent. Had that political system endured, women would never have become such important political actors. However, when Emperor Qin Shihuang unified China, he swept away Zhou norms and replaced them with a novel imperial system that provided consorts with unprecedented opportunities. Under the new scheme of government, proximity to the emperor replaced genealogy as the prime factor determining power. Because mothers, wives, and concubines lived near the ruler and interacted with him frequently, they were well positioned to take advantage of this new form of power relations.

Some empresses exercised power on their own while others worked in conjunction with their kinsmen. During the Eastern Han dynasty in particular, empresses dowager and their male family members often cooperated to dominate the government. If an empress dowager's natal kin occupied high positions in the military and civil bureaucracy, a woman confined to the palace could extend her reach deep into the most important mechanisms of government. However, consort kinsmen were usually arrogant and extravagantly corrupt, and they aggravated the chaos that

CONCLUSION

ultimately led to the collapse of the Han dynasty. Subsequent empresses came to realize that much of the antipathy toward powerful consorts was actually a fear of their kinsmen. For this reason, from the Tang dynasty onward powerful empresses usually limited the privileges of their male kinsmen and sought to handle matters on their own. Also, from the mid-Tang onward emperors usually took wives from lower backgrounds so the kinsmen of empresses dowager were far less useful than before.

Powerful women attracted formidable enemies. Officialdom resented empresses who sidelined the regular bureaucratic procedures of government. Palace eunuchs considered them rivals because both sides pursued the same goal: usurpation of the emperor's prerogatives. The ruler's relatives feared that a domineering empress might overthrow the dynasty or weaken the imperial line. And literati gentry schooled in Confucian ethics felt repugnance toward powerful women for transgressing gender norms. Over time the various antagonists of empresses fashioned elaborate misogynistic ideologies and rules intended to curb female ambition.

Empresses had no natural allies except for their own kinsmen. Almost everyone else in government and at the top of society resented them and opposed their rise. Given the breadth of this antipathy and the daunting arsenal of tools deployed by their male foes, it seems remarkable that so many empresses nonetheless gained authority and influenced matters of public concern.

Although both men and women exercised political power, the ways in which they did so differed substantially. Whereas the rightfulness of male authority was never questioned, officialdom and the literati considered female power illegitimate and unseemly, and they contrived many ways to block female ambitions. The enemies of powerful women did not always succeed. Palace women were highly diverse. They came from different backgrounds, had various characteristics, and pursued a range of goals. The ideologies, rites, and regulations that men devised could not possibly thwart every empress. Some astute women found ways to circumvent these restrictions and gain power.[4]

Because men resisted overt female participation in administration, women and men pursued their goals differently. This study has described the many methods that empresses used to get what they wanted.[5] If

CONCLUSION

a woman felt herself to be in a position of strength, she expressed her demands directly. Alternatively, an empress dowager might employ the rhetoric of filial piety to demand obedience from a young or weak emperor. More often a woman would try to influence events obliquely by soliciting the support of the emperor and high officials.

An empress could wield far more power if she could find ways to justify her authority. Yet, because governance was grounded in patriarchal ideology, legitimating female power was always difficult. Max Weber divided legitimation into three types. The first of these, legal domination, encompasses the laws and rules that regulate government. In China, these included the provision that only male descendants of a dynasty's founding emperor could rule. Due to this ironclad tenet, a woman could not appeal to the standards of the Chinese political system to legitimate her authority.

Second, power can be legitimized by traditional domination, which is the body of established practices and beliefs affiliated with a political system. China's political traditions generally opposed female power. Ever since the emergence of the earliest states in high antiquity, only a man could serve as a rightful sovereign. This deeply rooted convention explicitly prohibited female rulership. Nevertheless, some women managed to gain considerable power, and their actions served as precedents that helped legitimize episodes of female authority. Most influentially, the actions of Empress Lü, the wife of the first Han dynasty emperor, led people to regard the role of empress dowager as potentially powerful. The new imperial system had not had time to establish firm institutions and principles. The mechanics of governance were still highly malleable, and Empress Dowager Lü exploited this ambiguity. The precedent that she established at the beginning of the imperial era showed the political elite that the wives and mothers of emperors might possibly wield power. Numerous subsequent instances of rule by empresses dowager further legitimized female rule.

Charisma, Weber's third type of domination, was a particularly useful tool for ambitious palace women. Chinese empresses were not chosen for their abilities, and most were unremarkable. Even so, a minority of consorts happened to be unusually likeable, intelligent, talented, virtuous, educated, or sly. A woman with special qualities could sometimes use them to legitimize her exercise of power despite institutional restrictions. Although elaborate court decorum constrained most empresses, they nevertheless had control over certain aspects of their own person and immediate environment, and some were able to manipulate these factors to assert legitimacy and gain support. Empresses often stressed symbolism, employing religious emblems and images to compare themselves to holy figures.[6] A consort might dress opulently to inspire awe or wear deliberately simple garments to project an image of principled modesty. She could show devotion to her parents, weave a token amount of cloth, or undertake benevolent acts to claim exceptional virtue. Displays of charisma by empress dowagers were particularly useful when the ruler was young, weak, sickly, or incompetent. In these sorts of situations, high officials might even welcome a woman's involvement in matters of state to stabilize the government and accomplish pressing policy objectives.

Although Weber's typology of legitimation accounts for some of the actions of Chinese consorts, it does not account for all of the ways they justified their authority. Empresses also manipulated filial piety to claim legitimacy. This distinctive form of legitimation emerged due to the importance of filial piety in China—perhaps the most fundamental principle of kinship and ethics. While filial piety is present in almost all cultures to some degree, the Chinese took this virtue to an extreme by demanding that adult sons show lifelong deference and even obedience to their mother. The submission of sons to mothers and surrogate mother figures effectively placed the empress dowager above the reigning emperor in rank. Women often made use of this ethical imperative to legitimate their authority. So, in addition to the three forms of domination in the Weberian model found worldwide, China had a fourth type, moral domination, that sometimes allowed women to arrogate the emperor's powers.

Because Chinese empresses usually pursued their goals obliquely and were hidden from public view, their influence is easy to discount. But the sociologist Talcott Parsons put forward a pragmatic definition of power that can help historians grasp the fundamental nature of female authority in China. Parsons described power very broadly as the ability to get things done.⁷ Using this definition, if an empress managed to accomplish a goal, regardless of means, she was exercising power. Although men could use conventional institutions and ideologies to exercise power, women often had to circumvent the ordinary channels of administration to achieve their ends. If power is the ability to do things, then by this definition many Chinese consorts should be considered powerful to some extent. Over time, however, restrictions on palace women intensified, ideologies hardened, and palace women found it increasingly more difficult to pursue their aspirations.

Chinese women and men tended to use power differently. Emperors could benefit themselves by strengthening institutions and consolidating rules and norms. In contrast, women usually gained power by undermining the usual channels of administration so they often ended up degrading the quality of governance. Because empresses did not personally benefit from institutional integrity, they usually directed their powers toward narrower goals. Most often, when a woman gained power she used it to interfere in the imperial succession, benefit favored people and interests, or aggrandize herself. Otherwise, politically active empresses usually just enjoyed the exercise of power for its own sake.

A few extraordinary empresses stand out for using their authority to transform the government and state in ways that historians consider positive. Empress Wenming aggressively Sinicized the Tuoba people and strove to make the Northern Wei dynasty more culturally Chinese. Wu Zetian opened up the civil service to men from humble backgrounds, bringing talented administrators into the government. And during the twilight of the imperial system, Cixi undertook cautious reforms intended to strengthen China and respond to domestic and foreign challenges. However, these sorts of activist empresses were relatively few. Most consorts had limited ambitions and used their authority cautiously.

The conservatism of empresses does not imply that they were less competent than men. Most emperors also had very limited goals, and few stand out as reformers or visionaries. If a ruler took his duties seriously, he usually just tried to keep the system functioning smoothly. Because powerful women always had doubtful legitimacy, they had good reason to be even more cautious. An empress who suddenly altered the status quo would upset special interests, inciting a backlash that might bring her down. For this reason, powerful empresses usually accomplished little. It was safest for them to uphold existing policies while pursuing their personal interests behind the scenes.

Some historians have claimed that the most puissant women, such as Fu Hao and Wu Zetian, were feminists.[8] This assertion exaggerates their goals. Feminism is a contemporary concept that was absent in China before the late Qing dynasty. A woman who had no notion of feminism would not direct her power to achieving this ideology's goals. Accordingly, no empress ever sought universal female liberation. Even if one of them had tried, she would surely have failed. A social movement can only succeed when the time is right, but until the final decades of the imperial era, China's political, economic, social and cultural characteristics were all opposed to a feminist program.[9] For this reason, it is not surprising that there was never a feminist empress. Even if a woman had sufficient imagination to conjure up this idea, anyone who tried to implement a feminist agenda would have been destroyed.

Notes

1. Tajfel and Turner, "An Integrative Theory of Intergroup Conflict," 33–37.
2. Burn, Aboud, and Moyles, "The Relationship between Gender Social Identity and Support for Feminism," 1081–89.
3. Ortner, "Gender and Sexuality in Hierarchical Societies," 359–409.
4. Ortner, "Gender Hegemonies," 78.
5. Erler and Kowaleski, "Introduction," 1–2.
6. Cohen, "Political Anthropology," 215–35.
7. Parsons, "On the Concept of Political Power," 237.
8. Lu, "Shangdai nüjie Fu Hao," 94–96. Bokenkamp, "A Medieval Feminist Critique," 383–92; Chen, "Empress Wu and Proto-Feminist Sentiments," 77–116.
9. Lemert, *Social Things*, 103.

Glossary

Ai (emperor)	哀
Ai Jiang	哀姜
An Lushan	安祿山
Anle	安樂
Bai Juyi	白居易
Ban Gu	班固
Banpo	半坡
bao	保
baojun	暴君
Bi	妣
Bi Geng	妣庚
Bi Xin	妣辛
bin	賓
binü	俾女
bo	伯
Bo (empress)	薄
Cao (empress)	曹
Cao Cao	曹操
Cao Fang	曹芳
Cao Mao	曹髦
Cao Pi	曹丕
Chabi	察必
Chang (empress)	常
Changyi	昌邑
chen	臣
Chen (empress)	陳

Glossary

Cheng (emperor)	成
Chenghua	成化
Chengtian	承天
Chengzi	呈子
Chi (empress)	郗
Chong (emperor)	沖
Chongqing	重慶
Chu	楚
Chu Suanzi	褚蒜子
Chunqin	淳欽
Chunqiu	春秋
ci	次
Cui Guang	崔光
cuju	蹴鞠
da	大
da sima	大司馬
Da yun jing	大雲經
Dadianzi	大甸子
Daozong	道宗
Daowu	道武
Deng (empress)	鄧
Deng Sui	鄧綏
Di	帝
di taihou	帝太后
Dong (empress)	董
Dong Zhongshu	董仲舒
Dong Zhuo	董卓
Dongyangcun	東楊村
Dou (empress)	竇
Dou Wu	竇武
Dou Xian	竇憲
Dou Yifang	竇猗房
Duzhong	篤忠
er	二
er sheng	二聖
Erlitou	二裡頭

Famen	法門
Fan Ye	范曄
fang	方
Fazang	法藏
fei	妃
Feng (empress)	馮
fu	婦, 帚
Fu	傅
Fu Hao	婦好
Fu Ji	婦姬
furen	夫人
Gao Yun	高允
Gaozu	高祖
gong	公
Gong (prince)	恭
Gong Jiang	公姜
Gongyang zhuan	公羊傳
Goryeo	高麗
Gouyi	鉤弋
gu	姑
Guanglie	光烈
Guangwu	光武
Guangxu	光緒
Guanlong	關隴
guidao	鬼道
Gundai	袞代
Guo (empress)	郭
Hanshu	漢書
he	赫
He (emperor)	和
He (empress)	何
Hong Taiji	皇太極
Hongwu	洪武
Hongxi	洪熙
hou	后
Hou Hanshu	後漢書

Hou Ji	后稷
Hou Mu Xin	后母辛
Hu (empress)	胡
Huan (emperor)	桓
huang baba	皇爸爸
huang guifei	皇貴妃
huang taihou	皇太后
huangdi	皇帝
huanghou	皇后
Hui (emperor)	惠
Huo Guang	霍光
Huo Qubing	霍去病
Ji (king)	季
Ji (surname, concubine)	姬
Ji (empress)	紀
Ji Dan	姬單
Jiaguan	甲觀
Jiang Yuan	姜嫄
Jiangzhai	姜寨
Jin	晉
Jing (emperor)	景
Jingtai (emperor)	景泰
Jingzhao	京兆
Jiu Tangshu	舊唐書
jun	君
Kang Youwei	康有為
Kangxi	康熙
Li (imperial clan, empress)	李
Li Hua	李華
Li Tangmei	李唐妹
Li Yuan	李淵
Liang (empress)	梁
Liang Ji	梁冀
Liang Na	梁妠
Liangzhu	良渚
Ling (duke)	衛靈公

Glossary

Ling (emperor, empress) 靈
Liu (empress) 劉
Liu Bang 劉邦
Liu He 劉賀
Liu Xiu 劉秀
Longshan 龍山
Lü Buwei 呂不韋
Lü Zhi 呂雉
Ma (empress) 馬
Majiayao 馬家窯
Mao 毛
ming 名
Ming (emperor) 明
Mingshi 明史
mingtang 明堂
minghun 冥婚
mu 母
Nanzi 南子
neichao 內朝
nü 女
nüshi 女史
Nüze 女則
Peiligang 裴李崗
Pingyang 平陽
qi (wife) 妻
Qi (state) 齊
Qianjin 千金
Qianlong 乾隆
qie 妾
Qijia 齊家
Qin 秦
qin baba 親爸爸
Qin Shihuang 秦始皇
renjun 仁君
Ruizong (emperor) 睿宗
san cong 三從

Glossary

Shandong	山東
Shangguan	上官
Shao (emperor)	少
Shen	慎
Shen Wuhua	沈婺華
Sheng Jiang	聲姜
Shengzong (emperor)	聖宗
shengmu	聖母
Shiji	史記
Shijing	詩經
Shizu (emperor)	世祖
Shun (emperor)	順
Shunzhi (emperor)	順治
si	司
Silla	新羅,
Sima Qian	司馬遷
Sima Shi	司馬師
Sima Zhao	司馬昭
Song Yingzong	宋英宗
taihuang taihou	太皇太后
Tai Ren	太任
taihou	太后
Taiping (princess)	太平
Taizong (emperor)	太宗
Taizu (emperor)	太祖
Tang (king)	湯
Taosi	陶寺
Tongzhi	同治
waichao	外朝
wang	王
Wang (empress)	王
Wang Baoming	王寶明
Wang Mang	王莽
Wang Yao	王姚
wanghou	王后
wangqi	王妻

Wanli	萬曆
Wei (family, empress)	韋
Wei (empress)	衛
Wei Qing	衛青
Wei Ran	魏冉
weiqi	圍棋
Weishu	魏書
Wen (king, emperor)	文
Wen Mu	文母
Wende	文德
Wenming	文明
Wenxian	文獻
Wu Ding	武丁
Wu Zetian	武則天
Wu Zhao	武曌，武瞾
xia	下
Xian (emperor)	獻
Xianfeng	咸豐
Xianming	獻明
Xianwen	獻文
Xianyang	咸陽
Xiao	蕭
Xiao Yan	蕭衍
Xiaoding	孝定
Xiaojing	孝經
Xiaoming	孝明
Xiaowen	孝文
Xiaowu	孝武
Xiaozhen	孝貞
Xiaozhuang	孝莊
Xin	新
Xin Tangshu	新唐書
Xiwangmu	西王母
Xizong	熙宗
Xu (concubine)	徐
Xu Hui	徐惠

Xuan (emperor, queen)	宣
Xuande	宣德
Xuanwu	宣武
Xuanyi	宣懿
Xuanzong	玄宗
Yamatai	邪馬台
Yan (empress)	閻
Yan Ji	閻姬
Yang (emperor)	煬
Yang (empress)	楊
Yang Guang	楊廣
Yang Guifei	楊貴妃
Yang Guozhong	楊國忠
Yang Jian	楊堅
Yang Yuhuan	楊玉環
Yelü	耶律
yi	邑
Yin (empress)	陰
ying (sororal polygyny)	媵
Ying (surname)	嬴
Yingzong	英宗
Yiren	異人
Yixin	奕訢
Yongzheng	雍正
yu	御
yuan	元
Yuan (emperor)	元
Zeng (marquis)	曾
Zhang (emperor)	章
Zhang (empress)	張
Zhangsun	長孫
Zhao (emperor)	昭
Zhao (empress)	趙
Zhao (lady)	趙
Zhao Feiyan	趙飛燕
Zhao Hede	趙合德

Glossary

Zhao Ji	趙姬
Zhao Jieyu	趙婕妤
Zhao Yi	趙翼
zhaomu	昭穆
Zhaoxiang	昭襄王
zheng	烝
Zhenzong	真宗
Zhi (emperor)	質
Zhongzong	中宗
Zhou li	周禮
Zhu Yuanzhang	朱元璋
Zhuangxiang	莊襄
zhuanlun wang	轉輪王
zi (honorific)	子
zi (style name)	字
zongfa	宗法
Zu Ding	祖丁
Zuozhuan	左傳

Index

accompanying concubinage (*ying* marriage), 70–71, 209
Aceh (kingdom), 14
agency, of women, 2–3
Agrippina (royal mother), 16
Ai (emperor), 109–10, 234
Ai Jiang, 239
Akhenaten (husband of Nefertiti), 20
An (emperor), 114–15
ancestors, 63, 76, 85n54
ancestral cult, 28
ancestral sacrifices, 60–61
ancestress (*bi*), 70
ancient classics, political thought founded in, 233
Anle (princess), 23
An Lushan, 158–60
aristocracy, 139, 144, 167; polygyny among, 70; queens compared with, 75; of Shandong province, 146; during Tang dynasty, 169; wives of, 75; during Zhou dynasty, 106, 120–22, 215
al-Attar (theologian), 19

augusta (wife of Roman emperor), 32
Augustus (emperor), 18–19
Austria, 20
authority, 147; empresses justifying, 250; female power distinguished from, 3–4; marriage not imbuing, 25; men gaining, 46–47; of queens, 13; women gaining, 231; of Zhou queens, 73, 80
Avatasaka school (philosophy), 154

Babur (emperor), 36n97
Bai Juyi, 159
Ban Gu, 58, 98, 234
Banpo site, 44
bao (character), 217
Bao Si (consort), 234, *235*
Benedict, Ruth, 7
benefices (*yi*), 92–93
bi. See ancestress
bigamy, 162n57
big man, 50
bin sacrifice, 64
binü. See slave

biological determinism, 11
Bo (empress dowager), 101
Book of Documents (*Shangshu*), 234
Boudicca (queen), 33n2
Boxer Rebellion, 198
Bright Hall (*mingtang*), 155
Bronze Age, 9, 52–53, 58
Buddhism, 133, 138–39, 154–55, 222–23
Buddhist relics, 155
Buganda (kingdom), 18
burials, 54n5, 146; changing patterns in, 45; in Liangzhu culture, 49; of Tang consorts, 165n125; of Western Zhou, 71; of women, 43–44, 51–52. *See also* tombs
Byzantine empire, 16

Cao (empress), 38n145, *173*, 174
Cao Cao (warlord), 127, 210
Cao Pi (warlord), 127, 241
Caroline of Ansbach (wife of George II), 15
ceremonial objects, weapons as, 48–49
ceremonies, queens participating in, 18
Chabi (consort), *182*, 182–83
chakravartin (*zhuanlun wang*), 154–55
charisma, 5, 250–51
Chen dynasty, in China, 229n145
Cheng (emperor), 109, 239
Cheng (empress), 107

Chengtian (empress dowager), 177
Chengzi site, in Shandong province, 51
Cherokee women, 13–14
Chi (empress), 161n35
childbirth, by consorts, 64–65
China, 29; ancient, 5, 47; Chen dynasty in, 229n145; Chunqiu period in, 89n156; Gansu in, 43; Henan province in, 11; Jin dynasty in, 179, 207–8, 216–17; Jurchen nomads conquered by, 191; Liang dynasty in, 161n35, 216; Liao dynasty in, 22, 174–76; Liu Song dynasty in, 131, 203; Lu in, 88n124; Neolithic era of, 10, 41–42, 45–46, 58; Qi dynasty in, 224n7; Qin dynasty in, 91, 210, 213–14; Qin Shihuang unifying, 91; religion in, 49; Shandong province in, 42, 51, 146; Song in, 89n158; Sui dynasty in, 22, 133, 143, 216; Toba clan settling, 133–34; Xiongnu nomads invading, 105, 111; Yangtze valley in, 52; Yuan dynasty in, 180, 208. *See also* governments; Han dynasty; imperial China; Ming dynasty; Qing dynasty; Shang dynasty; Song dynasty; Zhou dynasty
Chong (emperor), 116
Chongqing (empress dowager), 193

Christianity, queenship altered by, 19
Chunqin (empress), 175–77
Chunqiu. See Springs and Autumns
Chunqiu period, in China, 89n156
Chu Suanzi (empress dowager), 132
civil service examination, 150–51
Cixi (empress dowager), 193, *194*, 199, 252; Confucianism represented by, 196; eunuchs depended on by, 196; Kang competing with, 197–98; regents deposed of by, 195
Classic of Changes (*Yijing*), 241
Classic of Filial Piety (*Xiaojing*), 28–29, 102–3, 129–30, 134, 183
Classic of Poetry (*Shijing*), 28, 218, 233, 236–37
Claudius (emperor), 16
concubinage, accompanying, 70–71, 209
concubines (*qie*), 53, 84n29, 133; children born to, 33, 38n143; imperial, 224n28; ranks of, 227n91; wives contrasted with, 38n143, 71–72, 209. *See also specific concubines*
conflict theorists, functionalist approach contrasted with, 3
Confucianism, 104, 106, 133–34, 160, 168, 178; Cixi representing, 196; empresses admonished by, 120; mothers empowered under, 121; Song dynasty influenced by, 171–72; Tang dynasty reviving, 240
consort kin, 81, 107, 119, 131; from elevated backgrounds, 110; emperors and, 100; governments impacted by, 109; mésalliance disempowering, 184
consorts, 210; administration participated in by, 66, 80–81; behavior of, 138; childbirth and, 64–65; from Chunqiu period, 89n156; female power of, 1; governments participated in by, 66; imperial Chinas empowering, 121–22; imperial honored, 218; Liao dynasty empowering, 176; during Ming dynasty, 189, 202n76; of Shang kings, 49, 58; social identity of, 63; Tang, 165n125; titles for, 58–60; tombs of, 63; virtuousness portrayed by, 18–19. *See also specific consorts*
consort system, during Qin dynasty, 91
Constantine (emperor), 19
culture: Dawenkou, 42, 44; Liangzhu, 49; Longshan, 10, 51; Majiayao, 42, 50; of nomads, 138, 177; Peiligang, *43*; Qijia, 53; Yangshao, 42
cwén (Anglo-Saxon word), 30

Daoism, 106, 155, 156; Dou (empress) practicing, 104; Jing backing, 101; Tang dynasty employed by, 222–23
Daowu (emperor), 136–37
Daozong (emperor), 178
da sima. *See* grand marshal
Dawenkou culture, 42, 44
Da yun jing. *See Great Cloud Sutra*
Den (king), 16
Deng (empress dowager), 114
Denmark, 9
determinism, biological, 11
Di (god), 64
di taihou. *See* empresses dowager
divinations, 64–65, 84n51
division of labor, gendered, 46, 54n12
domains (*yi*), 62
domestic sphere, female power in, 6, 9
Dong (empress dowager), 118
Dong Zhongshu, 238–40
Dong Zhuo (warlord), 119
Dou (empress), 105, 118, 147–48; Daoism practiced by, 104; eunuchs supporting, 113–14; tomb of, *102*; virtuousness demonstrated by, 101–2
Dou Wu (regent), 118
Dou Xian (grand marshal), 113–14
dowager, queens, 17, 75–76, 92
dowager, successor to emperor chosen by, 26

duke (*gong*), 70
Duzhong site, in Henan province, 11

Eastern Han dynasty, in China, 111, 128; emperors of, 113; empresses of, 120; Southern Dynasties contrasted with, 131–32
Eastern Zhou dynasty, 79–80, 87n118, 209, 213
education, of palace women, 221–22
egalitarian societies, 8, 34n39, 42, 51–52
Egypt, 14, 16, 19–20, 30
Eleanor of Aquitaine (wife of Henry II), 17, 36n77
Elizabeth I (queen), 31
emperor (*huangdi*), 32, 91–92, 148
emperors, Chinese: consort kin and, 100; of Eastern Han dynasty, 113; empresses dowager in relation to, 101, 129–30; during Han dynasty, 96, 210; Liao empresses advising, 176–77; monogamy binding empress and, 94; mothers of, 32–33; status of empresses decreased by, 166n162; succession of, 26; during Tang dynasty, 146, 207; weddings of, 38n137, 38n139; Wei, 135; women terrorized

INDEX

by, 243; during Yuan dynasty, 182. *See also specific emperors*
empresses (*huanghou*). *See specific topics*
empresses dowager (*di taihou*) (*huang taihou*), 92; edicts regarding, 199n4; emperors in relation to, 101, 129–30; female power demonstrated by, 120; as figurehead, 132; filial piety empowering, 178–79; kinsmen of, 248–49; as regents, 26, 104, 168; succession decided by, 99, 108, 147; wet nurse and, 163n63. *See also specific empresses dowager*
England, 31
entertainers, in the palace, 210, 221
er sheng. *See* two saints
eunuchs, 195, 217–18; Cixi depending on, 196; Dou (empress) supported by, 113–14; Dou W., opposing, 118; empresses opposed by, 189, 249; against gentry, 116–17; governments and, 118–19; Liu (empress) relying on, 173; Ming dynasty empowering, 189; Shun elevated, 116
exogamy, 62, 179; in kin-based societies, 45; during Shang dynasty, 84n36; surname, 72, 79

Famen Temple, 155

Fan Ye, 120
Fazang (monk), 154–55
feasting rituals, 74
fei. *See* secondary wives
female power: authority distinguished from, 3–4; of consorts, 1; control of resources and, 7; in domestic sphere, 6, 9; dynastic decline and, 14; empresses dowager demonstrating, 120; Han dynasty impacted by, 120; in imperial China, 9–10; through marriage, 15; Parsons describing, 251–52; public image and, 18; social structure and, 4; during Tang dynasty, 157; through financial resources, 17–18; traditional domination legitimizing, 250
female power relations, gendered, 8
female scribes (*nüshi*), 218
feminism, 253
feminist theory, 247–48
filial piety, 27–28, 33, 120–21, 129, 183; empresses dowager empowered by, 178–79; ideology of, 29; mothers emphasized in, 102–3
First Dynasty, of Egypt, 16
Five Dynasties and Ten Kingdoms, 174
fraternal succession, Tuoba practicing, 135–36

269

fu (titled wives), 61–62, 69–70, 78, 82n6, 82n17; gifts given by, 65; in networks of exchange, 65; of Shang kings, 58

Fu Hao (consort), 60, 253; posthumous wedding of, 64; tomb of, 65, 67–69, *68*, 83n27; warfare participated in by, 66

Fu Jing (consort), 66–67

functionalist approach, conflict theorists contrasted with, 3

furen. See lady; madam

Gallienus (emperor), 33n3

Gansu, in China, 43

Gao Yun, 120

Gaozu (née Li Yuan) (emperor), 103–4, 144, 147–49, 224n28; empress named by, 93–94; Guangwu contrasted with, 111–12; harems of, 206; titles given by, 32

gender, social identity and, 247–48

gendered female power relations, 8

gender hierarchy, Kutse Bushmen lacking, 8–9

gender norms, 41

gender relations, society reorganized by, 10

gentry, eunuchs against, 116–17

George II (king), 15

Giant Wild Goose Pagoda, 155

gifts: *fu* giving, 65; noblewomen giving, 88n125; Zhou queens giving, 74

Go (*weiqi*) (board game), 222

Gongyang Tradition (*Gongyang zhuan*), 27

Goryeo (Korean kingdom), 208

governments, of China: consort kin impacting, 109; consorts participating in, 66; empresses transforming, 252; eunuchs and, 118–19; increasing scale of, 52–53; Lü Z., controlling, 92; of Ming dynasty, 185; during Qin dynasty, 81, 91; religion justifying, 49; during Song dynasty, 167; of Tang dynasty, 29, 218; women impacting, 157–58

grand marshal (*da sima*), 113

graves, heterarchy exhibited by, 42–43

Great Britain, 15

Great Cloud Sutra (*Da yun jing*), 154

gu. See mother-in-law

Guanglie (empress), 111–12

Guangwu (emperor), 111–12, 125n62

Guangxu (emperor), 196–97, 199

guidao. See way of demons

Han (ethnicity), 140, 190

Han dynasty, in China, 102–3, 119, 206, 237–39, 243–44; collapse of, 127; emperors during, 96, 210; empresses during, 93, 108; female

INDEX

power impacting, 120; Liu B., reuniting, 92; Lü Z., empowered during, 95; monogamy during, 209; the palace during, *207*. *See also* Eastern Han dynasty; Western Han dynasty
Han Gaozu (née Liu Bang), 32, 92, 93, 95
Hanshu. *See Records of the Han*
Han system, 122
Hapsburg empire, 20–21
harems, royal: of Gaozu, 206; history of, 204; Jurchen nomads and, 216–17; organization of, 207–8
harem women, 123n6, 185, 221; background of, 206; officials compared with, 214; the palace managed by, 218; ranks classifying, 214–15; religion and, 223; of Wu (emperor), 216. *See also* concubines; consorts; wives
Hatchepsut (queen), 19–20, 30, *31*
Hazda nomads, 14
He (emperor), 113, 114
He (empress), 118
He (empress dowager), 119
Helena (wife of Constantine), 19
Henan province, in China, 11
Henry II (king), 17, 36n77
hereditary monarchy, 14–15, 50
heterarchy, 9, 42–43

hierarchies: agency contrasted with, 3; gender, 2, 8–9; women impacted by, 46. *See also* ranks; titles
Himiko (shaman), 13–14
Historia Augusta, 33n3
Hoelun (mother of Khan, G.), 181
Hong Taiji (emperor), 191
Hongwu (née Zhu Yuanzhang) (emperor), 184
Hongxi (emperor), 187
hou (title), 32, 60, 215
Hou Hanshu. *See Records of the Later Han*
Hou Ji (deity), 72
Hou Mu Xin "*Bi Xin*" (née Fu Hao), 60
Huan (emperor), 116, 117–18
huangdi. *See* emperor
huang guifei. *See* imperial honored consort
huanghou. *See* empresses
Huanglao, 101, 106
huang taihou. *See* empresses dowager
Hui (emperor), 96, 99, 124n33
Huizong (emperor), 221
human sacrifice. *See* sacrifice, human
hunting, men monopolizing, 11
Huo Guang, 108

ideology, 5, 12, 29, 244n6

INDEX

imperial China, 119; consorts empowered by, 121–22; empresses elevated by, 248; female power in, 9–10; mothers venerating, 27; women empowered in, 232
imperial concubines (*ji*), 224n28
imperial honored consort (*huang guifei*), 218
inequality, 3, 10–12, 51–52
informal political systems, queens in, 13–14
inner court (*neichao*), 105
Isabella of Castile (queen), 17

Jahangir (emperor), 18
Japan, 197–98
ji. See imperial concubines
Ji (empress), 187
Ji (king), 72
Jiang Yuan (archetype), 72
Jiangzhai site, 42
Jin dynasty, in China, 179, 207–8, 216–17
Jing (emperor), 101, 103–4
Jingdi (emperor), 104
Jingtai (emperor), 187–89
Jiu Tangshu. See Old Tang Records
Joseph (son of Maria Theresa), 20
jun. See lady
Jurchen nomads, 189–90; China conquering, 191; harems and, 216–17; wives of, 179–80

Kangxi (emperor), 191

Kang Youwei, 197–98
Khan, Genghis "Chingghis Khan," 181, 183
Khan, Ögedei, 181
Khitan people, 174, 177–78
kin, of consorts. *See* consort kin
kin-based societies, exogamy in, 45
king (*wang*), 70
kings: mothers of, 16, 29–30; wives of, 215; women as, 30–31; of Zhou dynasty, 40n192. *See also* Shang kings; *specific kings*
kinship customs, palace organization impacted by, 215
Korea, 14, 57, 208
Kutse Bushmen, gender hierarchy lacked by, 8–9

lady (*furen*) (*jun*), 78–79
Latter Zhou dynasty, 221, 224n7, 224n17
legal domination, 5
legitimation, 5
levirate marriage (*zheng*), 79
Li (empress), 168
Liang (empress), 115–16
Liang dynasty, in China, 161n35, 216, 219
Liangzhu culture, burials in, 49
Liao dynasty, in China, 22, 37n127, 174–77
Liao empresses, 176–77
Liao princesses, 37n127
Li family, 144–47

272

INDEX

Li Hua, 124n28
Ling (duke), 80–81
Ling (emperor), 118
Ling (empress), 163n80, 163n92
Ling (née Hu) (empress dowager), 141–43, *142*
Li Tangmei, 187
The Literary Mind and the Carving of Dragons (*Wenxin diaolong*), 242
Liu (empress), 168, 170–73, *172*
Liu Bang, 92
Liu family, 100
Liu He "King of Changyi" (emperor), 108
Liu Song dynasty, in China, 131, 203
Liu Xiang, 124n30, 237
Livia (wife of Augustus), 18–19
Longmen Grottoes, 154
Longshan culture, 10, 51
Louis VII (King), 17
Lu (state), in China, 88n124
Lü family, 100, 107
Lü Zhi (empress), 122–23, 250; government controlled by, 92; Han dynasty empowering, 95–98; violence by, 153

M5 (tomb), 83n27
Ma (empress), 113, 185, *186*
madam (*furen*), 219
Majiayao culture, 42, 50
Manchu emperors, of Qing dynasty, 25

Manchus, 25, 190, 209, 217
Mandate of Heaven, 236, 239
Maria Theresa (empress), 20, 32
marriage, 42, 128, 133, 146, 190; authority not imbued through, 25; female power through, 15; levirate, 79; of princesses, 21–25, 37n122; during Shang dynasty, 60–61; in Song dynasty, 89n158; sororate, 79; during Southern Dynasties, 130; among steppe peoples, 134; virilocality and, 45–46; *ying*, 70–71, 209. *See also* mésalliance; political marriage
Maya (society), 48
Memoirs of the Historian (*Shiji*), 94
men: authority gained by, 46–47; hunting monopolized by, 11; prestige acquired by, 44; warfare and, 47. *See also* emperors; kings
Mencius, 39, 89n171
Meritneith (Queen), 16
mésalliance: consort kin disempowered through, 184; Wei emperors pursing, 135; women disempowered by, 242–43
Mesopotamia, Uruk period in, 48
metaphysical theories, women disparaged by, 238
military, 73, 196
ming. *See* personal name
Ming (emperor), 113

273

Ming dynasty, in China, 184, 208, 217, 219, 222; consorts during, 189, 202n76; eunuchs empowered during, 189; governments of, 185; palace women during, 224n16
Ming History (*Mingshi*), 185
minghun. *See* posthumous weddings
Mingshi. *See Ming History*
mingtang. *See* Bright Hall
Mississippian society, 9
monarchy, 57; hereditary, 14–15, 50; patrilineal, 13; rulers elevated in, 52–53
Mongols, 180–83
monogamy, 93; Dawenkou cemetery reflecting increase in, 44–45; emperors and empresses bound through, 94; during Han dynasty, 209
mortuary treatment, social status reflecting through, 41–42
mother (*mu*), 59, 70, 78, 83n21
mother, sacred (*shengmu*), 153
mother-in-law (*gu*), 70
mothers, royal, 129–30, 136–37; Confucianism empowering, 121; of emperors, 32–33; filial piety emphasizing, 102–3; imperial China venerating, 27; of kings, 16, 29–30; Mencius mourning, 89n171; morning for, 28–29; mourning of, 29; policy influenced by, 81; of Qin Shihuang, 92; as regents, 16–17, 36n97; son intertwined with, 16, 27–28, 36n97, 39n150, 120; succession manipulated by, 16. *See also* empresses dowager mourning, 28–29, 161n22
mu. *See* mother
Mughal Empire, 30, 36n97
music, 234, 244n21

names: for empresses, 123n9; during Shang dynasty, 62; for women, 58, 78, 82n17. *See also* titles
Nanzi (lady), 80–81
Nefertiti (queen), 20
neichao. *See* inner court
Neixuni. *See Teachings for the Inner Quarters*
Neolithic era, of China, 10, 41–42, 45–46, 58
Neolithic societies, as egalitarian societies, 42
nephew, relationship between uncle and, 121
Nero (emperor), 16
New Tang Records (*Xin Tangshu*), 145
Ningzong (emperor), 168–69
noblewomen, 75; ceremonial duties of, 79–80; gifts given by, 88n125; status of, 76
nomadic women, 134–35
nomads: culture of, 138, 177; Hazda, 14; Xianbei, 133, 139;

Xiongnu, 105, 111. *See also* Jurchen nomads
Noor Jahan (queen), 18
Northern Dynasties, 138
Northern Wei dynasty, 133, 137–39, 143, 206–7
nü (character), 59
nüshi. *See* female scribes
Nüze. *See* Rules for Women

officials, harem women compared with, 214
Old Tang Records (*Jiu Tangshu*), 145, 147, 157
Ottoman system, 36n97
outer court (*waichao*), 105

padishah begum (title), 30
the palace, 203, 228n136; administration of, 217–18; entertainers in, 210, 221; during Han dynasty, *207*; harem women managing, 218; during Jin dynasty, 207–8; during Qi dynasty, 224n7; during Qing dynasty, *211*; during Song dynasty, 218–19; during Western Han dynasty, 226n67; women serving, 211, 225n40
palace organization, 227n97; kinship customs impacting, 215; during Qing dynasty, 217; during Six Dynasties, 215–16; women staffing, 219
palace women, 207, 212–13, 223; education of, 221–22; during Ming dynasty, 224n16; of Qin Shihuang, 205–6; rules and principles limiting, 241; seclusion of, 220; status and role impacting, 219–20; succession interfered with by, 168; sumptuary campaigns targeting, 240; as tribute, 208. *See also* harem women
Palmyra (kingdom), 17, 33n3
Parsons, Talcott, 251–52
patriarchy, 34n35; ideology bolstering, 12; inequality and, 10–11; women restrained by, 239–40
patrilineal monarchy, 13
patrimonialism, 6, 12–13
pattern (*wen*), 124n28
Peiligang culture, *43*
personal name (*ming*), 70
Ping (emperor), 110–11
Pingyang (princess), 23, *24*, 144
political marriage: interstate relations and, 78; by Shang kings, 61–62; during Zhou dynasty, 72
political system, warfare transforming, 48
political thought, ancient classics as foundation of, 233
polygyny, 70–71, 134, 174–75, 203–4, 209
popular culture, 7

275

posthumous weddings (*minghun*), 64
power, female. *See* female power
prestige, 6, 44
primary wife (*qi*), 70
prince, mother of, 136–37
princesses: Liao, 37n127; marriage of, 21–25, 37n122; Tang dynasty empowering, 23. *See also specific princesses*
property rights, 47, 51

qi. *See* primary wife
Qianjin (princess), 22
Qianlong (emperor), 193
Qi dynasty, in China, 224n7
Qijia culture, tombs of, 53
Qin (state), 120
Qin dynasty, in China, 81, 91, 210, 213–14
Qing dynasty, 81; empresses degraded during, 190–91; Manchu emperors of, 25; the palace during, *211*; palace organization during, 217; woodblock illustrations from, *110, 142*
Qinghai, Majiayao culture in, 50
Qin Shihuang (emperor), 97, 106, 122, 214; China unified by, 91; mother of, 92; palace women of, 205–6
queen (*wanghou*), 78, 91
queens: as ambiguous term, 32; aristocracy compared with, 75; authority of, 13; ceremonies participated in by, 18; dowager, 17, 75–76, 92; female power exercised by, 20; in informal political systems, 13–14; kinsmen of, 15–16; patrimonialism and, 12–13; status of, 76; of Zhou, 72–73. *See also* Zhou queens; *specific queens*
queens dowager (*wang taihou*), 17, 75–76, 92
queenship, Christianity altering, 19
quern (tool), *43*

ranks, 218; of concubines, 227n91; titles demonstrating, 217; of women, 71–72, 79, 213
Rebellion of the Seven Kingdoms, Western Han dynasty threatened by, 103–4
Records of the Han (*Hanshu*), 94
Records of the Later Han (*Hou Hanshu*), 94, 120
Records of Wei (*Weishu*), 134, 138
Reform Movement (1898), 197
regents, 38n145, 110–11; Cixi deposing, 195; empresses dowager as, 26, 104, 168; Liao empresses as, 177; Liu as, 170–71; mothers as, 16–17, 36n97. *See also specific regents*
religion, 57, 154; in China, 49; empresses turning to, 189;

governments justified with, 49; harem women and, 223; royal women advantaged by, 19–20. *See also* Confucianism; Daoism
religious rites, women participating in, 65
Renzong (emperor), 170–71, 174
rights, property, 47, 51
Rites of Zhou (*Zhou li*), 228n136
rituals, feasting, 74
Roman emperors, 32
royal women, religion advantaging, 19–20
Ruizong (emperor), 150, 157
rulers: empresses degraded by, 136; monarchy elevating, 52–53; widows of, 175–76; women as, 1–2. *See also* emperors; empresses dowager; kings; queens
Rules for Women (*Nüze*), 148

sacred mother (*shengmu*), 153
sacrifices, ancestral, 60–61
sacrifices, human, 214, 244; *bin*, 64; of widows of ruler, 175–76; women as, 53–54, 213; *yu*, 64
sacrificial cult records, 61
Sage Mother (goddess), 171
san cong. See three followings
scribes, female (*nüshi*), 218
secondary wives (*fei*), 53, 70, 79
servant, terracotta figure of, *102*
Seti II (king), 14

Shandong province, in China, 42, 51, 146
Shang dynasty, 12; exogamy during, 84n36; marriage practices of, 60–61; names during, 62; Zhou dynasty contrasted with, 66, 69
Shangguan (empress dowager), 108
Shang kings, 205; consorts of, 49, 58; of *fu*, 58; political marriage by, 61–62
Shangshu. See Book of Documents
Shao (emperor), 119
Shen (lady), 102
shengmu. See sacred mother
Shiji. See Memoirs of the Historian
Shijing. See Classic of Poetry
Shima Kunio, 83n21
Shizu "Kublai Khan" (emperor), 182–83
Shun (emperor), 115–16
Shunzhi (emperor), 191
Silla kingdom, of Korea, 14, 57
Sima Qian, 96–99, 236–37
Sima Shi, 128
Sima Zhao, 128
simplified weddings, during Zhou dynasty, 210
Six Dynasties, 28–29, 127, 162n57, 203–4, 215–16
slave (*binü*), 106
social identity, gender and, 247–48
social mobility, in Western Han dynasty, 106

social status, mortuary treatment reflecting, 41–42
social stratification, 3
social structure, female power and, 4
society, gender relations reorganizing, 10
son, mother intertwining with, 16, 27–28, 36n97, 39n150, 120
Song dynasty, 27, 145, 207, 216–17, 241, 242; Confucianism influencing, 171–72; ethical views shifting during, 169–70; governments during, 167; marriage in, 89n158; the palace during, 218–19
Song Yingzong, 38n145
sororal polygyny (*ying* marriage), 70–71, 209
sororate marriage, 79
Southern Dynasties, 128, 130–32, 138
Springs and Autumns (Chunqiu), 239
states, development of, 52
status, of women, 45–47
steppe peoples, marriage among, 134
Stone Age, 8
stone roller (tool), *43*
stratification, social, 3
style name (*zi*), 69
substance (*zhi*), 124
succession, royal: Chunqin unable to control, 177; of emperors, 26; empresses dowager deciding, 99, 108, 147; fraternal, 135–36; hereditary monarchy stabilizing, 50; Lü empowered through, 95; of Mongols, 181; mothers manipulating, 16; palace women interfering with, 168; during Tang dynasty, 23, 147; Wenxian interfering with, 144; women excluded from, 13–15
successor to emperor, dowager choosing, 26
Sui dynasty, in China, 22, 133, 143, 216
Sun (empress), 187–89, 242
surname exogamy, Zhou practicing, 72, 79
surnames, 83n18

Tabgach clan. *See* Toba clan
Taiping (princess), 23, 157
Tai Ren "Mother of Wen" (Wen Mu), 72–73
Taizong (emperor), 147, 148, 168
Taizu (emperor), 176–77, 208, 216
Tang (king), 64
Tang consorts, burials of, 165n125
Tang dynasty, 22–23, 145, 158, 216, 220–22, 237–38; An rebelling against, 159–60; aristocracy during, 169; Confucianism revived by, 240; Daoism employed by, 222–23; emperors of, 146, 207; empresses of, 147; female power

during, 157; governments of, 29, 218; princesses empowered during, 23; succession during, 23, 147; Zhou kings elevated by, 40n192
Tang Taizong (emperor), 225n39
Taosi site, 52–53
Tawoset (regent), 14
Teachings for the Inner Quarters (Neixuni), 189
terracotta figure, of servant, *102*
Theodora (empress), 16
three followings (*san cong*), 235
Three Obediences (Thrice Following) (schema), 27
Thrice Following. *See* Three Obediences
titles, 29–30, 216; for consorts, 58–60; Gaozu giving, 32; ranks demonstrated through, 217; for wives, 32; of Wu Zetian, 153; under Zhou dynasty, 69. *See also fu* (titled wives)
Toba (Tabgach) clan, 133
tombs: of consorts, 63; of Dou (empress), *102*; of Fu Hao, 65, 67–69, *68*, 83n27; of Fu Jing, 67; of Qijia culture, 53
Tongzhi (emperor), 195, 196
traditional domination, 5, 250
Tuoba (people), 135–37
Tuoba Wei regime, 137, 141
two saints (*er sheng*), 171

uncle, relationship between nephew and, 121
Uruk period, in Mesopotamia, 48

virilocality, marriage and, 45–46
virtuousness, 18–19, 101–2

waichao. See outer court
wang. See king
Wang (empress dowager), 109–11, 148–49
Wang Baoming (empress dowager), 132
wanghou. See queen
Wang Mang (regent), 110–11
wang taihou. See queen dowager
Wanli (emperor), 189
warfare: Fu Hao participating in, 66; Liao empresses participating, 177; men and, 47; Pingyang participating in, 144; political system transformed by, 48; Zhou queens not involved in, 87n118
warrior women, 17
way of demons (*guidao*), 13
wealth, 18
weapons, as ceremonial objects, 48–49
Weber, Max, 4–5, 251
weddings, 38n137, 38n139, 64
Wei (empress), 150, 157
Wei (lady), 105, 107
Wei emperors, mésalliance pursued by, 135

Index

Wei family, Li family intermarrying with, 146–47
weiqi. *See* Go
Wei Qing (general), 105
Wei Ran, 81, 120
Weishu. *See Records of Wei*
wen. *See* pattern
Wen (king), 72–73, 76
Wen (née Yang Jiang) (emperor), 101, 164n97, 203, 212; behavior and lifestyle of, 103; sons of, 203, 224n17; Yang J., styling himself on, 143
Wende (emperor), 161n35
Wenming (née Feng) (empress dowager), 139–40, 252
Wenxian (empress), 143–44
Wenxin diaolong. *See The Literary Mind and the Carving of Dragons*
Western Han dynasty, 111, 236; intellectual traditions of, 106–7; the palace during, 226n67; Rebellion of the Seven Kingdoms threatening, 103–4; social mobility in, 106
Western Zhou, burials of, 71
Western Zhou dynasty, 213, 234
wet nurses, 163n63, 212
widows, of rulers, 175–76
wife, of Roman emperor, 32
wife, primary (*qi*), 70
wives, 112; of aristocracy, 75; blood kin and, 78–79; concubines contrasted with, 38n143, 71–72, 209; high-status families, 137; of Jurchen nomads, 179–80; of kings, 215; natal family prioritized by, 145–46, 162n47, 182; secondary, 53, 70, 79; status of, 179–80; titles for, 32. *See also fu* (titled wives)
womanhood, ideal, 77–78
women, 127–28; agency of, 2–3; authority gained by, 231; burials of, 43–44, 51–52; Cherokee, 13–14; emperors terrorizing, 243; governments impacted by, 157–58; hierarchies imparting, 46; imperial China empowering, 232; as kings, 30–31; mésalliance disempowering, 242–43; metaphysical theories disparaging, 238; names for, 58, 78, 82n17; nomadic, 134–35; palace organization staffed by, 219; the palace served by, 211, 225n40; patriarchy restraining, 239–40; religious rites participated in by, 65; ritual canon restraining, 235; royal, 19–20; as rulers, 1–2; as sacrifices, 53–54, 213; status of, 45–47; succession excluding, 13–15; warrior, 17. *See also* concubines; consorts; empresses dowager; harem women; palace women; queens

Index

woodblock illustrations, from Qing dynasty, *110, 142*
Wright, Arthur, 164n97
Wu (emperor), 104, 106, 108, 125n50, 206, 241–43; harem women of, 216; inner court empowered by, 105; superstition influencing, 107
Wuding (king), 214
Wu Ding (king), 60, 61, 65, 66–67
Wu Zetian (empress), 29, 148–49, 155, 160, 165n122, 252–53; Buddhism practiced by, 154; legacy of, 151; titles of, 153; violence of, 152; Xiwangmu cult promoting, 156

Xian (emperor), 119
Xianbei nomads, 133, 139
Xianfeng (emperor), 193, 196
Xiang Yu, 123n6
Xianwen (emperor), 140
Xiao (clan), 175
Xiao (imperial line), 22
Xiaoding (empress dowager), 189
Xiaojing. See *Classic of Filial Piety*
Xiaoming (emperor), 141
Xiaowen (emperor), 139–40
Xiaowu (emperor), 203
Xiao Yan, 132
Xiaozhen (emperor), 193
Xiaozhen (empress dowager), 196
Xiaozhuang (empress), 191, *192*
Xin Tangshu. See *New Tang Records*
Xiongnu nomads, 105, 111

Xiwangmu "Queen Mother of the West," cult of, 156, 166n153
Xiyin "Prince Gong" (nobleman), 195
Xizong (emperor), 216–17
Xu (née Xu Hui) (lady), 148, 219, 229n143
Xuan (emperor), 108–9, 136, 243
Xuan (queen dowager), 81, 95, 120
Xuande (emperor), 187, 242
Xuanwu (emperor), 141
Xuanyi (empress), 178
Xuanzong (emperor), 158–59
Xunzi (thinker), 77–78

Yan (empress), 115
Yang (emperor), 144
Yang (empress), 168–69, 200n14, 220
Yang Guifei (née Yang Yuhuan), 158–60, *159*
Yang Guozhong, 158–59, 160
Yang Jiang, 143
Yangshao culture, 42
Yangshao era, 11
Yangtze valley, in China, 52
Yan Kejun, 123n16
Yan Shigu, 224n28, 227n91
Yao people, 187
Yelü (clan), 175
Yelü (imperial line), 22
yi. See benefices; domains
Yijing. See *Classic of Changes*
Yin (empress), 114

ying marriage. *See* accompanying concubinage; sororal polygyny
Yingzong (emperor), 174, 187–89
Yongzheng (emperor), 193
Yuan (emperor), 219
Yuan dynasty, in China, 180, 182–84, 208
yu sacrifice, 64

Zeng (Marquis), 213
Zenobia (queen), 17, 33n3
Zhang (emperor), 113
Zhang (empress), 124n33, 187, *188*
Zhangsun (empress), 148
Zhao (emperor), 107
Zhao (empress), 131
Zhao (lady), 107
Zhao Feiyan (concubine), 109, 110, *110*
Zhao Hede (concubine), 109
zhaomu system, in Lu, 88n124
Zhaoxiang (king), 81
Zhao Yi, 25, 164n97, 238
zheng. See levirate marriage
Zhengde (emperor), 208–9
Zhenzong (emperor), 168, 170, 200n14
zhi. See substance

Zhi (emperor), 116
Zhongzong (emperor), 147, 150, 151, 157
Zhou (king), 234
Zhou dynasty, 12, 37n122; aristocracy during, 106, 120–22, 215; Eastern, 79–80, 87n118, 209, 213; kings of, 40n192; Latter, 221, 224n7, 224n17; political marriage during, 72; Shang dynasty contrasted with, 66, 69; simplified weddings during, 210; surname exogamy practiced during, 72, 79; titles under, 69; Western, 213, 234; *zongfa* kinship system of, 38n143
Zhou li. See Rites of Zhou
Zhou queens, 72; authority of, 73, 80; Eastern, 77; gifts given by, 74; warfare not involving, 87n118
zhuanlun wang. See chakravartin
zi. See style name
zongfa kinship system, 38n143, 71, 95
Zu Ding (king), 61
Zuo Tradition (*Zuozhuan*), 27, 234–35

www.ingramcontent.com/pod-product-compliance
Lightning Source LLC
Chambersburg PA
CBHW020111010526
44115CB00008B/791